How to Recognise and Support Mathematical Mastery in Young Children's Play

This exciting book explores young children's fascination with all things mathematical. Drawing on the 'Talk for Maths Mastery' initiative, it helps practitioners to understand early mathematical development and recognise the maths taking place in children's play. Emphasising the importance of starting from children's existing mathematical interests, it shows how adults can build on these starting points to gradually introduce new concepts and address misconceptions as they arise.

The book considers how mathematical development and learning is embedded within children's dispositions and mindsets. Including case studies, links to practice and reflective questions, the chapters reveal what mastery orientation looks like from the children's perspective in their learning and covers:

- children's serve and return conversational talk
- mathematical babies and their developmental momentum
- schematic patterns of thinking
- mathematical mark-making
- child-led play
- problem solving
- creative and critical thinking
- how adults can support children's mathematical talk, thinking and mastery

Featuring children's learning stories and full-colour photographs throughout to illustrate practice, this book is essential reading for all early years practitioners and teachers working with children throughout the EYFS and KS1 as well as students on early years courses.

Di Chilvers is an advisory consultant, author and trainer at WatchMeGrow and the Development Map, UK.

How to Recognise and Support Mathematical Mastery in Young Children's Play

Learning from the 'Talk for Maths Mastery' Initiative

Edited by Di Chilvers

Routledge
Taylor & Francis Group

LONDON AND NEW YORK

First published 2022
by Routledge
2 Park Square, Milton Park, Abingdon, Oxon OX14 4RN

and by Routledge
52 Vanderbilt Avenue, New York, NY 10017

Routledge is an imprint of the Taylor & Francis Group, an informa business

British Library Cataloguing-in-Publication Data
A catalogue record for this book is available from the British Library

Library of Congress Cataloging-in-Publication Data
Names: Chilvers, Di, editor.
Title: How to recognise and support mathematical mastery in young children's play : learning from the 'talk for maths mastery' initiative / edited by Di Chilvers.
Description: Abingdon, Oxon ; New York, NY : Routledge, 2021. |
Includes bibliographical references and index.
Identifiers: LCCN 2020052008 (print) | LCCN 2020052009 (ebook) |
ISBN 9780367133566 (hardback) | ISBN 9780367133573 (paperback) |
ISBN 9780429026072 (ebook)
Subjects: LCSH: Mathematics—Study and teaching (Early childhood) |
Mathematics—Study and teaching (Early childhood)—Activity programs. |
Early childhood education.
Classification: LCC QA135.6 .H69 2021 (print) | LCC QA135.6 (ebook) |
DDC 372.7—dc23
LC record available at https://lccn.loc.gov/2020052008
LC ebook record available at https://lccn.loc.gov/2020052009

ISBN: 978-0-367-13356-6 (hbk)
ISBN: 978-0-367-13357-3 (pbk)
ISBN: 978-0-429-02607-2 (ebk)

Typeset in Univers
by Apex CoVantage, LLC

Contents

Introduction   1

1   What is Talk for Maths Mastery?   7
DI CHILVERS

2   Maintaining the momentum of children's mathematical development   27
DI CHILVERS

3   What does mathematical mastery mean for young children?   55
DI CHILVERS

4   Documenting children's mathematical talking and thinking through observation, learning stories and floor books   81
KATIE HULME

5   Building mathematical thinking through whole-class child-led learning   109
AMY PARKER

6   Making their mathematical mark: understanding and supporting children's mathematical mark-making and thinking   137
DAVID YATES

7   How do adults support children's mathematical talk, thinking and mastery?   169
KATH PRIESTLEY

8   Maintaining children's mathematical momentum into Year 1 – a case study   198
NATALIE REILLY AND DAVID YATES

vi Contents

Final thoughts   221
Appendices   223
List of figures   234
References   237
Index   247

Detailed Contents

Introduction   1
   Contributors   3
Acknowledgements   5
   The children   5
   The Talk for Maths Mastery partners   6
   Notes   6

1   What is Talk for Maths Mastery?   7
   DI CHILVERS
   What is Talk for Maths Mastery?   7
   What is an extended professional development initiative?   8
   How to get started with Talk for Maths Mastery   11
   How to use the Talk for Maths Mastery tools and strategies
   in practice   12
      Observation using narrative learning stories   13
      Maths Is Everywhere review   15
      Hot and Cold Spot audit   17
      Mathematical learning environment audit   18
      Action planning   19
      Timelines   19
   What should you do with your research findings?
   What do they tell you about practice?   20
   Talk for Maths Mastery – our story   21
   An even bigger question!   22
   The principles underpinning continuous provision   23
   Bringing our themes and questions together   24
   Summary   26

2   Maintaining the momentum of children's mathematical
   development   27
   DI CHILVERS
   What do we mean by 'learning momentum'?   28
   The number line discussion – the transition of pedagogy   29
   Helpful number line tips   32
   Maintaining momentum, a mathematical journey . . .   32
      Mathematical babies – developmental momentum   33

Mathematical toddlers – developmental momentum 34
Mathematical young children – developmental momentum 36
Mathematical talk – maintaining the momentum 38
Talking and thinking 39
Schema and mathematical development 40
What are schema? 40
What are figurative schema? 42
What do schemas tell us about young children's mathematical thinking? 48
What should adults do? 48
How do schemas underpin children's mathematical concepts? 48
What are concepts? 48
Embodied learning and mathematical development 52
What is spatial reasoning? 53
Summary 54

3 What does mathematical mastery mean for young children? 55

DI CHILVERS

Reflecting on this chapter's question 55
What is mastery orientation? 57
What is mathematical mastery? 65
Seeing children's mastery orientation – a way of looking 68
Children's conversational talk – serve and return 72
Child-led play and activities 73
Sustained shared thinking 74
Characteristics of effective learning 77
Self-regulation and meta-cognition 78
Children's agency and self-belief 79
Summary 80

4 Documenting children's mathematical talking and thinking through observation, learning stories and floor books 81

KATIE HULME

Key questions 81
Why is documentation important, and how can we use it effectively to support mathematical talking, thinking and mastery? 82
What is documentation? 82
Documentation through learning stories and floor books 82
The process of using floor books 84
Seeing mathematical mastery in the documentation? 87
Problem solving 87
Fluency 87

Reasoning 88
How can children's serve and return interactions support
their learning? 92
How language deepens understanding – the role
of the adult 96
How talk and play can reveal misconceptions 96
Case study: only big things are heavy (children aged
3 and 4) 97
How do we address children's misconceptions? 98
How do we follow children's mathematical interests? 99
What is an interest? 99
How does children's schematic thinking and learning
support their early mathematical development? 100
Planning for children's interests 103
Mastery and meta-cognition 104
Summary 107

5　Building mathematical thinking through whole-class
child-led learning 109
AMY PARKER

Key questions 109
1. What is the place of play in developing mathematical
mastery? 110
The Ofsted definition of teaching 113
Maths Is Everywhere 117
2. How do we follow children's interests and build
mathematical thinking and mastery? 119
How do we teach? 119
How many whole-class sessions do we teach? 120
How much child-led time is there? 120
3. What does mathematical mastery through whole-class,
child-led learning look like in practice? 121
Love Monster – a whole-class learning story 121
Problem solving is a key disposition and skill in
mathematical mastery 123
What is sustained shared thinking? 123
Creating a maths mastery enabling environment 124
Reflection and meta-cognition 125
Authentic contextual experiences 127
Reflecting on our mathematical thinking and learning 132
Why whole-class learning stories? 134
Summary 135

6 Making their mathematical mark: understanding and
supporting children's mathematical mark-making
and thinking   137

DAVID YATES

Building on early mark-making experiences from birth to 3   138
  Continuous provision and the under-threes   139
  Continuing learning at home   140
The developmental progression of mathematical mark-making   142
  Peyton – mark-making at 2 years old   142
  Extending thinking for mark-making   145
Mathematical mark-making with 3- to 4-year-olds   146
Children's mathematical conversations   148
  Sensitive adult interactions   148
  What adults do to support children's mathematical
  mark-making is vital in building sensitively upon their
  developing interests and experiences   149
Building on the enabling environment   150
The influence of the wider environment on mathematical
mark-making   153
  Maths in 'real-life' contexts   153
Mathematical mark-making at 3–4 years old: Meryam   153
Mathematical mark-making with 4–5 year olds   156
  Mathematical mark-making at 4–5 years old: Aadam   156
  Boys and mark-making   159
  Mathematical mark-making at 4–5 years old: Meryam   159
  Mathematical mark-making at 4–5 years old: Aadam
  and Farhaad   161
Mathematical mark-making into Year 1 (5+ years old)   163
Summary   167

7 How do adults support children's mathematical talk,
thinking and mastery?   169

KATH PRIESTLEY

What do young children need to support their
mathematical thinking and learning?   169
My maths story   171
  So why am I writing a chapter in a book about
  maths mastery?   171
The role of the adult: "My mathematical thinking is supported by . . ."   172
  1. Adults who can identify children's mathematical
    thinking and see the potential for mathematical
    opportunities in many different situations   173

2. Adults who allow children time to explore, develop
and revisit their own problem solving and pursue
their own interests and fascinations 177
3. Adults who provide an appropriate combination of
child-initiated and adult-focused teaching and learning
to get the balance right 181
Example 1 182
Example 2 183
4. Adults who value and create opportunities for
children's talk 186
5. Adults who have a secure knowledge of child
development and how children learn 191
6. Adults who know how to observe 192
Through observation . . . 194
Summary 197

8 Maintaining children's mathematical momentum into
Year 1 – a case study 198
NATALIE REILLY AND DAVID YATES
1. Having a strong overall vision 199
2. Implementing the vision into Year 1 202
3. What were the challenges? 207
4. What about the role of the adult in Year 1? 208
5. How are children's interests followed? 210
6. Continuing continuous provision 214
7. Partnership between home and school 215
The Early Years Foundation Stage meets the National
Curriculum 215
Summary 220

Final thoughts 221
Appendices 223
List of figures 234
References 237
Index 247

Introduction

Being curious about how young children learn, watching and listening as they play and trying to understand what it all means is an intriguing, exciting and worthwhile undertaking that is not without its challenges. Crucially, we need to know about child development in order to tune into and value what it is we are seeing, then offer the right support and teaching. Understanding children's mathematical development is all part of this worthwhile pursuit but can be the area of learning that adults find difficult to come to grips with, often because of their own feelings about maths. So this book is for everyone who wants to find out more about how young children develop mathematically in their earliest years, as babies, toddlers and older children, whilst at the same time build their understanding, knowledge, experience and confidence of engaging in early mathematics.

Through sharing our experiences of the Talk for Maths Mastery initiative (what we did, how we engaged with the children and learned from them through their child-led play), we show how our *research* informed and empowered us to have a much deeper, clearer understanding of how mathematical development progresses. However, there are also many other connections as to how young children learn overall, which this book explores in detail. For example, children's talk is fundamental for all development and learning not just mathematics. Communication and language are how children make their thinking and learning visible; they are also among the most significant and reliable indicators of their development and later progress (National Literacy Trust, 2019; Bleses et al., 2016; Romeo et al., 2018; Hirsch-Pasek at Temple University, USA; Harvard University Center on the Developing Child, USA) and give us a real insight into their mathematical understanding, skills and knowledge.

Talk for Maths Mastery (TFMM) began as a year-long initiative with 12 primary schools in Sheffield to ensure that firm foundations for mathematical development and learning were laid from the start. It focused on how we could support children's progress and attainment through the adult's knowledge and understanding of children's early mathematical development and increase parental involvement as part of the process.

After two years of working together, we had refocused our understanding of children's mathematical development and learning, seeing it in a much broader context, embedded within child-led play and connected to deeper levels of thinking and wider dispositions for learning, where we could clearly see their understanding and mastery of mathematical concepts and skills.

For young children, mathematics is a part of their everyday world, not a separate enterprise; their learning and development are connected in complex sequences and patterns, as their brains and bodies begin to make sense of experiences and actions through play. Birth to 6 years old is a critical period for children as they develop positive dispositions, attitudes and skills to become lifelong learners; so the more we can understand this complex stage of human development, the better able we are to *teach* through informed practice and focused support.

This has been significant in moving our own mindsets from seeing maths as a 'tricky' area of learning to teach to realising that we are all mathematicians in our daily lives and clearly seeing and appreciating the rich mathematical potential of young children, including babies and toddlers. Consequently, we now work from the principle that maths is happening everywhere at any moment; we just need to keep an open mind, open eyes, and listen.

It is time to share this work more widely and place children's mathematical development, play and learning within the context of their lives as babies, toddlers and older children, with the direction of travel commencing from their unique starting points and *not* from the top down. Our concerns are about the overuse of prescriptive mathematical programs, designed for older children, being used in a formal way with young children, with a narrow view of mathematics, which only focus on numeracy and leading to younger children's wider mathematical experiences being overlooked or dismissed at a time when these skills are the very ones which are required for the future world of science, technology, engineering (arts) and maths (STEM or STEAM).

Throughout this book, we look at the way in which mathematical development and learning are embedded within children's dispositions and mindsets and particularly how this relates to mastery orientation. The chapters explore what this looks like from the children's perspective in their learning, including children's serve and return conversational talk, following their interests and ideas, their schematic patterns of thinking, mathematical mark-making, child-led play, problem solving and creative and critical thinking.

Through the many learning stories and examples of children deeply engaged in their child-led play, included in this book, we see the multi-faceted ways in which they are, from the start, competent and capable thinkers and learners through:

- developing positive growth mindsets
- concepts, dispositions, attitudes and skills
- being deeply involved and engaged
- Playing and Exploring, Active Learning and Creating and Thinking Critically
- sustained shared thinking
- self-regulation and meta-cognition
- children's agency and self-belief

All these aspects, which can sound complicated, are fully explained; we look at what they mean and their part in children's development, how they are underpinned by theory and research, what they look like in practice, how we can observe them and importantly how they relate to and underpin mathematics in its broadest sense.

At the end of the TFMM initiative, we saw a significant change in attitudes towards mathematics in both the children and the adults:

> Children are much more confident to talk about the maths they are doing. They are able to solve mathematical problems themselves and see themselves as able to do this. They really feel in charge of their own learning and love thinking of what to do next.
> (Amy Parker, TFMM Partner, July 2017)

And:

> This initiative has enabled me to shape my philosophy of what I truly feel is best practice. At the heart of this lies child-led learning, the importance of developing talk through an approach which is shared and taken on by parents; the importance of structuring the day in a way which gives children time to follow and develop ideas and thinking. I wish I had such a clear philosophy when I was working in KS1 in the past.
> (Y1 Teacher, TFMM Partner, July 2017)

We hope that you will also notice a change in your confidence and practice and be inspired by young children's mathematical interests and creativity.

Five of the TFMM partners have written chapters in this book, specifically about their work during the initiative and how it has continued to inform their thinking and practice. They each bring a wealth of knowledge and experience of working with young children, leading creative practice and forming strong partnership with parents, families, colleagues and other professionals.

Contributors

Di Chilvers: Advisory consultant in early childhood education

Di was the external adviser leading the TFMM initiative, providing pedagogical leadership and training, links to research, reading and theory. Her focus on making the connection between practice and theory is critical for everyone involved in early childhood education, particularly regarding how children develop and learn. Di's chapters concentrate on this and how mastery orientation underpins children's mathematical development and much more (Chapters 1, 2 and 3).

Katie Hulme: Nursery teacher and curriculum coordinator at Prince Edward Primary School, Sheffield

Katie explains how she followed children's interests, questions and thinking, using creative ways to document this through learning stories, floor books, films, and the class blog. These all offered the children and adults an opportunity to revisit and talk about their mathematical learning together, supporting children to reflect on and deepen their meta-cognitive thinking (Chapter 4).

Amy Parker: Reception teacher and Foundation Stage Lead at Prince Edward Primary School, Sheffield

During the Talk for Maths Mastery initiative, Amy became interested in how to develop whole-class child-led learning projects and ways to document the process rather than just the outcome. The Love Monster learning story is the culmination of this work and shows how mathematics woven into everyday meaningful contexts reveals children's deeper understanding and mastery (Chapter 5).

David Yates: Reception and Nursery teacher at Tinsley Meadows Primary Academy, Sheffield

David has focused on the link between drawing and writing and how children use mark-making to explore and show their developing understanding of maths. mathematical mark-making is a fascinating way of considering children's thinking and learning and how they make this visible. His chapter explores what this can tell us about children's understanding and mastery of maths (Chapter 6).

Kath Priestley: Reception teacher and Early Years Specialist

Kath has worked across the early years sector in a range of settings and schools with very young children and their families. She never ceases to be amazed by the complex and fascinating ways in which children learn and the part that a skilled adult can play within this. Having lacked confidence in maths as a child, she is determined that children and the adults who work with them should not have to feel anxiety or 'fear' about maths (Chapter 7).

Natalie Reilly: Senior Assistant Head and Phase 1 Leader, Fordbridge Community Primary School, Solihull, Birmingham

Natalie explains how Talk for Maths Mastery became the key to Year 1 children deepening and mastering critical thinking in their mathematical development. This was achieved through the team's observations, interactions and discussions with the children in their independent learning. The learning stories in Year 1 show how children think critically and the depth and mastery in their understanding and, most importantly, in their mathematical talk (Chapter 8).

Other contributors

With many thanks to the following partners who have shared their practice, experience and knowledge:

Clare Richmond, owner/manager, Rainbow Nursery, Kentish Town, London

Iva Faltyskova, Deputy Head, Puss in Boots Nursery, Camden

Astrid Binkle-Newby, Ready Steady Go Pre-School, Camden, London

Jayne Weaver, Dawn Scrimshaw, Claire Green and Hayley Tufft, Fordbridge Community Primary School, Solihull, Birmingham

Acknowledgements

The children

Most importantly, a huge thank you to all the children involved in TFMM and to their learning stories, which have opened our eyes to their thinking, talking, inspiration and creativity in mathematics and in many other aspects of learning. We have seen how their innate drive and interests spur them on to find answers to their questions through play, collaboration with others and fantastic conversations. The best way to really know children, child development and their learning, mathematical or otherwise, is to take time to observe, think about what we see and then put that understanding to good use:

> Stand aside for a while and leave room for learning, observe carefully what children do, and then, if you have understood well, perhaps teaching will be different from before.
> (Loris Malaguzzi, in Edwards, Gandini and Forman, 1998, p. 57)

Writing a book about the Talk for Maths Mastery initiative was an inevitable challenge after all the hard work, commitment and thinking by the partners. We always said, "No one knows as much as all of us" (McNicoll, 2008), and this has been very true in terms of co-constructing our thinking and understanding. The 'hidden' compelling outcomes being that, in working together, collaborating and sharing practice, the participants' confidence, self-awareness and advocacy for children grew through their deeper understanding of how children learn best and knowing how child development informs teaching and learning. The TFMM partners' chapters have evolved from this continued co-construction (serve and return) which has taken considerable time but which has led to thoroughly informed explanations of children's mathematical development and learning in practice (as well as many other aspects of their learning). It has been a sheer pleasure to work with everyone in the initiative, and thanks must go to them and everyone else who has been involved in some way or another.

The Talk for Maths Mastery partners

Twelve primary schools from the Sheffield South East Learning Partnership (SSELP), a collaborative partnership who have worked together for 19 years, having started as an Education Action Zone (EAZ). Some of the schools are situated in socio-economic areas of deprivation, several with high levels of children who have English as an Additional Language (EAL). The schools face various challenges as they work together to raise attainment, aspiration and life chances for every child in the partnership.

Each school had a TFMM lead, usually the Foundation Stage Coordinator, and a second colleague who attended three full days training across the year (autumn, spring, summer) and six twilight seminars (one each half term). Teachers from Year 1 became involved as we focused on the transition between the Early Years Foundation Stage (EYFS) and the National Curriculum. Di Chilvers was the external adviser leading the TFMM initiative, being a mentor and critical friend to the partners, challenging thinking in a supportive and respectful way.

Notes

There are many professionals working with young children in schools and other settings, all of whom have various titles, from *practitioner* to *pedagogue*, so throughout the book we have described all those who work with young children as the 'adult'.

We also use the term *child-led* and *child-initiated* interchangeably. Amy Parker takes a deeper look at this in Chapter 5.

1 **What is Talk for Maths Mastery?**

DI CHILVERS

This chapter looks at how the Talk for Maths Mastery initiative can help you to develop good mathematical practice with your children, whilst at the same time furthering your own understanding and confidence.

This means taking a good look at what the children are doing and saying, what the adults are doing and saying and what the enabling environment is doing and saying, then bringing this all together and prioritising what you need to do next to move things on.

We explain the TFMM initiative, sharing our questions, observations and findings, along with the 'tools' and strategies we used to help us to stop and think about what we were already doing, how we looked deeply at our practice and reflected on what we saw.

> What is Talk for Maths Mastery?
> What is an extended professional development initiative?
> How to get started with Talk for Maths Mastery?
> How to use the Talk for Maths Mastery tools and strategies in practice?
> What should you do with your research findings? What do they tell you about practice?
> Talk for Maths Mastery – Our story

What is Talk for Maths Mastery?

Talk for Maths Mastery has evolved from its beginnings into a way of working with young children which brings together the following strands:

- Recognising that young children are competent and capable learners with their own learning momentum, intrinsically motivated to actively play, explore and engage in creative and critical thinking
- Supportive adults who know and understand how children develop and learn, including mathematical development from birth to 6+
- Providing an enabling environment which tunes into young children's mathematical lines of development and their interests in ways that connect to familiar real life, authentic contexts
- Collaborative partnerships with parents and families based on real-life, everyday home learning experiences and culture

This book explores all these strands in depth. However, in practice with young children, the strands are all woven together as they all interweave and connect, creating a holistic approach which supports children's development, thinking, talking and learning. Together they create a mathematical pedagogy:

> 'Pedagogy' is what we know about children and how they learn, together with the experiences and responses we provide. It describes our methodology and our understanding and beliefs of what is right for young children.
>
> In determining the nature of our pedagogy, we need to consider the child, the experiences we provide, our interactions, the environment, the family and their community and how these factors influence each child's holistic development and progress in learning.
>
> (Education Scotland, 2020)

The emphasis is on *Talk*, *Maths* and *Mastery*. Whilst children's talk, communication and language are probably, for most, a familiar concept, *mathematics and mastery* are often viewed as an unknown, scary prospect to delve into, and only if we really must! Kath Priestley (Chapter 7) raises the persistent issue of adults' confidence in mathematics, usually a leftover from poor teaching at secondary school. However, one of the 'hidden outcomes' of TFMM, and working together with others, was the development of professional confidence and understanding, through observing children and talking together about what they were doing. It was empowering, with many light bulb moments, which revealed, "Oh *that's* what is happening!" and, "Now I understand why they did/said that".

Feedback from the TFMM partners, at the end of year one, was extremely positive, as adults said they were "more confident at recognising, facilitating and deepening children's mathematical learning". TFMM strategies had "opened their eyes to mathematical opportunities", and they "felt empowered to support children's mathematical development". Building professional confidence and self-awareness takes time, which is why *extended professional development initiatives* are so valuable in growing adults' knowledge, experience and practice.

What is an extended professional development initiative?

One of the most effective ways of developing your thinking and practice is to become part of an extended professional development initiative (EPDI), which simply means working together, collaboratively as a group or community of learners, over a period of time. It is a highly effective way to develop thinking and professional learning because the 'community' becomes a forum for developing ideas, sharing good practice and raising the quality of learning and teaching. Siraj-Blatchford and Manni (2007), in their work on effective leadership, talked about "A community of learners with a common commitment to reflective, critical practice and professional development" (p. 16). Wenger-Trayner (2015) explain:

> Communities of practice are groups of people who share a concern or a passion for something they do and learn how to do it better as they interact regularly.

Working together as a community of learners in the TFMM initiative was an inspiring experience for the practitioners and teachers as they developed their thinking and practice together, sharing ideas and co-constructing good early years pedagogy. When everyone comes together, there is a great deal of knowledge and experience in the room to share; the group/community can learn from one another. It is certainly true that "*No one knows as much as all of us*" (McNicoll, 2008); together the group can generate a huge amount of thinking.

There is a research element to this, where you can pose questions about what you want to explore and find out. In our case, it was children's mathematical development, but the process is the same for any inquiry. It is called research-in-action but is more commonly known as practitioner action research, research-based-pedagogy or practitioner inquiry, where:

> Teachers/practitioners make opportunities to 'really deeply' look at what is 'going on' in their settings/schools including observation of children and talking about their thinking through pedagogical conversations.
>
> (Peacock, 2018)

This kind of in-practice, evidenced-based research keeps the focus in everyday, meaningful, contexts, with those involved observing, investigating, exploring, enquiring, questioning and reflecting on what is happening by asking questions such as:

> Why are we doing this?
> Why are we doing it this way?
> What difference will it make?

For example, one of the everyday practices we should all be familiar with is observation, but would we recognise this process of watching children to find out what they are doing and learning as a form of research? In TFMM narrative observation, using learning stories was

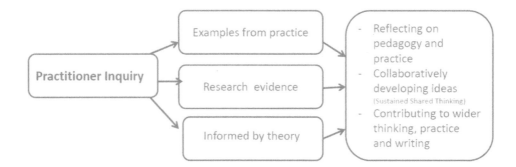

Figure 1.1 Process of practitioner inquiry used in the New Zealand Educational Leadership Projects

one of our key tools for research, which ultimately helped us to identify when children were displaying mastery orientation, as well as many other things.

In academic fields, this kind of research is known as 'grounded theory' where evidence is gathered 'in action' at ground level and used to inform thinking, alongside looking at wider research and informed theories. This, in effect, triangulates the whole process and strengthens the development of pedagogy and practice. It is a highly reflective process which is used widely in the New Zealand educational leadership projects (Figure 1.1) where schools and early years settings, as part of the Education Ministry's Teaching and Learning Research Initiative (TLRI Programme, www.tlri.org. nz/tlri-research), follow a yearly research focus, supported by an external mentor and then disseminate the outcomes nationally and internationally (Carr and Lee, 2012).

Practitioner(s) gather information about their current practice through observation and various other strategies (see the following section on 'tools' and strategies); they look for further evidence from research, and they also find out about theories which relate to the aspect of inquiry. These are all brought together, shared, discussed and analysed through reflection, collaboration and co-construction, pulling out the threads and ideas to develop stronger, effective early years practice. This can lead to the development of wider thinking, practice and writing, which is exactly what happened with the TFMM initiative.

The TFMM initiative involved everyone in this reflective process through:

- working collaboratively as a community of learners
- talking, discussing and thinking together – engaging in our own sustained shared thinking (SST)
- having time to reflect together on what we do and why we do it that way
- sharing practice, ideas, stories
- co-constructing good practice
- making partnerships, networks, support, buddying, solidarity, friendships

Communities of practice do not have to be as large as the TFMM group, they can be much smaller, for example, staff in a setting, nursery and reception class, or working together with a colleague. What makes a huge difference though, is that you have the backing from your manager, head teacher, foundation stage coordinator or key lead person, as this will be a crucial support to help you change and embed new practice.

How to get started with Talk for Maths Mastery

Starting any kind of initiative or project can be a bit overwhelming in deciding what to do first and how to get going. So, as with children's starting points, begin where you are 'at', find out what you are already doing well, what you know and how successful it is. Then you can build on firm foundations.

There are various ways of taking stock and gathering evidence of where you are, stepping back to reflect on practice and having time to investigate, explore and examine what you are doing. Kolb (1984) refers to this as a cycle of reflection; as you reflect on an experience, consider how effective or worthwhile the experience is and think about what to do next (Figure 1.2a).

This should be a familiar, everyday process used in early years practice with children, as you observe in order to 'describe' what you are seeing, then analyse what you have seen and 'decide' what it tells you. Finally thinking about 'what's next' and planning for further development (Figure 1.2b).

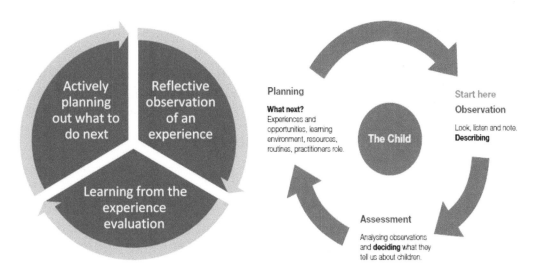

Figure 1.2 (a) Kolb's experiential cycle of reflection; **(b)** observation cycle from Development Matters

Source: Kolb (1984), Development Matters (Early Education, 2012, p. 3)

Reflection point

Think about a time in your work with children when you have taken a step back and thought about what you were doing and why you were doing it?

When was this?

As you played and talked with a child or children?
Talking with colleagues or with the child or children's parents?
During training or a planning meeting?
While you were you reading something?

Whom were you with?

A child or children?
A colleague/s or parents?
On your own?

Did this help you?

What happened to your thinking/practice?

What became clear, as we began to look at our starting points, was the amount we could learn from the children and to look at mathematics from *their* perspective rather than from a structured mathematics programme with prescriptive and narrow outcomes. There was an initial need in the group to 'clear the fog' and take an informed in-depth look at children's mathematical development. This involved being able to acknowledge that children are already competent and capable mathematicians in their every-day lives and to understand that if we start with observing children in their child-led play, we will actually see maths happening in all sorts of places, ways and thoughts, rather than assuming that they know nothing until they are gathered together around a table or carpet and taught by an adult.

How to use the talk for Maths Mastery tools and strategies in practice

There are various 'tools' and strategies to help identify your starting points and 'take stock' of what is already happening with regard to children's mathematical learning. One of the main strategies to use is observation of children, particularly **narrative learning stories**, as they help you to look more deeply into children's contextual engagement in mathematical play. Observation should already be something you are involved in as part of your everyday practice, so this is also a good opportunity to build and share your skills with each other.

Other tools are:

- 'Maths Is Everywhere' (Appendix 1) and 'Maths Talk Is Everywhere' reviews (Appendix 2)
- Hot and Cold Spot audit from Every Child a Talker (DCSF, 2008c)
- Maths audit from Numbers and Patterns – Laying Foundations in Mathematics (DCSF, 2009b) (Appendix 3)
- Action plan (Appendix 4)
- Learning stories (Appendix 5)

Remember, you do not need to use all these tools. Choose the best ones for you in your context. Take your time with this and involve everyone, so that they can all 'have a go'.

Observation using narrative learning stories

Observation is one of the most effective ways to fine-tune your knowledge of child development and how children think and learn. This is a sensible place to start when trying to find out if mathematical talk, thinking and learning is happening, through watching and listening to the children as they engage in their child-initiated play and activities. Both Malaguzzi (Edwards, Gandini and Forman, 1998) and Dewey (1933) see observation as a mixture of many things, including making children's learning visible, understanding their learning and as a reflective tool to improve the quality of pedagogy and practice. Malaguzzi's wise advice is to:

> Stand aside for a while and leave room for learning, observe carefully what children do, and then, if you have understood well, perhaps teaching will be different from before.
> (Edwards, Gandini and Forman, 1998, p. 82)

As the TFMM partners observed children engaged in child-led play, the mathematical fog began to clear, and they began to draw meaning from the children as their play unfolded. Taking photographs and quickly writing down the children's talk, then turning this into a learning story showed their ideas, thinking and talk as it grew, often in collaboration with other children, as they co-constructed their play together. You can see this in action in the learning stories throughout this book, including Go Compare (Chapter 6) and Numbered Footballs (Chapter 3). Superficial snapshot type observations do not give the full picture, whilst narrative observations, through a combination of photographs and words, show the complexity of children's mathematical engagement and the deep understanding they have. This is a window into mastery orientation and the complex strategies children are using in their play (see Chapter 3, 'What does mathematical mastery mean for young children?').

Observation should be a central part of everyday professional practice when working with young children, so integrating this within TFMM is a *smart* use of time and can be used for multiple purposes (see Appendix 5: '101 Uses of Learning Stories'). Learning stories sharpen our professional knowledge and understanding of children's development and learning; if we want to see and understand children's mathematical mastery, we need to look closely and carefully at what they are doing, saying and thinking. Jill Goodhand, Foundation Stage Coordinator, explained the value of using learning stories:

> Learning stories come out of something quite ordinary like playing with the play dough or sitting at the snack table with friends. It is the place to hear children's talk and listen to their ideas, interests and responses. This is certainly a window into children's thinking which the children express through their conversational language.
>
> What does the Learning Story tell us? Apart from the child's thinking, it tells us about ourselves as practitioners/teachers, the difference we made by asking a question, our ability to see a mathematical opportunity and possible next steps. How will we follow this up? What do we need to change in our provision? Who would think that one rhyme like 5 Little Ducks, made from 20+ different sized and shaped ducks, could lead to so many stories in so many directions with different children?

In summary, narrative learning stories help you to:

- keep an open mind and learn from the children and their play
- see children's everyday mathematical interests and thinking unfolding in their child-led play and activities
- see children making sense of maths in wider, meaningful contexts, embedding their understanding and learning
- focus on deeper levels of involvement in your observations and assessment for learning
- sharpen your professional knowledge and understanding of children's development and learning
- develop an informed understanding of how to maintain the momentum of children's learning through supporting their child-led play/activities
- recognise and understand mastery orientation

As Katie Hulme explains, in Chapter 4, documenting children's learning in this way has many values, not just as part of a professional development initiative. In Chapter 8 we see how a school in Solihull has continued to use learning stories to document mathematical thinking and learning in Year 1.

Reflection point

It takes practice to move from using single snapshot observations to narrative learning stories, which will have several photographs showing the child(ren)'s play as it unfolds. Start small and slowly build as your confidence grows.

Stories/observations happen anywhere and at any time, so keep alert and capture them when you can. They may not be obviously mathematical at the time, but as you discuss them with colleagues, you will be able to focus on the maths and the child's language/talk. Keep an open mind; this dialogue is important and develops your knowledge and understanding.

Having an observation 'buddy' means that you will always have someone to talk to, especially if they are more experienced. You can share your knowledge and thinking.

Maths Is Everywhere review

The Maths Is Everywhere review (Appendix 1) was created as a reflective observation to remind all adults that maths can happen anywhere, at any time and not just in a dedicated maths area! There can also be an assumption that maths only occurs when there is an adult 'teaching' or through a mathematical adult-focused activity, e.g. using Numicon or working on simple addition. It is important to look forensically at what is *actually* happening and not at what you *think* is happening, as this could inadvertently lead to a view that children are not engaging in any mathematics at all. This can often be the case in Reception classes when the adults can be constantly engaged in adult-directed activities without having any opportunity to observe and interact with children in continuous provision. Unfortunately, this also means that they will never see if their teaching has been fully understood by the child(ren) as they replay and embed what has been taught in their child-led activities.

Use the review at different times of day, indoors and outdoors, with all the staff team involved; then discuss your findings together. This will tell you a great deal about what is actually happening throughout the day indoors and outdoors. Looking at the similarities and differences and making notes of any key themes, along with the levels of involvement of the children and adults, will tell you a great deal. You can then prioritise what you need to do next and make an action plan. The whole process becomes an opportunity for everyone to contribute and learn from one another as well as giving support to any staff who are newly qualified or need further professional development.

An additional review was created to focus specifically on listening to children's mathematical talk (Appendix 2) and serve and return conversations (see Figure 1.3).

Name of practitioner: *Kirsty (2 – 3yr old room)*   Setting: Date:

 Maths <u>talk</u> is everywhere!

Spend 10 minutes and have a look around the setting and the outdoor environment.
Where can you <u>hear maths talk</u> happening? What sort of <u>maths talk</u> is it?
E.g. About the Characteristics of Effective learning e.g. problem solving, reasoning, ideas etc? About number, shape, space and measures? Serve and return conversations? Anything else?
*Remember children communicate what they are thinking in other ways not just through talk – can you see this? *
Turnover/ get more paper if you need to!

What can you hear? What are the children saying?	Where is it happening?	What type of maths is it?
Bouncing on trampoline – 2 children decided they will take a turn each. Katie: "1,2,3,4,5 your turn Emi Li". Emi Li did only 4 jumps and left Katie: "Again, one more jump" (5 jumps altogether ☺)	Trampoline, Physical area	Counting Repetition Taking Turns Adding (one more number)
Mohammed looking through box with magnetic letters M: "I have one" – showing me numeral 2 M: "and another one. We got many of them" Adult: "this is number 2" M: "2" repeating after adult. "I have two 2" lifting them in the air Adult: "we can put them on your board" M: Placed his two numerals 2 on the magnetic board…then he found more and placed them in the line. Then he carried on with other numerals.	Exploration area – magnetic numbers	Matching numerals to correct number More or less Learning new words (non-English speaker) by repeating by teacher Making connections
Ruby: "It's too big." Meaning the toilet "I went like this, forward". Adult: "No, you went back, backwards" showing the direction to the child Ruby: "I can do it too; back, front, back, front" – while rocking on the toilet. "I need only 1 toilet paper. 1,2,3…" Adult: "Isn't it too much?" Ruby: "I have enough now, I have 5"	Bathroom/ toilet	Directions Learning new words Describing what she is doing Saying & counting out numbers 1-5

Figure 1.3 Maths Talk Is Everywhere – an example

Hot and Cold Spot audit

This audit was originally developed as part of the Every Child a Talker (ECAT) project (DCSF, 2008c, p.15) to evaluate how effective the enabling environment is in supporting children's mathematical engagement and talk. You can use the audit to zone in on the potential opportunities for mathematical talk and ask the following questions:

- Are serve and return conversations taking place between children as they become involved in their child-initiated play active learning, and creative and critical thinking?
- Can you hear and see children using the mathematical language, skills and concepts that you have taught in adult-focused activities? (See Chapters 2 and 3)

The answers to these questions will tell you how effective your enabling environment is in supporting and extending mathematical thinking, learning and teaching.

Enabling environments are frequently interpreted through 'continuous provision' and what is provided both inside and outside for the children. It can sometimes become predictable and overly organised or taken for granted if we don't keep thinking about how it is meeting and supporting children's needs, interests and development. Signs which declare mathematics will happen in a designated area are limiting, both to the children, who will engage in mathematical play wherever they choose (often outdoors), and adults, who end up thinking that this is where they can only *teach* maths without looking anywhere else. The danger is that we miss the child's real mathematical potential rather than being inspired by it.

Enabling environments and continuous provision should be spaces and places where mathematical play happens all the time in one way or another. Using this type of Hot and Cold Spot Audit raises awareness across the team that mathematical play and conversations can happen anywhere, at any time and with any child(ren), as long as you look.

All you need to do is:

- make a drawing of the layout of your setting, including the inside and outside spaces
- observe the children over a period of time e.g. 45 minutes (observing every 5/10 minutes)
- use a red pen to record the maths 'hot spots' including where children are engaging in conversations with one another and/or adults (add one cross if talking and play takes place sometimes, and more crosses if it takes place there a lot)
- use a blue pen and mark with a circle the places where mathematical play, activities and talk could take place but are not actually happening at that moment in time

It is interesting for every adult to undertake a Hot and Cold Spot observation and then discuss this together as a team. The discussion in itself will be extremely valuable in reflecting on practice and supporting continual professional development (CPD). Again, you will need to prioritise your findings and create an action plan to make the changes to practice together.

Mathematical learning environment audit

An audit or self-evaluation is a helpful tool to take a snapshot overview of the enabling environment and the opportunities for children to become involved in mathematical play and activities. It is quite easy to become complacent and think that having a maths area and a number line will cover the curriculum along with a daily maths input of some sort. Doing a 'stocktake' refreshes everyone's practice and thinking and can lead to some very interesting findings, as we found out in our work, especially related to number lines and games (see Chapter 2).

The maths audit (Appendix 3) was adapted from *Numbers and Patterns: Laying Foundations in Mathematics* (DCSF, 2009c) and takes a broad look at the quality of opportunities to support and extend mathematical development indoors and outdoors for older children, rather than for babies and toddlers. In the TFMM initiative, we used the audit to focus our thinking on continuous provision and the crucial part this plays in supporting and embedding children's mathematical learning.

The audit questions are there to make you think and reflect on practice rather than a shopping list to be ticked. As you work through the audit, think about the age of the children you are working with and whether the question is appropriate, e.g. are the resources clearly labelled? This could be interpreted for younger children, under three, as having a few photographs which help them to match where the books belong or where the tray for beakers is kept. The key here is not to go mad with laminated labelling of everything; children's brains will tune out if there is an explosion of labelling on every wall, window and cupboard.

Always ask yourself the following questions as you use the audit:

> What will the child actually see here?
> Will it make sense to them?
> Is it meaningful to them?

If it doesn't/isn't, talk about this with your team and think of another/better way which is appropriate for your children.

The best way to undertake the audit is in collaboration with your colleagues/team so that everyone is fully involved and has a voice. This TFMM way of working, as a community of learners, means that everyone has to think about and consider the effectiveness and quality of the mathematical experiences you are offering. Discussing this together is all part of the learning process and ensures that there is shared commitment, understanding and ownership of any changes that are made.

The columns for 'Areas for Development' and 'Comments and Next Steps' are there to *document* what is in place as well as your thoughts and possible next steps. Having some notes, as a record to look back on and refer to, is helpful so that you can see what is going well and where changes need to be made. It doesn't mean writing an essay. Use bullet points, as they are a quick way of making brief notes, and you can always colour-code if you want to be even more organised. Remember it is your audit, so use it in a way which is helpful and meaningful to you and your team. When you have completed the audit, it's time to get together and think about your priorities in order to create an action plan.

Action planning

Making an action plan is a great way of keeping focused on a few, manageable priorities over a period of time and not becoming overwhelmed with trying to do everything at once. It is far better to work on a manageable plan, with everyone taking part in the process and actually enjoying it, rather than becoming stressed. In TFMM, we used the Action Plan (Appendix 4) with only three lines for actions; one which focused on the children; one related to practitioner development of some sort (including the learning environment); and one which involved the family and home learning. The action plan should be shared with the team and reviewed periodically (e.g. termly) though this was entirely up to the TFMM Lead as some actions are quick wins whilst others take longer. Remember that an action plan is not a race to the finish but something which supports change, guides you and your team and helps you to keep on track. When you reflect, you will see the impact of your endeavours, which is a great feeling. Keep it where everyone can see it; it should look well-worn rather than pristinely kept in a file!

Timelines

Timelines are helpful if you want to work towards a specific end date by which the action is completed. Having set the time scale, work out the weeks or months in the form of a grid, and then break down what needs to happen each week/month, by whom, when you need to meet to discuss progress etc. This makes everything clear and is particularly helpful for good communication when there is a large team. It is important to be realistic about time scales and how they sit alongside all the other routines and actions that are taking place. The aim is to make sure there is enough time to keep everyone on board so that any changes to practice become well embedded and sustainable. Remember that taking it slowly is a very helpful option. The timeline in Figure 1.4 is an example from one of the TFMM partners, but you may have other ideas for and ways of doing this.

Foundation Stage and Y1 TFMM Timeline	
October	M.H Meeting with FS 2 and Y1 staff to complete Maths Environment audits. FS 1 Maths Environment audit to be completed.
November	• Hot and Cold Spot results from FS 1, 2 and Y1 (N.H) • Action plan set up (M.H) • Learning stories (N.H. M.H) • Evaluating/enhancing ways of working (N.H. M.H)
December	<u>Baking workshops</u> launched with student/parental involvement. Rota devised – Nadia, Cordy and Student
January	<u>Display ideas</u> • Handwritten numerals • Numerals reflecting cultures • Vocabulary/concept prompts (FS 1, 2 and Y1) <u>'Big maths' resources</u> in end classroom plus role-play area reflecting real maths contexts e.g. post office, Lidl shop etc. (Y1) <u>Maths games</u>-in carrier (FS1, 2 and Y1)

Figure 1.4 Example of a timeline from Pipworth Primary School, Sheffield

What should you do with your research findings? What do they tell you about practice?

It is well worth spending time gathering your 'research' findings and including different perspectives, since what you find from children, adults and the enabling environment provides the evidence for what you need to do in order to move forward and build great practice whilst, at the same time, developing your own pedagogical knowledge and understanding. As the TFMM learning community, we became very excited about what we found, but as a large group we also had to do some sifting and sorting to look for recurring themes and make our own connections in order to make it manageable. This is all part of following a practitioner inquiry action research model; it is about looking at and listening to the evidence that is in front of you and then reflecting on what it all means for practice and young children's mathematical development and learning.

> In reflective practice there is a need to slow down, stand back and watch, in order to find out what is really happening in children's learning and how we can teach them more effectively. It includes discussion, responding to each other's thinking, agreeing and disagreeing, listening and being open to discover and create new ideas and thinking.
>
> (Chilvers, 2002, p. 32)

The following is our TFMM story: an explanation of what we saw, what we read and what we discussed, and, above all, how it widened our understanding of children's mathematical development, learning and mastery orientation.

Talk for Maths Mastery – our story

After bringing together all the key findings from the Mathematics Learning Environment Audits, we identified several themes/questions which needed further development and unpicking, including:

Is there enough mathematical talk?

- Everyday mathematical language, talk and conversation
- Opportunities for mathematical talk in continuous provision and other activities
- The characteristics of effective learning and mathematical language
- Modelling language
- Talk which builds and extends thinking – co-construction

- Did we have a range of books (fiction and non-fiction), stories, rhymes and poems which encapsulate maths and create contextual understanding?
- How were questions being used including 'possibility questions' linked to Creating and Thinking Critically? (See Appendix 6)
- Are there regular opportunities for baking and cooking – 'The Great British Bake Off'?
- Are we reflecting the culture and languages of all children with a wider range of books displaying many languages and cultures, patterns and numbers?
- Can children independently access games and have frequent opportunities to create and make their own games?
- Are we engaging with parents and families through real-life, authentic partnerships?

After discussing these themes, we needed to draw them together in a manageable way, remembering that it was better to look at a few of them in depth rather than all of them superficially. We ended up reframing them into the following questions.

Was there enough mathematical talking and thinking, including . . .

- everyday mathematical language and conversation in natural contexts – e.g. child-led play including outdoor play, story time, singing and at snack times?
- opportunities for mathematical talk in continuous provision and other activities?
- talk which builds and extends thinking leading to co-construction and sustained shared thinking?

- talk linked to the characteristics of effective learning, particularly Creating and Thinking Critically?
- adults' use of possibility questions to extend mathematical thinking?

Reflection point

Are we asking the right questions?

Using questions in this way helps you to reflect on practice by making you think, just as we use open-ended questions to extend children's thinking. For example, look at the difference between the following questions:

What mathematical talk can you use with babies and toddlers?
Or:
How can we build interesting mathematical opportunities for serve and return conversations with babies and toddlers?
Which of these questions make you think more? Why?
(This is why there are so many questions in this book!!)

An even bigger question!

We were looking at our questions in the context of children's mathematical development, particularly the relationship between their talking and thinking. However, as we began to deepen our research, through observing what we saw children doing in their child-initiated play, we were faced with an even bigger question:

> How do we make sure that we maintain the momentum of children's mathematical development and learning from 2-year-olds[1] to 6+ (Y1) building firm foundations on children's starting points?

We arrived at this big question after focusing on the child(ren)'s perspective as they initiated and led their play and explorations. We listened carefully to their conversational talk, particularly their serve and return conversations (see Chapters 2 and 3) and reflected on this through the 'lens' of the 'Characteristics of Effective Learning' (Appendix 6). What we saw was children, of all ages, engaged in complex, deep levels of problem solving, reasoning and sustained shared thinking that frequently surprised us in their complexity and creativity. They were experts at communicating their thinking through their child-led play either by themselves or collaboratively and through their actions, expressions and talk. In the context of their play, we began to see how mathematical they were and just how much they truly understood.

As we followed the children's lead, we started to look closely at the balance between child-led play and adult-focused teaching (DCSF, 2009a; Chilvers, 2012, 2013, 2015; Ofsted, 2015) and how this supported Creating and Thinking Critically, including the thinking of ideas, problem setting, problem solving and sustained shared thinking, as these are inherently mathematical dispositions and skills (see Chapters 2 and 3). For this to happen effectively, children need to have access, all the time, to high-quality continuous provision, which enables them to confidently and independently control (self-regulate) their own play, thinking and talk, and, importantly, set (and take) their own next steps without always being reliant on an adult. Continuous provision plays a critical part in how children learn, supporting the three characteristics of Play and Exploration, Active Learning, Creating and Thinking Critically, and their integral aspects, all of which contribute to the development of mastery orientation, which will be investigated much further in Chapter 3.

Our thoughts were that exemplary continuous provision should work as the 'third teacher' based on the following principles:

The principles underpinning continuous provision

1. A place where we can see children's *real* understanding, embedded learning and developing thinking: *how* they are learning
2. Time, space and opportunity for child-initiated/led play, thinking and learning for children to become engrossed, involved and excited
3. Where we can often see sustained shared thinking (but only if we look using good observation)
4. Where children can replay, reflect and revise, in independent and collaborative ways, becoming self-regulated thinkers and learners
5. A place and space which inspires in creative and imaginative ways, with open-ended, creative materials
6. Where children can grow in confidence, self-belief and resilience as mathematicians
7. With adults who know when and how to sensitively intervene and 'teach' using a range of strategies, including playful teaching (Ofsted, 2015, p. 5)

Continuous provision is not something that is there as a time-filler to occupy children until the adult becomes available or as a reward when children have completed their 'work'. For mathematical development and learning children, both young and older (including 5- to 7-year-olds) rely on this as a place to practice, embed and develop their deep understanding of key concepts and skills. Without it, they are often rushed onto the next learning objective before consolidating the previous one. As Julie Fisher (2010, p. 134) explains:

> Continuous provision in Year 1 looks pretty much the same as it does in the Foundation Stage (it is the increased challenge

that children bring to using the resources, the increased mastery of play itself and the increase in challenge from the adults that support the play that differentiates it appropriately for older learners).

We were heavily influenced by Julie Fisher's work because it made so much sense, as we explored our own themes and questions. Could we be sure that there was progression in continuous provision, and did the adults see these opportunities to build and extend children's current levels of development and thinking? Seeing children's mathematical potential in their play from a very young age and knowing that children are born with an innate drive to be mathematical (see Chapter 2) made us begin to wonder how well this instinct or momentum to learn, find out and explore was maintained as they developed, flowing from the ground up through their motivation, eagerness and enthusiasm for learning via Playing and Exploring, Active Learning and Creating and Thinking Critically. We needed to look at how we could maintain this momentum in relation to mathematical development.

Bringing our themes and questions together

The challenge that faced us was how to use all our evidence, questions and thinking to find some answers or theories as to how young children's mathematical talk and mastery develop and are best supported by all adults. The children's learning stories continued to guide our way as we talked about what we were seeing children do in their child-initiated play and activities, *how* they were learning and what they were thinking whilst they were deeply involved in their mathematical play and inquiry. The children's mathematical momentum was clearly visible, which made us reflect on how adult-focused teaching could be woven into child-initiated play and activities.

Carruthers (2017) refers to an approach called 'Open Mathematics', which follows the same starting points as TFMM through adults "listening to understand children's mathematical meanings" who "genuinely want to know the mathematical culture that surrounds the children's thinking" and who are "constantly aware of the potential of mathematical learning and not restricting the mathematics" (p. 3).

Gradually, as described in the practitioner inquiry process in Figure 1.1, we wanted to contribute to wider thinking and practice and brought everything together into an exemplification document (Chilvers and SSELP Schools, 2017) to look more deeply into certain areas and share our findings more widely with others who work with young children.

The exemplification showed the progression and momentum of mathematical development and learning in six areas:

1. Mathematical mark-making (Chapter 6)
2. Construction

3. Sensory materials
4. Games
5. Creativity and Critical Thinking: problem-solving (Chapters 2 and 3)
6. Following children's interests (Chapters 4 and 5)

And two additional themes:

7. Floor books and documentation (Chapter 4)
8. A whole-class approach to building on the mathematical thinking in child-led interests (Chapter 5)

Each area mapped out possible lines of progression to maintain the momentum of children's mathematical development and learning, starting with 2-year-olds. It is important to note that we were very aware that mathematical development does not begin at 2 years of age. Developmental psychology shows that newborn babies can distinguish elements of shape and pattern and have innate 'numerosity' as they are drawn to objects, patterns and sequences (see Chapter 2). However, some of the schools had 2-year-olds in their Foundation Stage, which is why we needed to look more closely at the development of mathematical thinking and understanding at this age.

The six areas were framed under four headings, all focusing on the child's perspective:

> **The Child's Perspective** (I like to learn by . . .)
> **The Role of the Adult** (You can support my mathematical thinking by . . .)
> **The Enabling Environment and Continuous Provision** (To develop and extend my learning, I need . . .)
> **The Home Learning Partnership** (My home learning helps me when . . .)

Each area is informed by children's learning stories across the age ranges, illustrating their mathematical talking, thinking, learning, understanding and mastery. They make the link between theory and practice, highlighting the connection to the characteristics of effective learning (Playing and Exploring, Active Learning and Creating and Thinking Critically), schematic development, sustained shared thinking and mathematical mastery. Examples from the exemplification are included throughout this book.

As we worked together to shape the exemplification, we came to a clearer understanding of the way in which children engage in mathematical talking, thinking and learning through their child-initiated play and how we can best support, teach and extend this learning. We were able to look more deeply into the meaning of mathematical mastery and what this actually involved with young children. This was not a neat process, as children's development is far from linear, but once we started looking, reflecting, discussing and thinking from the children's perspective, it became much clearer, as the following chapters explain.

Summary

Undertaking a professional development initiative has many advantages, especially when you are part of a group of people working together in the form of a learning community. There are many benefits for everyone involved, particularly the children. This chapter has shown through the TFMM case study and following the process of practitioner inquiry how engaging in action research and reflecting on practice can lead to many positive outcomes, including:

- deepening practitioner/teacher's knowledge, understanding and experience of children's mathematical development and learning
- seeing young children's early education from a broader and more informed perspective, based on theoretical principles, research and evidence from a wide range of sources
- taking time to 'stop and think', reflect on practice with others in large or small groups, which increases professional confidence and the leadership of exceptional early years practice
- ensuring that young children's early education and mathematical experiences are relevant, finely tuned to their needs, interests and developmental momentum

Note

1. Remember that the schools had taken 2-year-olds into the Foundation Stage, which is why we began here. See Chapter 2.

2 Maintaining the momentum of children's mathematical development

DI CHILVERS

This chapter focuses on children's mathematical development from birth, looking at the complex ways in which their talking, thinking and understanding unfolds through play and exploration and being active learners. Understanding mathematical development is a fundamental part of working with young children and a professionally informed skill which supports and extends children's mathematical momentum. However, young children's development is not a neat and tidy process but more of a weaving together of developmental theories, research and pedagogy which connect in many ways and are not just mathematically related. This chapter explores some of them, including:

- what we mean by 'learning momentum'
- maintaining momentum, a mathematical journey – babies, toddlers and older children
- mathematical talking and thinking
- schema and mathematical development
- how schema underpin children's mathematical concepts
- embodied learning and mathematical development
- spatial reasoning and mathematical development

Through our observations and the learning stories, we could clearly see children's innate motivation, curiosity, reasoning and problem solving as they played and talked together. This strong intrinsic drive to make sense of everything that they experienced was visible in the youngest of children as they researched how to balance bricks, line up the animals in the right order or follow a rhythm beating on a basket (see the example of Jacob in Figure 2.1). Gopnik et al., in their in-depth work *How Babies Think* (1999), talk about children's "drive to understand the world in its purest form" saying: "Human children in the first three years of life are consumed by a desire to explore and experiment with objects" (pp. 85–6).

We frequently talked about maintaining children's natural developmental momentum from the minute they are born and ensuring that we recognised

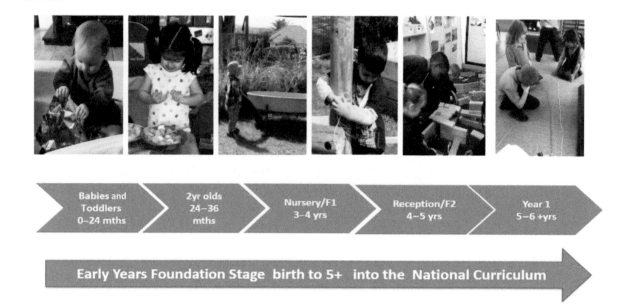

Figure 2.1 Maintaining children's learning momentum

this by tuning into their thinking – supporting, building and extending without slowing them down or coming to a halt. In our heads, we imagined going up the escalator together, starting from the ground, going upwards rather than coming at them from the opposite direction or the 'top down'. The question we asked was:

> How do we make sure that we maintain the momentum of children's mathematical development and learning from 2 years[1] old to 6+ (Y1), building firm foundations on children's starting points?

When you observe a child's developmental momentum, it is clear that the direction of travel begins at birth, with their starting points, wherever they are, and builds from there (see Figure 2.1). This is the natural evolutionary process of children's development, where new thinking and learning connect to existing understanding, making strong links between each aspect until they are fully mastered and not the other way around, i.e. from the top down! Fisher's (2016) work summed up our thinking:

> By tuning in to the child's thinking, the practitioner is helped to focus on the right subject matter, to follow the connections that the child is making in their thinking, and to respond appropriately with conversational turns that maintain the child's learning momentum.
> (p. 79)

What do we mean by 'learning momentum'?

Fisher (2016, p. 79) uses the term *learning momentum* to describe how adults keep the child's talking and thinking flowing, by tuning into where they are, seamlessly supporting and extending their learning in a collaborative partnership rather than taking over. Jill, the teacher in Go Compare, is doing just this as she observes the children and then asks, "Can you order them from the longest to the shortest?" (see Chapter 6). We then see how, through the use of a possibility question,[2] the children's learning momentum gathers pace and excitement. Teaching is responsive in that the child's momentum is maintained and developed through a 'serve and return' approach often leading to sustained shared thinking.

Learning momentum also applies to the longer-term view of children's development (as shown in Figure 2.1) beginning the moment a child is born and starts to experience the world around them – they are learning all the time. As we talked about children's developmental momentum, we began to see how crucial it was for the adults to maintain this through the transition of pedagogy, supporting children's next steps and progression in appropriate ways and building on what has come before. Particularly important is to ensure that there is continuity as children move from one setting/room/key person to another, especially when they transfer into a new key stage such as Year 1 of the National Curriculum. It is about making sure that the adults do not drop the *baton*, causing children's development to slow down or even stop.

For example, a discussion about number lines helped our thinking and understanding of the *transition of pedagogy* and making the links across children's mathematical development, ensuring that the next steps of learning and teaching build on the children's current understanding and support their progression in appropriate ways:

The number line discussion – the transition of pedagogy

The discussion began as a result of the following gap task:

> **Gap Task...**
>
> Take an aspect of continuous provision e.g. water/sand play, construction, malleable materials, role play etc and.....
>
> Observe how the children are playing from the youngest to the oldest (child-led play/activities)......document what you see and what the children are doing and saying particularly focusing on mathematical development and the Characteristics of Effective Learning;
>
> How is the play different for the children?
> What do you do to support the children and build on their current play?
> How do you make the continuous provision meet the needs of all your children from the youngest to the oldest?
> What does this tell you about continuous provision?

In the discussion that followed, one of the TFMM partners had considered the use of meaningful number lines in continuous provision which really stretched thinking and understanding about children's development, especially when we posed the question, "What would a number line look like for a 2-year-old?" The partners needed to understand what came before the children were 2 years old, in the first 24 months of a child's life, and all the earlier experiences of 'number lines' they had encountered as they played and explored. This momentum had to be maintained when the children came in to school to make sure that the progression of development and the continuum of learning was connected, gradually becoming more complex, stretching children's thinking through the zone of proximal development rather than being repeated as they move from class to class (see the examples in Figure 2.2).

	At 9 months, Jacob is matching the pattern of the drumbeats that Emily is modelling as they play together. His learning is embodied through his physical actions as he tunes into the rhythm and sequence of the beat, focusing on Emily, listening and copying. He starts to say "ba, ba, ba", following Emily's voice as she says, "bounce, bounce, bounce". The beat becomes internalised and builds from a simple tapping to a pattern of beats one after the other. Clapping is another embodied way of following a sequence or pattern.
	Elsie at 2 years old was playing with the wooden bricks. Building towers of different heights, she said "This one is getting really big". Her Mum talks about them being "tall towers". After lots of playing, building towers and then knocking them down, her brother Henry joins in as a play partner. He shows her how to build the towers (a vertical line) and make a row adding one more brick each time from one to four (horizontal line). Elsie's thinking is supported by Henry and her Mum, and she becomes focused on the number of bricks in each tower, counting them and adding a chick in a basket on each one.

Figure 2.2 Maintaining learning momentum with number lines

Figure 2.2 (*Continued*)

	The children in the nursery class had been reading the story of *Spinderella* (Donaldson, 2016) and had become interested in counting. They counted themselves in a line, then the wellington boots (in pairs and in a line), and designed a game using a line of plastic outdoor markers with chalked numbers next to them. Jamil said he was keeping score by making a line for each point as a tally and then adding them up to 3. Other children had drawn a number track to calculate the total, which was 18.
	Callum and Joey (in Reception) have been playing with the dough, carefully making footballs and lining them up. "We got to line the footballs up ready for the goalie," says Callum. "Yeah he's got to get them in the order so he can save them," replies Joey. As the play progresses, the boys decide that it would be helpful for the goalie to number each ball. They fetch the wooden numbers but run out at 10. The problem is quickly sorted out as they find paper, scissors and felt pens to make the missing numbers, as their number line develops (Read the full story in Chapter 3).
	In Go Compare (read the full story in Chapter 6), Bailey and his friends are busy making Superworms after studying the story (Donaldson, 2012). They line the worms up next to each other and talk about them being "level" and start to order them as suggested by the teacher. They talk at an abstract level about order, length, reoccurring patterns and make comparisons using their prior knowledge and understanding. The children co-construct their mathematical thinking together and use complex language. Bailey's reflections on his mathematical thinking and learning show how he has really mastered these concepts.

Reflection point

Talk together with colleagues about the developmental progression of the number lines and how they support children's mathematical understanding of number.

How does Jacob's interest in rhythm and beating a pattern help him to become involved in counting and understanding number?

How does Elsie's play and interest in building towers show her mathematical thinking? What kind of maths is she engaged in?

Come back to this reflection point after reading the whole chapter, especially Figure 8 Schema into concepts. What can you see happening in the children's play as it progresses to the more abstract mathematical thinking in Go Compare?

Helpful number line tips

- Number lines should reflect children's interests. They should be displayed at child height and include the children's interpretations of the numbers in different forms
- A blank number line can be displayed with numerals, pictures and other materials for children to create their own
- Number lines in the construction area reflect children's interests, e.g. dinosaurs, tall buildings
- Make interactive number lines/boards available
- Number lines at child height with photos of children which might include photographs of children showing the number of fingers starting from zero
- Ask the children which themed number lines they would like – encourage them to help create a number line, give ownership, e.g. Peppa Pig, Spiderman
- Provide children with as many open-ended creative materials, both indoors and outdoors (can be a on a much larger scale) and observe as they play. How do they use the materials? Do they line up and order materials? This could be the start of a number line!
- Read stories and sing songs which all connect in some way to making a number line, e.g. 'Five Little Speckled Frogs' and *Spinderella*

Maintaining momentum, a mathematical journey . . .

In TFMM, we viewed children as inherently mathematical from birth; competent and capable and full of potential rather than taking a view of the child waiting to be instructed into the adult-led world of mathematics though a narrow set of knowledge presented in a prescribed, linear programme of learning to be acquired by a certain age. This shift in perspective makes the practitioner much more aware of *how* children are thinking, making their learning visible, including what they bring from home and their 'funds of knowledge'(Chesworth, 2016) drawn from their everyday lives in their family and community.

Mathematical babies – developmental momentum

Even before babies are born, their brains are busy developing, especially in the final trimester, when they become more aware of all kinds of sounds and rhythms, including the pattern of sounds and intonation of the mother's voice and heartbeat. This all becomes stored in the memory ready to be retrieved through positive attachment, attunement and communication outside the womb when they are born (Karmiloff-Smith, 1994; Trevarthen, 2018).

As newborn babies, they instinctively seek eye contact, and faces become very important, so much so that when they are shown paddles with spots arranged in the pattern of a face, they consistently show preference to this by looking longer and gazing. It is this innate patterning, whether visual, auditory or sensory, that provides the deep foundations on which to build. For example, we see how Jacob (in Figure 2.3) is continuing to show a deep interest in rhythms and sound patterns by following the adult and copying her exact beats on the basket.

Figure 2.3 Jacob following a rhythmical pattern

Babies are also experts at mouthing everything that comes into their grasp in the first weeks and months of life. What they are doing here is mouthing the texture, size and shape of objects, playing and exploring and beginning to recognise the qualities and attributes of these objects. Babies' brains are at their busiest in this sensitive period between birth and 2 years old, absorbing every experience, making connections and building their brain architecture (Harvard University, Center on the Developing Child, https://developingchild.harvard.edu/science/key-concepts/brain-architecture/).

Gopnik, Meltzoff and Khul (1999) refer to babies as 'scientists in the crib,' as they have a similar exploratory drive to experiment, find out, test and create theories in order to learn, which is why play is so critical for young children. In fact, the relationship between science and mathematics is a strong one:

> A key aspect of our developmental picture is that babies are actively engaged in looking for patterns in what is going on around them, in testing hypotheses, and in seeking explanations. They aren't just amorphous blobs that are stamped by evolution or shaped by their environment or moulded by adults.
>
> (p. 152)

Babies are great thinkers. They notice things about themselves and others and become fascinated in hands, fingers, toes, eyes, noses etc. Fingers and toes are their first mathematical tools to which they and the adults around them pay great attention, counting toes and fingers, singing rhymes, clapping, kicking legs and feet, taking first steps and jumps. All these everyday interactions involve mathematical talking and thinking, which become more complex as the baby asks, verbally or otherwise, for 'more' or 'again'. In fact, mathematics becomes one of the children's "One hundred languages" (Malaguzzi in Edwards, Gandini and Forman, 1998) an integral part of their play, communication, talk and thinking, rather than something which is disconnected and taken out of context.

Other contextual mathematical experiences for babies and toddlers happen throughout the day, including regular routines following each other in sequence; becoming aware of the spaces around them; exploring materials and textures; beginning to learn about cause and effect, e.g. dropping the toy for you to pick up and hidey-boo (both early serve and return games); testing out how far they need to stretch to grasp the toy and communicating their feelings if they can't; learning to eat small chunks of banana or peas one at a time; listening to the language around them, e.g. "Just one more spoonful then it's all gone!" There are so many rich experiences that we would not necessarily associate with becoming mathematical, but that is what they are, the initial small steps all contributing to building their learning momentum.

Reflection point

Take some time to observe babies in their first 12 months.
Watch what they are doing, their actions, movements, facial expressions and interests.
Listen to their voices, communication, expressions and feelings.
How are they playing? What is happening as they are exploring? Think about how the babies' actions, communication and interests have their roots in early mathematical development.

Mathematical toddlers – developmental momentum

As babies become toddlers, learning to walk and talk, their developmental momentum is working at full speed with huge potential and opportunities for learning. Child development is not a neat and tidy process, as every child will do this in their own unique way. This is why young children are so interesting and also why a predetermined set of outcomes in a scheme of work or programme will not support their learning in the same way as bespoke interactions with practitioners who skilfully observe, model, encourage, communicate and talk. Babies and toddlers construct their early mathematical thinking and knowledge primarily through interaction with the adults around them and their environment, although there are some actions which appear to be innate as we can see with Leo in his explorations with the trucks.

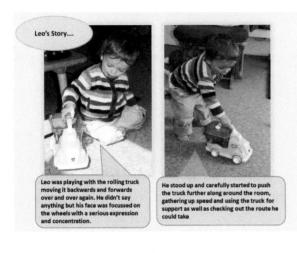

Leo's Story....

Leo was playing with the rolling truck moving it backwards and forwards over and over again. He didn't say anything but his face was focussed on the wheels with a serious expression and concentration.

He stood up and carefully started to push the truck further along around the room, gathering up speed and using the truck for support as well as checking out the route he could take

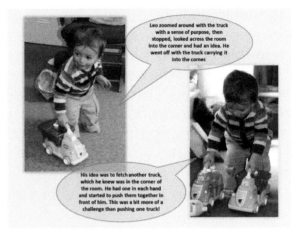

Leo zoomed around with the truck with a sense of purpose, then stopped, looked across the room into the corner and had an idea. He went off with the truck carrying it into the corner.

His idea was to fetch another truck, which he knew was in the corner of the room. He had one in each hand and started to push them together in front of him. This was a bit more of a challenge than pushing one truck!

He levelled up the trucks to give him more balance and with deep concentration, tongue out, and careful precision he transported the two trucks forwards and back across the room, looking for more space and turning when he needed to.

What did we see?

Leo has been toddling confidently for a few weeks and is steadier on his feet; he really likes to push something along and particularly chooses the pram and the trucks. We think Leo has a trajectory and transporting schema as we have seen this frequently in his play – he also likes to push the pram.

He had an idea a few days ago to use two trucks together and keeps practicing this getting more proficient and confident at keeping the trucks in line and pushing them along.

He suddenly seems to have an idea, you can see this in his face through his expression, and then he is on a mission to find what he needs and follow it through. He has set his own challenge and sets about solving the problem through his play. He becomes very involved in this and spends up to 15 minutes concentrating, being absorbed and not easily distracted.

It seems like all his energy goes on this and he doesn't say very much at all but you can see him communicating his ideas through his actions and facial expression. His creative and critical thinking is clear as he tests his idea, uses cause and effect to trial his movements and balance and changes his strategy along the way taking into account balance, special awareness and direction

Further possibilities for Leo?

Leo has an interest in trajectories and transporting so we could try the following with him,

- Rolling balls down guttering or drain pipes
- Using the wind-up cars and trains to provoke more interest and ideas
- Use larger sit on trucks outside for Leo to push along with his legs and feet
- We also need to encourage Leo to talk about his ideas and express his thoughts, so we could try the following,
  - Model possible language whilst playing alongside Leo and making a commentary on what he is doing
  - Show Leo his story of the trucks and 'read' it to him. Listen to his responses and record what he says
  - Sing some action rhymes with him that have up and down movements e.g. incey, wincy, spider

This informed review of Leo's development and learning documents his progress, recognising that he has become more confident in his walking and that he likes to play with wheeled toys, repeatedly pushing them from one point to another at various speeds. His key person, having observed his play regularly, thinks that he is showing a trajectory and transporting schema and that he may even be interested in the rotation of the wheels (see section Schema and mathematical development).

Leo's play tells us a good deal about his mathematical thinking and his complex ideas as he:

- follows his own ideas which appear to be rooted in schematic patterns of thinking (see section Schema and mathematical development)
- problem sets and problem solves
- makes his own decisions about what to do next and how to do it
- uses reasoning, trial and error (cause and effect) and persists even if it doesn't work
- experiences spatial awareness (see section Schema and mathematical development), movement in space, fast and slow, direction, stopping and starting
- actively engages in play-based, hands-on, concrete, real-world, contextual experiences, which build his understanding and "*working theories*" (Wood, 2019)
- shows his own "*funds of knowledge*" and has a "*sense of agency*" which builds his confidence, self-belief and intrinsic motivation (Wood, 2019). "Children's funds of knowledge in their play are sources and areas of knowledge, that have movement and direction over time" (Chesworth, 2016)

Chapter 3 explores these ideas in depth and how they all contribute to the development of mathematical mastery and mastery orientation.

Mathematical young children – developmental momentum

What became clear from the many observations and learning stories undertaken during the TFMM initiative was that children's development was not a neatly ordered, linear process of learning one thing and then another as part of a prescribed programme. A narrow *one-size-fits-all* approach to teaching mathematics (or any other area of learning) does not meet the complex, developmental momentum of children under the age of 60 months, where the model of their learning is more like *spaghetti* interwoven, connected and messy; which is completely normal and pedagogically known as holistic development (see Chapter 7, 'How do adults support children's mathematical talk, thinking and mastery?').

What all young children require is a more bespoke approach to teaching mathematics which is informed by observing their current unique experience, skills and understanding and developing this through providing a rich, play-based curriculum, enabling environment, authentic real-life experiences and experienced adults, who support them to make the connections between their concrete, action-led play and exploration. Then they will gradually progress into a more abstract world of internalised thinking, symbolic representation and "sophisticated understanding" which involves "making sense of and using mathematics across physical, imagined, spatial, numerical, quantitative, particular and general contexts" (Thom, 2017, p. 17).

Figure 2.2 and Figure 2.8 (Schema into concepts) outline this developmental progression in detail, along with the children's learning stories included in this book. For example, we see Jacob, Dylan and Leo (this chapter) and Peyton (Chapter 6) actively learning in the here and now (concrete), whilst Bailey and his friends in Go Compare (Chapter 6) are working at a complex, abstract level showing their conceptual understanding of comparison; and Daisy, in One Is a Snail Ten Is a Crab (Chapter 8), uses resources to make her own equations including multiplication!

The observations and learning stories throughout this book show how young children, through a combination of following their interests and ideas in their child-initiated play, supported by informed, appropriate teaching, have crossed the bridge into mastery orientation. These aspects of development are unpicked in depth in Chapter 3, 'What does mathematical mastery mean for young children?'

Figure 2.4 Rainbows Nursery poses the question for their own reflections by asking, "Can you see the maths talk?"

Mathematical talk – maintaining the momentum

Children, including babies and toddlers, have many ways of communicating their mathematical ideas and interests, not just through talk but through their languages of expression, action, emotion and especially through the universal language of play (Chilvers, 2019, The Observation Tool Kit p. 29, https://watchmegrow.uk/observation-toolkit/).

The examples of the children in this chapter and throughout the book clearly demonstrate the creativity of children to communicate their thoughts and actions. They love language, especially mathematical vocabulary, which is expressive, imaginative and interesting. For example, a pumpkin or a turnip is not just 'big' or 'large'; it is 'enormous', 'giant', 'huge', 'massive', 'humongous', 'gargantuan', 'mammoth', 'colossal' and even 'titanic'. These are words which spark an interest and lead to mathematical 'serve and return' conversations and sustained shared thinking (all explained in Chapter 3).

Mathematical thinking and learning often create a language of their own, related to names, actions and abstract processes, such as addition, subtraction and multiplication. Children need to fully understand the deep meaning and processes of these terms in order to master them. For example, to understand what the symbol '5' or word 'five' really means, children have to be fully cognisant of the *fiveness of five* where they can recognise the quantity of 5 in any form (conservation of number), change the order (order irrelevance) and explain what happens if you take something away or add another one (addition and subtraction). It is a complex shift in children's thinking (see Figure 2.8) which is supported through plenty of meaningful play (baking, shopping, games, collage, box modelling, construction play etc.); conversations with one another and adults; real-life experiences and songs, rhymes, poems and stories, including their own learning stories.

The *Zero Project* at Puss in Boots Nursery, Camden, began after Iva, the Deputy Head, became involved in a Talk for Maths Mastery initiative which focused on the following question: "What kind of talk supports children's mathematical development?" She created an exploration table (Figure 2.5), and the children's talk flowed through using carefully posed, possibility questions by the adults, leading to a lot of inspired talking and thinking.

Iva asked the children: "Who knows what is zero?"
Max: "Zero is the end of all numbers".
Lucas: "No, it is a beginning of all numbers".
Fabian: "Zero is nothing".
Elan: "Less than zero is −1 and 1 is one bigger than zero".
Josie: "Zero looks like O [the letter]".
Lucas: "Zero is before 1".
Iva asked the children: "If I have zero friends what does it mean?"
William: "You are lonely. . . . "Don't you have really any friends, Iva?"

Figure 2.5 Exploration table

Iva: "I have many friends; I have all of you. Is zero friends a lot or not?"
William: "It means no friends!"
William counted loud for himself: "1, 2, 3, 4, 5, 6, 7, 8, 9 . . . I have 9 friends. How many friends do you have, Iva?"
Iva: "I have 7 friends [showing fingers]".
William: "I have much more than you".

Conversational talk, such as this, is embedded in real-life meaningful encounters where children can confidently express their thinking, draw on their own experiences and hypothesise, without being worried about getting it wrong or making a mistake. This early resilience, where young children will 'have a go' and persist at something, even if it is challenging, is a lifelong, positive disposition, which, along with confidence and self-belief, is fundamental to later mathematical development and learning (see Chapter 3).

Talking and thinking

It may seem obvious to say that children's talk is directly connected to their thinking, as cognitive development and language development grow simultaneously, rather like the individual threads in a rope spiralling around each other to make one strong, continuous length. However, this can often be missed, especially if adults are only looking for superficial evidence of learning, e.g. can count to 10 (which can be easily memorised by children) rather than deep understanding, where children communicate in other ways, e.g. through their play or through explanation, as we saw with the children talking about zero. What is needed is to observe children and listen to them through the powerful combination of:

Child-led play + Talk/interaction + Experiences + Time + Adults = Opportunities to think

For example, Bailey, at 5 years old, gave us great insight into his mathematical thinking as he reflected on his interest in making comparisons after some previous work on *Superworm!* (see Chapter 6 for the full learning story). This is what he said:

> All year I have been making things out of paper, sellotape and string. I know you have to make things the right size. If you want to change the size you can, but you do have to compare. I know that to make my worm the longest I need to know how long Carrigan's is. I can only know that if I compare it. But I remember you showed me how to make things level. Today I remembered myself.

Bailey's profound thoughts tell us a great deal about his knowledge, understanding and enjoyment of maths (and many other aspects of his learning) and his ability to articulate his thinking. He viewed his learning as an exciting challenge, a problem to be solved (having set it in the first place) through using his previous knowledge and discussing it with his friends in their collaborative, child-led play.

We can see how he has communicated his thinking through using open-ended materials like string and explaining his methods in a logical, reasoned way without worrying if he was wrong. These are all deep-level dispositions and skills which show how he has confidently mastered concepts around comparison, measurement and representation (see Chapter 3).

Schemas and mathematical development

Adults, as they observe children in their child-led play, will often recognise some repeatable patterns of actions (sometimes called behaviours) which give us an insight into their thinking (cognitive structures). This is the case with Leo, in his previous learning story, and the examples that follow, where we may see children keenly interested in everything which spins and turns, including the washing machine (rotation); or wrapping themselves in blankets, hiding in cardboard boxes (enclosure or envelopment), all *action schema*: or drawing circles, curves and spirals as we see with Peyton's *figurative schema* in Chapter 6.

What are schemas?

> Schemas are a form of thought that relate to cognitive structures. They are like pieces of ideas or concepts. Patterns in

children's actions, or in their drawings and paintings, indicate common themes or threads (schemas) of thinking running through them.

(Meade and Cubey, 2008, p. 3)

Athey (1990) clarifies this complex thinking in action as:

A pattern of repeatable behaviour into which experiences are assimilated and that are gradually coordinated. Coordinations lead to higher-level and more powerful schemas.

(p. 50)

This is an innate process of cognitive development, with the earliest schematic actions occurring when babies gaze and track people and as they mouth objects at a sensorimotor level (Piaget) through their bodily senses, actions and movements. Babies' instinctual serve and return behaviour, as they communicate face to face with an adult, taking turns (tracking eye and facial movements) is all part of this early schematic development which paves the way for more complex actions to grow.

As babies become more mobile and begin to crawl and walk, their world expands, and there is more to explore, investigate and find out, as Leo discovers. At this point, children are on a mission to make sense of everything that they encounter through their play and explorations. This is their research, gathering together 'bits and pieces', discovering how things work, their properties and making sense of them; they are *assimilating* new experiences and thinking in their brains. As they 'fit' the pieces together they *accommodate* new learning into their existing understanding, but this takes time and continues at different levels of development as children's learning becomes more complex.

It is crucial not to rush past this process of active learning as this is where the roots of mathematical development are taking hold, where actions become internalised, gradually becoming grouped together, connected and coordinated as they make sense, providing the foundational groundwork for later conceptual understanding and mastery. For example, as Leo continues his explorations into trajectories (horizontal and vertical straight lines) and transporting (moving things from one place to another), he is gradually coming to understand concepts of length, distance, spatial awareness, speed, motion, direction, time, pattern, order, angles, sequencing and weight. This can lead to the more complex conceptual understanding we see with Bailey and his friends in the Go Compare learning story in Chapter 6.

This foundational thinking in action is supported and extended through play, particularly *child-led play*, in *enabling environments* which are flexible and provide open-ended creative materials with many possibilities. A further factor is *talk*, especially serve and return conversations between adults and children (see above). With this combination of experience and support, children's schemas, over a period of time, become more sophisticated, moving from the concrete (motor or action level) to abstract, internalised thinking in their heads (brains). See how schema develop into concepts below in Figure 2.8.

What are action schemas?

> Action schema interests lead progressively to understanding about places and things, such as relationships and orientation of objects in space.
>
> (Meade and Cubey, 2008, p. 140)

Action schemas are clearly evident in Jacob's, Elsie's, Leo's and Dylan's play in this chapter; where the children are repeating their patterns of actions (physically) in their child-initiated play. This needs to be observed as a reoccurring, repeatable pattern, theme or thread of thinking which can happen anywhere, at any time in a variety of different situations. Importantly, this occurs most frequently in child-initiated play and can sometimes be mistaken for repetitive, aimless play or even as disruptive behaviour. For example, Katie, who has written Chapter 4, explained a 'problem' she was having with most of the boys who had only been in the nursery for a term. They were constantly moving materials/equipment from one side of the room to another in significant quantities and leaving it in piles. Tidy up time was becoming a challenge as they did not want to clear up the piles of materials that they had transported. This was repeated over several weeks. What Katie was explaining here was a group phenomenon where all the boys had strong transporting schemas which they kept repeating and applying to other aspects of their play most days.

Having shared this with the TFMM group, we started to look at how schematic patterns of behaviour were connected to mathematical development and learning. Katie talked with the children about their actions and what they could do together to move the play on into other aspects of trajectories, preferably ones that involved tidying up! They created a wonderful story based on the children's schematic patterns of play and called it 'The Room That Moved! The Story of a Classroom on the Move' (https://diamondclassfs1.wordpress.com/?s=The+Room+that+moved) (also see Chapter 4).

What are figurative schema?

Young children also express their schematic thinking through other representational forms such as painting, drawing, box modelling, sculptures in clay and dough (visual art) and through physical movements, dancing and music (physical arts). Athey (2007), after many years of studying children's play through observation, referred to this as children having 'figurative schemas' where they represented their thinking in many ways, a point Malaguzzi made strongly in his poem, 'The One Hundred Languages of Children' (Edwards, Gandini and Forman 1998).

Figure 2.6 George at 3.4 years old has carefully painted parallel lines, dots and circles in specific places which at first glance look like a pattern. When asked about his painting, he describes a busy junction that his mum uses when they come home in the car. The circle is the roundabout and the lines form the roads that intersect, with the dots being the road markings. This is all formed from a 'birds-eye' perspective above the roundabout which featured in other paintings, drawings and construction (see 'Embodied Learning and mathematical Development' and 'What Is Spatial Reasoning?').

Figure 2.7 Keeley and Ruby had spent all morning in the box modelling corner, having found a sturdy box which they covered and decorated. As they chatted together, the box became a boat which needed a carpet.

They embarked on cutting small paper shapes to make the carpet, making sure that they all fitted together and none of the box was visible. This involved a mosaic of interconnected pieces (tessellations) which took a long time to complete. This *infilling*, *connecting* and *enclosure* was a cluster of schemas which came together in *transforming* the box through a *complex, figurative* schema.

Thank goodness the adult had not suggested using a ruler to measure the space and cut one piece, as so much thinking, talking and learning would have been lost. This wasn't the time for adult intervention – it was time to observe.

The children's representations are dominated by patterns, actions and sequences that they have experienced and embodied (as discussed later in the chapter) through their play and other experiences. For example, Milo is representing his figurative thinking through the lines and grids he has created with the ruler; Dylan through his dots using the cotton buds and paint; Aadam (Chapter 6) is figuratively representing his whole story and imaginative thinking through patterns, drawing and writing which he then explains, "This line means half," and "Slow car and a long car on the road"; and Meryam (Chapter 6) comes to grips with her explanation of difference between 2D and 3D shapes.

Children's figurative schema representations become increasingly complex as they become woven into more abstract, symbolic thinking particularly related to mathematical understanding. David Yates explores this much further in Chapter 6, where:

> Figurative schema interests lead progressively to understanding symbolic representations – in drawing, constructions and written language.
>
> (Meade and Cubey, 2008, p. 139)

Reflection point

So how do schemas and children's threads of thinking connect to their mathematical development and learning?

> If you have a rich array of things that children can explore their interest with, then you will naturally get into mathematics and science. If you're trying to put a number of things in a small container and it's full, then you're getting the concept of fullness. Concepts of volume and capacity are taught more formally later, but these are the early and fun beginnings of those discoveries.
>
> (Nutbrown, https://famly.co/blog, accessed October 2019)

Can you see the connection as children play with water and sand pouring, filling and emptying (containment and enclosure) or the flow of water as it shoots from the hose pipe (trajectories)?

Think about horizontal, vertical and diagonal trajectories, and observe the children in construction play or outdoor play. Can you see the maths?

Clare Richmond at Rainbows Nursery in Camden captures Dylan's (2.11 years) schematic and mathematical thinking perfectly in this learning story. As Dylan lines up his figures (trajectories) and matches them into pairs (connecting), he then figuratively interprets the 'twoness' of the pairs by using the cotton buds to represent them stomping along. At the same time, he talks about what he is doing and his thinking.

Two by two......

Dylan sits down and lines up the figures he has been carrying, "Hulk, Hulk, Batman and Batman, Spiderman and Spiderman.

I comment that he has 2 of each, "They match" Dylan replies.

He moves the figures, so they pair up opposite each other.

Dylan takes a cotton bud and dips it into the ink and makes a series of marks, "Stomp, stomp, stomp". He then takes 2 cotton buds at a time and makes double marks.

Dylan talks quietly to himself, "There were lots of dinosaurs they go RAAAA"

He spontaneously shows me his fingers, "1,2,3,4,5" he counts.

What do we see?

Dylan's ongoing love of dinosaurs has expanded to include superhero characters; he is often to be found playing with these small world figures. Dylan shows real attention to detail –selective of the figures he has chosen to carry around. Dylan showed intention and care in the marks he made with an awareness of 'matching' and 1:1 correspondence (2 feet- 2 marks and 5 fingers-5 counts). Dylan has a rich imagination and develops storylines and narratives where he is increasingly able to express in words.

What we might do next

Provide a range of small world figures for Dylan to play with. We will support and document Dylan's narratives and provide a range of media and materials to make marks with. We will offer Dylan different objects to sort and match (e.g. the the 'gogo' figures.

Lachi (4.7 years) has been involved in sorting and classifying his beloved wild animals, lining them up in compatible groups based on his thinking and chosen criteria, e.g.:

- Lions, tigers, leopards and cheetahs all positioned facing the same direction
- Giraffes clustered together
- Elephants and rhinoceros lined up and facing in the same direction as the big cats
- Zebras in their own enclosure
- Sealions in their own enclosure with added sea to swim
- A stray ostrich (behind the cats but also facing in the same direction) and a kangaroo (with the giraffes)

How interesting it would be to talk to him about his reasoning for these groups. Why are they all facing the same way? Will all the cats get on together – are they all the same? Why is the ostrich next to the lions?

We need to wait for the right moment to ask such questions. However, simply saying, "How interesting. What is happening with your animals?" gives Lachi the space to share his thinking in his own way and will probably be a wonderful catalyst for sustained shared thinking through a serve and return conversation.

Milo uses the ruler while drawing roads on large sheets on the floor. "Look I can make straight lines" he tells his friends as he lines up the ruler and draws along it. "I can be the person who draws straight lines, I am the straight line person. "Do you need a straight line across that road?" he asks a friend.

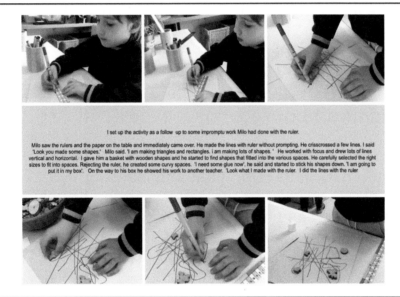

I set up the activity as a follow up to some impromptu work Milo had done with the ruler.

Milo saw the rulers and the paper on the table and immediately came over. He made the lines with ruler without prompting. He crisscrossed a few lines. I said 'Look you made some shapes.' Milo said. 'I am making triangles and rectangles. i am making lots of shapes.' He worked with focus and drew lots of lines vertical and horizontal. I gave him a basket with wooden shapes and he started to find shapes that fitted into the various spaces. He carefully selected the right sizes to fit into spaces. Rejecting the ruler, he created some curvy spaces. 'I need some glue now', he said and started to stick his shapes down. 'I am going to put it in my box'. On the way to his box he showed his work to another teacher. 'Look what I made with the ruler. I did the lines with the ruler

Milo's (4 years) interest in rulers and straight lines show how his complex figurative schematic thinking is developing. Astrid at Ready Steady Go! Pre-School in Camden, has observed and documented his fascination so that they can discuss this together, share it with the other children and his parents.

Milo's creative and critical thinking is in full swing as he makes the links between his ruler patterns crossing (bisecting, diagonals) each other in different directions and all types of spaces being revealed in between.

Astrid offers a possible next step with the basket of wooden shapes which Milo takes up, looking for small objects to carefully position in some of the spaces.

The intentionality of his actions and thinking show how he is mastering a range of concepts in unique and creative ways.

Soraya was inspired by Milo's ruler skills and began to have her own ideas. She drew vertical lines: "Look there is a square. Now I make a line and it turns the square into rectangles". She kept on working until she had created a grid with rectangles and began to fill them in with the wooden shapes.

What do schemas tell us about young children's mathematical thinking?

- How children think and structure their knowledge and understanding (cognitive structures) and the accumulative coordination of schemas as they build on firm foundations
- How they make sense of the world and the ways in which they need to do this through play, opportunities to explore, time to explore, time to experiment, time to revisit and repeat things
- The importance of Playing and Exploring, Active Learning and Creating and Thinking Critically – the characteristics of effective learning (see Appendix 6)
- Many underpinning mathematical structures which develop the brain 'architecture' for future complex processes
- Skilled problem setters and problem solvers from the beginning
- Logical thinking processes including reasoning, testing, checking, trying out, replaying and repeating thinking and ideas (meta-cognition)

These are all dispositions which underpin mastery orientation (see Chapter 3).

What should adults do?

- Be aware of the nature of schemas, how they underpin children's cognitive and mathematical development and learning
- Observe children and look for the patterns in their thinking as they play; remember schemas can be single or clustered
- Schemas are children's earliest, abiding interests; they should lead the learning with supportive, interested and playful adults. This is the starting point . . .
- Plan for children's next steps based on their schematic interests, but keep it natural and authentic
- Provide open-ended materials which connect to children's schematic behaviour and thinking and develop it further . . .

(Also see Chapter 7.)

How do schemas underpin children's mathematical concepts?

What are concepts?

Concepts are the ideas and understanding we each have which enable us to group together objects, events and abstractions. . . .

[They are] mental models we construct to explain the world around us, which help us to deal with things and events more efficiently".

(Robson, 2006, p. 129)

A concept, in a simplistic way, can be described as a grouping together of ideas/thoughts/actions which all have a connection; a way in which experience, thinking and knowledge can be grouped or organised. For example, the concept of the colour yellow ranges through every possible shade of yellow, which we have abstractly given the collective name of being 'yellow'. Children can learn the concept of yellow quite quickly through helpful adults talking and playing, "Shall we put on your yellow wellies?" or "Let's find the bright yellow socks today?" or 'Can you find something yellow before the music stops?" Or the difference between the concepts of 'hot' and 'cold' as you talk together about drinks, food, the weather or being careful near the cooker/heater they learn the difference between the concepts of hot and cold.

Many concepts develop out of children's real-life, authentic experiences, e.g. the difference between a dog and cat, or dark (night-time) and light (daytime). As with all learning, young children need to make the connections between all these experiences, make sense of them and begin to move from the concrete and wide-ranging to the more specific and abstract, especially where mathematical concepts are concerned.

Many concepts are formed from children's earliest schematic patterns of thinking as well as through a mixture of first-hand, real-life, meaningful experiences, e.g. routines such as shopping, dinner times, bath time, bedtime; *play* and knowledge (being taught). Figure 2.8 shows how children's schematic patterns of thinking, when supported, will maintain their mathematical momentum towards developing and understanding complex concepts and abstract thinking (mastery).

Reflection point conceptual understanding

Young children can represent their conceptual understanding of mathematics in many *different, unique* ways rather than in one *prescribed* or *preferred* way, which means that adults should be aware of *how* children are making sense of their learning, through careful observation of child-initiated play, e.g. Dylan's understanding of the twoness of two or Bailey's understanding of comparison (see Chapter 6 and Go Compare) are both unique, creative ways of expressing thinking and understanding.

When you observe children in their child-initiated play, can you see and understand their conceptual understanding?

Schemas into concepts			
Children developing their schematic thinking into internalised thought and understanding			
Motor or action level	**Symbolic representational**	**Functional dependency relationships**	**Abstract thought level**
Experienced through bodily senses, actions and movements in the here and now first-hand (action schema) Repeated patterns of action in play The child's innate first interests Helping to understand about people, places and things Actions begin to group together and coordinate in the brain becoming internalised and embodied (see next section) The foundations of cognitive development and thinking	Moving action into internalised, abstract and symbolic representations, e.g. re-presenting their thinking through talk, imaginative play, child-led play; also, through painting, mark-making, construction play, box modelling (see Figure 2.5) (figurative schema) Children look for creative ways to interpret their ideas and make them visible; see Dylan Two by Two and Milo The Straight-line Person. Symbolic/imaginative play becomes even more important in supporting this shift in thinking; it underpins the abstract cognitive structures for mathematics and literacy, e.g. using number symbols and signs.	Children become aware of the "effects of their actions on objects or materials" Athey (1990, p. 70 in Nutbrown, 1999), e.g. *knowing that if I do this, then that will happen*. This is the understanding of cause and effect. This links directly to children's problem setting and problem solving. Finding a solution to a problem, e.g. Callum and Joey (Figure 2.2), in the number line example and in Numbered Footballs (see Chapter 3), realise they have run out of numbers (cause) but know how to make some more (effect)	"Where a child (children) gives a verbal account of an experience in the absence of any material or situational reminder of the original experience" (Athey, 1990, p. 68 in Nutbrown, 1999). Children are now able to "imagine small numbers of objects and perform number operations on them in their heads" (Pound, 2006, p. 25). Concepts have formed as experiences and 'cognitive structures' have developed through play, adult support and plenty of talk.

Figure 2.8 Schema into concepts

Motor or action level	Symbolic representational	Functional dependency relationships	Abstract thought level
Playing and exploring is critical at all ages to enable this dynamic process to happen		Understanding the relationship between cause and effect is fundamental to mathematical thinking and learning.	We see this in Go Compare as the children show their understanding of the complex, abstract concept of comparison – it makes sense to them. They have mastered many aspects of measurement through their child-led, collaborative play.
See Jacob and Elsie in the number line example (Figure 2.2). See Leo's learning story.	See the children in the number line example (Figure 2.2). See Dylan and Milo's learning stories.	See Callum and Joey in Numbered Footballs (Chapter 3).	See Bailey and his friends in Go Compare (Chapter 6). The children's understanding of measurement in Let's Build a House (Chapter 8). Tristan and Daisy's mathematical problem solving in One Is a Snail Ten Is a Crab (Chapter 8).

Figure 2.8 (Continued)

As children's schematic thinking develops and schema become connected and coordinated, they go on to higher levels of thinking and understanding, eventually becoming further coordinated into systems of concepts (Kant, 1724–1804; Athey, 2007). This applies across children's holistic development and learning, not just in terms of mathematics, where schema "will act as 'developmental precursor' for more elaborate mathematical understandings related to length and measurement" (Brock and Siraj-Blatchford, 2015, p. 3). They go on to say;

> The mathematics curriculum is itself an elaborate figurative schema and if educators are to understand what constitutes mathematical learning, we need to consider these schemas and not just the children's most recently acquired schemes.
>
> (p. 3)

Embodied learning and mathematical development

Earlier in this chapter, we saw how Jacob, Leo and Dylan were physically moving both on the large and fine motor scales as they played. We also discussed how the concept of a *number line* begins with actual bodily movements, such as counting steps or jumps, and how babies mouth objects so that they can *research* the shape and texture of materials/toys. Interestingly, many of our observations and learning stories involved children playing outside on a large scale, for example, playing physical games involving speed, spatial awareness and balance; construction play with enormous cardboard boxes, drapes and tarpaulins and guttering; and negotiating timed turn-taking as they raced on the bikes. As Nutbrown (1999) suggests in her extensive observations of children, "Mathematics it seems, is never far away from young children's actions" (p. 64).

It is no coincidence that young children are inherently active and that playing and exploring are prerequisites of development. But for many children in school today, learning is most often associated with sitting down at a table with paper and pencil, completely detached from the physical movement of the body, with adults who have little awareness of how this internal embodiment underpins cognitive understanding, particularly mathematics. Mathematics teaching and learning have become a sedentary, disconnected activity for younger children, lacking in possibilities, Creativity and Critical Thinking through using programmes and tests which only accept prescribed ways of working things out. Thom (2017) describes what it means for young children to be mathematical, in the following way:

> (In)formal mathematics and thinking involves the entire body of the child, not just from their neck up. Consider the potential ways that a child's walking along the perimeter of a playground engages their senses and develops their awareness and knowledge of its 'squareness' – for example, its four straight sides of equal length and four right-angles corners.
>
> (p. 20)

Thom (2017) also makes the connection here with the development of children's spatial awareness and spatial reasoning and how this underpins science, technology, engineering and mathematics (STEM) with the additional perspective of the arts (STEAM). For young children, becoming mathematical encompasses all these aspects, but only if the adults around them are aware of the connections, e.g. between shape, space and measures, number, technology, expressive arts and design and physical development (EYFS, DfE, 2017). In the Love Monster learning story (see Chapter 5), the children are involved in many of these aspects through their baking, using recipes, the logistics of shopping, designing and making invitations and ensuring everyone has a bun! (See Chapter 6.)

What is spatial reasoning?

Spatial reasoning is a skill which develops from birth in much the same way that this chapter has discussed mathematical development, starting with sensory experiences such as using the mouth, lips, tongue, eyes and smell to explore objects and moving onto embodying, owning and coordinating body parts, hands, fingers (proprioception). It then becomes more internalised and conceptual.

> As a starting point, we can describe spatial reasoning as how in the mind's eye, we see the world around us, and how we can picture, understand and manipulate the locations and relative positions of shapes, objects or processes.
>
> (Thom, 2017, p. 21)

All the fundamental aspects of early development which underpin later more abstract learning when children can imagine, in their brains, mathematical problem solving and reasoning (what would happen if? and functional dependency), symbols (mathematics is full of symbols, e.g. $a^2 + b^2 = c^2$!), and processes of calculations and complex thinking. Thom's (2017) work also points out that "children's spatial skills prove to be a better gauge for their later mathematics performance than vocabulary and even mathematics tasks" after research "found the spatial thinking of the three-year-olds accurately predicted how well they performed in mathematics two years later at school" (p. 21).

Harry's (5.6 years) spatial reasoning is exceptional as he constructs his maps (see Chapter 7) in geographically correct drawings, where buildings and roads interconnect at specific points in relation one another. George at 3.4 years old (see Figure 2.4) also shows his understanding of roads and roundabouts and the spatial awareness of how they look and feel. They have both made a significant leap in their thinking from the actual experience to abstract thought level. Jacob at 9 months old is learning quickly about the way he can use his hands to beat a rhythm with the support of the adult, who repeats "bounce, bounce, bounce" as she taps the beat out. What you can't hear from the photographs is that he also accompanies his beats with "ba, ba, ba" doing his best to copy the sound.

Reflection point embodied learning and spatial reasoning

When you observe children in their child-led play, look closely at *how* they are learning: how are they using their bodies, senses and awareness to explore, find out and understand? For example, how is Leo's play with the cars helping to develop embodied learning and spatial reasoning?

Also, how do experiences like singing 'Two Little Dickie Birds' and 'Five Currant Buns in a Baker's Shop' support and extend children's embodied learning and spatial reasoning?

Summary

Being aware of young children's mathematical development and how this gradually progresses means that adults are better able to tune into and support learning, often as part of play and in-the-moment observation. The children's learning stories help us to see development and make sense of the complex processes of the brain and body, how they are learning and what they understand. We also see how creative and innovative children are in their problem setting and problem solving.

Recognising the part that schema have in laying the foundation to later mathematical concepts is often forgotten in practice or not completely understood; similarly with embodied learning and spatial reasoning. This chapter has given an insight into these critical developmental theories.

Chapter 3 will further explore children's development and learning, looking at how a combination of aspects, including child-initiated play, playful learning and sustained shared thinking, all weave together into mastery orientation.

Notes

1. We started at 2 years old because the schools all had younger children.
2. Chapter 3 looks at possibility questions, serve and return interactions and play.

3 What does mathematical mastery mean for young children?

DI CHILVERS

This chapter brings together the many aspects of *how* children learn and develop mathematical mastery, through analysing their learning stories, looking at wider reading and research as well as child development theory.

It looks particularly at *mastery orientation* an all-encompassing term from Dweck's (2000) extensive work on mindsets, which she directly connects to how children use problem-solving strategies when faced with difficulties or challenges. Also, research from the Effective Provision of Pre-School Education longitudinal study (EPPE, Sylva et al., 2004) which found that sustained shared thinking, when children were supported by adults to develop and extend their ideas, led to "mastery orientation", whereby children believed in themselves and their own efforts. They became more confident about themselves as resilient thinkers and learners, had feelings of high-self-esteem, high aspirations and secure feelings of self-efficacy.

Reflecting on this chapter's question

What does mathematical mastery mean for young children? Some of our initial thoughts were that it involved children in the following ways:

- Being able to do something confidently again and again and again (see Leo, Dylan and Miro in Chapter 2, as they followed their schematic patterns of thinking)
- Challenging themselves and one another (see Aadam and Farhaad as they explore Big Numbers in Chapter 6)
- Using the ideas, they have learned in new ways and in different contexts (see Callum and Joey in Numbered Footballs, this chapter)
- Seeing and understanding the 'whole' picture of a concept (as Bailey does with the concept of comparison in Go Compare, Chapter 6)
- 'Owning' the mathematical concept/idea and using it as part of their play and learning within a meaningful context (see Milo, The Straight-Line Person, and Dylan in Chapter 2; the children in As Tall as a Camel in Chapter 4 and Callum and Joey)

These explanations all have something significant in common, which is their positive view of all children (babies, toddlers and older children) as competent and capable learners, rich in potential who are fully involved in their thinking and learning (Malaguzzi in Edwards, Gandini and Forman, 1998). Redding, Morgan and Harmon (1988) describe this as 'mastery motivation' where:

> The competent toddler becomes readily and eagerly involved in a task, shows pleasure in task solution and in the face of frustration, remains involved.
>
> (p. 423)

The how and what of children's learning

The *how* of children's learning involves all the aspects of development which support them in becoming good thinkers and learners and learning how to learn. This includes the dispositions children will need to support mathematical learning, such as problem solving, exploring, asking questions and concentrating, many of which they develop through play, exploration and active learning (see Appendix 6). The *how* is also experienced and developed through mastery orientation, which is the focus of this chapter.

What children learn mainly consists of all the things they will need to know (knowledge); in England, this is found in the seven areas of learning of the Early Years Foundation Stage (DfE, 2017) and includes literacy (reading and writing) and mathematics (numbers, shapes, space and measures). Children also need knowledge to support their interests, such as knowing the difference between a *Velociraptor* and a *Diplodocus* or why warm water melts ice and spirals down the drain, and the skills they need to use scissors, hold a paintbrush or climb a ladder etc. It is much easier for them to learn knowledge and skills if they can do this through the *how* which, in the process, supports their confidence, self-esteem, well-being and, crucially, the development of a positive mindset.

It is essential that there is a strong connection and balance between the *how* and the *what* as children try to make sense of their experiences, thinking and learning, with the imperative being that it all leads to deep understanding.

> For young children, who are skilled knowledge seekers through their play and exploration, there is no real deep learning without *understanding*. Children have amazing memories, and absorb so many experiences, but these all need to be sifted and sorted in the short-term memory and connected to previous learning, which then forms the strong foundation of understanding in the long-term memory. When we observe children in their child-led play we look for real *understanding and mastery*, not simply memorised repetition of knowledge.
>
> (Chilvers, 2020)

What is mastery orientation?

For a child, **mastery orientation** is what Fisher (2017) calls the "Bob the Builder feeling of Yes, I Can!", through a strong sense of self-belief and the intrinsic drive or motivation to 'have a go'. As explained in Chapter 2, children are born with an innate intrinsic drive to play, explore and learn which involves hard work, struggle and challenge, like learning to crawl, toddle, balance and walk, overcoming any setbacks and difficulties with eager enthusiasm, persistence and resilience; their innate drive is definitely of the 'yes, I can' form. We see this enthusiasm, persistence and resilience in the children's learning stories where they are completely involved and in their 'element'.

> When children are in their element, they become active protagonists in their own learning, building confidence in themselves as learners and creative thinkers. This in turn strengthens their resilience and their ability to embrace the many changes they will inevitably face in their lives.
>
> (DCSF, 2010, p. 11)

This is what Dweck (2006) calls a "**growth mindset**" where children are active agents in the learning process with the ability to affect change, intrinsically motivated to find out, experiment and problem-solve, seeing themselves as competent and capable thinkers and learners – 'Yes, I can'.

However, Dweck (2006) also identified the impact on children's learning of having a "**fixed mindset**" where their 'capacity for learning is perceived as static and unalterable, regardless of effort', which she calls "learned help-lessness". The consequence of this being that some children quickly learn that others will tell them what to do and how to do it and that there is always a right answer; ultimately leading to a lack of confidence, courage and inclination to take a leap and try it for themselves. Children with a fixed mindset often "see learning as a risky business" and "have in effect set their own limits" (DCSF, 2010, p. 7). Eventually, 'I can' becomes 'I can't' (Fisher, 2017).

The research which underpins the theories of growth and fixed mindsets is complex and wide-ranging, though Carol Dweck, a professor in psychology, has been at the forefront in explaining how these impact on children's development and learning,

> Dweck (2000) suggests that children's sense of self-competence and self-efficacy, what she calls mastery, begins to develop from an early age and can have a significant impact on their attitudes to learning.
>
> (Robson, 2006, p. 52)

Figure 3.1 brings together key aspects of her work and others', as they describe the 'mindset behaviours' that we may see in children, even at a very young age.

Growth mindset – mastery orientation	Fixed mindset – learned helplessness
"Dweck suggest that the master learners develop a growth mindset; they wrestle with problems and delight in the effort of thinking and learning" (Dowling, 2013, p. 72).	Children . . . "stick to the familiar where they can feel safe and they know what to do – they are reluctant to try anything new . . . avoiding the challenge of uncertainty and initial confusion involved with thinking" (Dowling, 2013, p. 72).
"I can do it . . .", "I am good at this . . ." "I love a challenge . . ." "If it goes wrong, it doesn't matter. I can try again". Positive attitude: "A positive outlook that assumes problems can be resolved and that it is worth persevering" (Lindon, 2007, p. 92).	Lack of self-belief, constantly looking for approval and reassurance. "I can't' do it", "I am rubbish at maths", "I am no good at it". Negative attitude: "Children regularly give up swiftly, feeling that they are incompetent and cannot deal with new challenges" (Lindon, 2007, p. 92).
Intrinsic drive comes from within – self-motivated Children set their own *'learning goals'* and follow them to develop and master new skills.	Externally motivated by adults, constantly looking for praise and external rewards – extrinsic drive through external sources, e.g. stickers, prizes, awards Adults setting the *'performance goals'* with an emphasis on assessment, grades and performance
Enjoying the process of thinking, trying things out, problem setting and problem solving More likely to be self-regulated in their learning, independence and autonomy (Whitebread, 2012). Resilient and secure, can cope with change and uncertainty	Thinking and learning are risky and require confidence to 'have a go' and get started – less likely to set problems and engage in problem solving. More likely to be dependent on direction from adults, e.g. waiting to be told what to do next, unsure, not taking control of their own learning Lower resilience, feeling insecure, worried about change and uncertainty
Viewing children's "intelligence as an ever-expanding repertoire of skills and knowledge" (Carr and Lee, 2012, p. 23). Cognitive challenge is an integral characteristic of children's play and activities. It can be set by the children and adults, e.g. sustained shared thinking. Intelligence can be nurtured, developed, co-co- constructed	A belief that intelligence is fixed – you either know it or you don't (often reinforced by, e.g. Early Learning Goals, SATs[1]). Cognitive challenge set by the adult is at a low level, always adult-directed and not play based, leading to learning that is narrow and prescriptive Children know who the 'clever children' are!

Growth mindset – mastery orientation	Fixed mindset – learned helplessness
Being ready, willing and able (Carr, 2001) (see the 'What Are Dispositions and Attitudes?' box). Having ownership of their learning Taking responsibility: A disposition included in the Te Whariki learning stories (see Figure 2.2).	Do not have ownership, so unable to make a difference or an investment, e.g. only one set way to do an activity "In effect, a child stops trying because experience has taught them that their actions will not be effective" (Stewart, 2011, p. 41).
Children are more likely to be influenced by: • challenging open-ended activities • uninterrupted opportunities for playing and exploring • engaging in self-assessment • flexible curriculum • making choices and decisions • autonomy, independence and following interests • adults scaffolding teaching and learning • balance of child-initiated and adult-led activities	Children are more likely to be influenced by: • tight planning/programmes • restricted timetables • little or no choice • all adult-led teaching • "[r]estricted types of activities with limited choices" (Whitebread, 2012, p. 147)

Source: Drawn from: Bloom (1968) in Emery et al. (2018), Carr and Lee (2012), Dowling (2013), Dweck (2000, 2006), Elliott and Dweck (1988), Lindon (2007), Parker-Rees (1997), Stewart (2011), Whitebread (2012), www.tauckfamilyfoundation.org/outcomes/child-outcomes/mastery-orientation

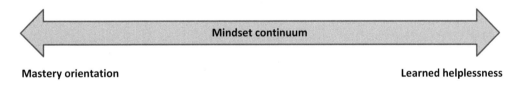

Figure 3.1 Describing some mindset behaviours we may see in young children

Research (Heyman, Dweck and Cain, 1992; Dweck, 2000, 2006) into younger aged children at 3 and 4 years has shown that the type of behaviours listed in Figure 3.1 will influence where they 'sit' along a continuum between mastery orientation and learned helplessness, in terms of their 'approach to learning', their attitudes, dispositions and the progress they make throughout school. It is not the case of children being in either one mindset or another or that mindsets are fixed and unchangeable; much will depend on their early experiences at home, including good attachment and attunement from birth, social relationships, opportunities for serve and return conversations and talk, plenty of time to play and explore, building their confidence and self-belief as thinkers and learners – competent and capable.

We see many of these early experiences, dispositions and attitudes in the children's learning stories throughout this book, where babies, toddlers and older children are self-motivated and well-supported to maintain their developmental momentum, growing a positive mindset and a love of learning.

What are dispositions and attitudes?

Children and adults can often be described as having a *happy, cheerful disposition* or, conversely, an *unhappy, sad disposition*, which is used as a reference to their character, personality or mood. Looking at Callum and Joey in the football learning story, we can see their dispositions in the way that they are *self-motivated, involved, concentrating, persisting and inventing*, as they *enthusiastically* decide how to help the goalie. These are all positive 'learning or thinking dispositions' (Carr, 2009), which are also described as "learning orientations" and "enabling attitudes" (Pascal and Bertram, 1997), "learning power" (Claxton, 2000), "mind-set behaviours" (Dweck, see Figure 3.1) and "habits of mind",

> Dispositions are a very different type of learning from skills and knowledge. They can be thought of as *habits of mind*, tendencies to respond to situations in certain ways.
> (Katz, 1988, p. 30 in Carr, 2009, p. 95)

Children's dispositions and attitudes are all inherently connected to the development of mindset behaviours (Figure 3.1) and mastery orientation, serving as further evidence of the fundamental and complex nature of child development and how children learn in general. This is especially critical to how children see themselves in relation to their mastery of mathematics and ensures that positive dispositions and firm foundations are well embedded at a young age, to underpin their progress through school and into lifelong learning, as Kath Priestley explains in Chapter 8.

Dispositions are woven into the core of Te Whariki, the New Zealand Early Childhood Curriculum (https://tewhariki.tki.org.nz/en/early-childhood-curriculum/) through pedagogy which focuses on the holistic development of children and fostering positive dispositions for learning. Carr (2001) describes this as children being *Ready, Willing and Able*:

Being Ready:
A disposition where children want to express and communicate their ideas, feelings, thoughts etc.
They have the inclination, predisposition or inner, innate urge to be curious explorers and finder-outers.
They want to PLAY and EXPLORE (see Chapter 4 and the children in Here, There and Everywhere).

Being Willing:

A disposition where children want to have a go; they recognise and make their own opportunities,

Are motivated to express their ideas and share/communicate them with others...

Through PLAY and ACTIVE LEARNING.

Being Able:

A disposition where children know the right skills to use, can put their ideas into action, try things out and have the confidence to do that

They are self-regulated thinkers and learners

Through being CREATIVE and CRITICAL THINKERS.

Dispositions are central to observation in Early Childhood Education in New Zealand and form the key focus of assessing children's development and learning, through narrative learning stories, which pay attention to deeper levels of understanding rather than superficial outcomes. When Te Whariki was launched in 1996 (Ministry of Education, New Zealand), "five domains of learning dispositions" (Carr, 2001) were drawn from the curriculum and became the framework for learning stories; see the example in Figure 3.2.

The five domains of *Taking an interest*; *Being involved*; *Persisting with difficulty*; *Expressing an idea or a feeling*; and *Taking responsibility* can all stand alone as dispositions, but when they work together, they lead to a depth of thinking which can be described as mastery orientation, as the child/children ultimately takes/take responsibility in leading, sharing and owning their own learning. For example, the children in the Love Monster learning story (see Chapter 5) have *taken an interest* in the Love Monster's story and how to make him happy; they are in effect 'hooked' as a whole class! Consequently, they become *deeply involved* listening to one another's ideas and suggestions, then planning together, which involves setting tasks, finding strategies and looking for solutions (problem solving) and *persisting with difficulty*. It is a challenge which they are all enjoying. They *express their ideas and feelings* in many ways, not just through talk, and have whole-class *responsibility*, which they take very seriously, especially when they have too many buns!

The Five Domains have many other dispositions embedded within them, which is why they were chosen to be the key inclusive themes in the Te Whariki curriculum. Assessing children's thinking and learning through these dispositions, rather than areas of learning like mathematics, literacy etc., means that we have a much broader,

Learning Story

Child's Name:

Child's Age:

Date:

	Dispositions	Examples or cues	A LEARNING STORY
Belonging Mana whenua	**Taking an Interest**	Finding an interest *here* – a topic, an activity, a role. Recognising the familiar, enjoying the unfamiliar. Coping with change.	
Well-being Mana atua	**Being Involved**	Paying attention for a sustained period, feeling safe, trusting others. Being playful with others and/or materials.	
Exploration Mana aoturoa	**Persisting with difficulty**	Setting and choosing difficult tasks. Using a range of strategies to solve problems when 'stuck' (be specific)	
Communication Mana reo	**Expressing an idea or a feeling**	In a range of ways (specify). For example: oral language, gesture, music, art, writing, using numbers and patterns, telling stories	
Contribution Mana tangata	**Taking responsibility**	Responding to others, to stories, and imagined events, ensuring that things are fair, self-evaluating, helping others, contributing to programme	
Short Term Review			**What Next?**
Question: What learning did I think went on here (i.e. the main point(s) of the learning story)?			**Question**: How might we encourage this interest, ability, strategy, disposition, story to: • Be more complex • Appear in different areas or activities in the programme. How might we encourage the next 'step' in the Learning Story Framework?

Figure 3.2 New Zealand learning story – learning dispositions

holistic view of a child's development and progress as they connect and weave together with one another. As Carr (2001, p. 22) suggests, using "learning dispositions will contribute to developing understandings in a range of school curriculum areas" and at a much deeper level.

Reflection point

Dispositions and attitudes explain *how* children learn. Claxton (2000) calls them 'learnacy skills' or essential lifelong learning dispositions.

Have a look at the characteristics of effective learning in Appendix 6. Can you see the Five Domains of Learning Dispositions as they are broken down into aspects which all connect?

How does this connect with mastery orientation?

Evidence from the HighScope Perry Preschool longitudinal study (Schweinhart and Weikart, 1993), a well-known and successful early intervention programme in the United States, showed that:

> Children with high aspirations, independence and who experience an early education curriculum that encourages a mastery orientation are significantly more effective learners and achievers in the long term.
>
> (Pascal and Bertram in Abbott and Moylett [Eds.], 1999, p. 99)

The HighScope curriculum builds on children's strengths, interests and abilities enabling children to co-construct their own learning by following a 'plan, do, review' approach and by being actively involved in working with materials, people and ideas. All essential dispositions and skills for developing children's mastery orientation and fostering a growth-mindset.

Reflection point

Look at the learning story Numbered Footballs below with Callum and Joey. The boys are following their interest in football. Their teacher, Miss Mercer, is observing and documenting their serve and return talk as they follow their line of mathematical thinking.

What is this child-led play telling us about their mindsets and mastery orientation?

As you observe your children in their child-led play, including babies and toddlers, can you see any of these mindset behaviours?

How are you ensuring that children are growing positive, growth mindsets when they are with you?

Numbered Footballs with Callum and Joey

Callum and Joey have been carefully rolling and making balls with the playdough and lining them up.

We got to line the footballs up ready for the goalie.

Yeah he's got to get them in the order so he can save them.

Miss Mercer: I wonder how many you have made...?

We've made loads look 1,2,3,4,5... (Callum counts the 23 footballs)

Callum then stops and runs to the maths area and comes back with some wooden numbers..........

The boys set to work adding the numbers onto their footballs. They order up to 5 very quickly and then begin to check which number is needed next by recounting the footballs they have already numbered.

1,2,3,4,5,6,7,8, 9,10

Let's do this then he (the goalie) knows which one comes next

Yeah I'll line them up and the numbers can go up....

But we've still got these...!

1,2,3,4,5,6,7,8... 9 now

Then one more is 10

Miss Mercer: Oh no what are you going to do now then?

Callum goes to the writing area and brings back a pencil and some paper and sets about drawing around a cutter. He then cuts out his circles ready to continue numbering the footballs.

Let's do this and it will be a circle like these ones

Ok you do the circles and I'll do the numbers

The number elevens next....

Here then you can do the number 11 one, I'll cut another for the 12..

1,2,3,4,5,6,7,8,9,10,11, 12,13..we need a 14 now. That's a 4 and a 1.

Yeah it's a 1 and a 4 the 4 comes last

Callum then goes to another part of the classroom and check this out on the number line

Miss Mercer: Hmmm I wonder if it will have a 10 and then a 4 like the number 11 is a 10 and a 1.
How could you check?

Summary of Learning:

Callum and Joey have followed their interest in football. Using the dough they have created a system of numbering the footballs so that the 'goalie' knows how many are going to be kicked into the goal! This is their idea, a problem set by them, which they then set about problem-solving together. Through their sustained shared thinking they:

- decide to order the footballs to make it easier for the 'goalie', lining them up checking their order by counting them and conferring with each other.
- set about adding the number label to each of the footballs and then run out! They quickly think of a way to make their own numbers and set up a system with Callum drawing the circles and Joey writing the numbers.
- use their previous mathematical knowledge of numbers to help each other.
- keep checking and reviewing what they are doing, chatting together and helping each other.
- concentrate and work together sharing the planning, decision making, problem solving and reviewing how well it is going.

Next Steps:

- Ask Callum and Joey to share their learning story with the class, explain their thinking and reflect on what they have done, e.g. what about 14?
- Are there more football problems to be solved? Create some scenarios for the boys to follow and look at the league tables!

What is mathematical mastery?

Maths mastery programmes, in England at Key Stage 1 (5–7 years) and Key Stage 2 (7–11 years), have been developing over the last five or six years after teacher exchanges to Shanghai and Singapore, where outcomes for children's mathematical learning were high. After significant government interest, and a drive to improve the maths outcomes for children in England, many schools adopted programmes that were based on the teaching in Shanghai and Singapore, using a mastery approach where:

> programmes see mastery as a 'journey and long-term goal, achieved through exploration, clarification, practice and application over time' and 'not about just being able to memorise key facts and procedures' as this is 'superficial and can be easily forgotten'.

And:

> No pupil should be left behind. The focus is keeping up over catching up. By making high expectations clear and emphasising the value of mathematics education, pupils are encouraged to build confidence and resilience.
>
> (www.tes.com/teachingformastery)

The maths mastery programmes are sequenced following a set approach, with specific 'components' or key principles and aims which include the following:

● All children are capable of understanding and doing mathematics given enough time and nurturing a positive mindset. Children's abilities with maths are not fixed; they can be developed with 'practice, support, dedication and hard work'

- 'Children build their understanding in small, logical steps. Each step must be secure before moving on to the next. It is critical that no gaps in understanding are left unfilled'
- A 'set of mathematical concepts and big ideas for all' children which they need to fully understand and transfer into other aspects of their learning
- Whole-class, adult-directed teaching with children working together on the same focus/topic ensuring 'greater depth' and understanding rather than superficial learning
- 'Teaching is focussed, rigorous and thorough, to ensure that learning is sufficiently embedded and sustainable over time'
- The focus is on number and numeracy: 'reinforcing number to build competency and fluency' including 'committing key facts, such as number bonds and times tables, to memory'
- Problem solving, reasoning and procedural fluency are key skills
- Structured classroom activities should include 'back and forth interactions, questioning, short tasks, explanations, demonstrations and discussion'
- The development of understanding through using **concrete** representations of maths with objects (often called manipulatives), **pictorial** representation and **abstract** symbols and representations (see Figure 2.8)

(Drawn from National Centre for Excellence in the Teaching of Mathematics, www.ncetm.org.uk; Teaching for mastery in primary maths, www.tes.com/teachingformastery)

The aim is that through these carefully planned, adult-directed daily maths lessons using the preceding principles and practices, all children will build their mastery of mathematics along with their confidence and self-belief. Drury (2014, p. 9) explains what mathematical mastery looks like for the child:

> A mathematical concept or skill has been mastered when, through exploration, clarification, practice and application over time, a person can represent it in multiple ways, has the mathematical language to be able to communicate related ideas, and can think mathematically with the concept so that they can independently apply it to a totally new problem in an unfamiliar situation.

This is a clear explanation of mastery in relation to mathematics, with many similarities to our thoughts and findings from the Talk for Maths Mastery initiative about what mastery means and looks like for young children. This particularly applies to children being able to transfer and connect their thinking and ideas to other aspects of their play and activities, as we saw with Callum and Jamie, and in how the children show their mastery in their child-led play through exploration, clarification, practice and application particularly in continuous provision.

Reflection point

So, what is the difference between *mastery* as described by the mathematical mastery programmes and *mastery orientation*?
Is mastery only about mathematics and numbers, or does it have a bigger part to play in children's development, thinking and learning?

However, despite these connections, there is a significant mismatch between the way in which young children (particularly those under 5) learn and actively participate in mathematics and the pedagogy that supports that learning, and the teaching methods (see the preceding list of principles and practices) used in the maths mastery programmes. For example, young children's learning is best supported through active, play-based, contextual experiences with opportunities to follow their interests and co-construct their thinking, language and learning alongside other children and adults. Mathematics embedded in children's play takes a much wider perspective of maths rather than simply numeracy, and we have already seen in Chapter 2 how children's early mathematical development is underpinned by their schematic lines of thinking, especially connected to shape, space and measures.

Whole-class, adult-directed teaching sessions, lasting longer than 15–20 minutes will not engage *all* children as their attention and concentration differ vastly at an early age, when some children in the class are just 4 years old and others are 5 years old. The emphasis on recording in workbooks takes children rapidly into an abstract level of representation before fully experiencing more contextual, concrete, in-the-moment interpretations (see Chapters 2 and 6), particularly when they should be using serve and return conversations to extend their language and thinking.

mathematical mastery programmes have been developed from KS2 (7- to 11-year-olds) into KS1 (5- to 7-year-olds) and are now starting to become widely used in Reception classes with young children, who are within the Early Years Foundation Stage (EYFS). The direction of travel here is from the 'top down' rather than the 'ground up' where children's mathematical momentum is built on the firm foundations of child development (see Chapter 2). How do the two opposing directions of travel meet so that they make sense to young children and support their mathematical learning and mastery in the best ways possible?

The answer lies in the interpretation of mastery as "mastery orientation" (Dweck, 2000; Sylva et al., 2004), which connects to children's dispositions and attitudes towards learning as well as their sense of self-competence and self-efficacy, as we can see from Figure 3.1, looking at mindsets rather than teaching for mastery using a 'set of components' and 'practices' for teaching and learning (Boylan et al., 2018, p. 25). Mastery orientation, as we discovered in the TFMM initiative, offers us a pedagogical approach informed by child development theory and research which applies to all learning and not just mathematics. There is also the following concern regarding prescriptive programmes of teaching, especially for young children:

> Mastery learning is currently having such a big influence on maths teaching generally and teachers can be less able to try out different more open mathematics; encouraging teachers to look at the curriculum rather than the child. Current mathematics professional development is born out of learning how to teach the current "approach" and there are fewer opportunities for early years teachers and practitioners to research, in greater depth, the complexities of how young children learn.
>
> (McCarthy and Redpath, 2017, p. 12)

Seeing children's mastery orientation – a way of looking

Through our observations of the children, using narrative learning stories and becoming much more aware that mathematical opportunities happen anywhere and at any time, we began to build a much clearer picture of children's development, especially where this involved mastery orientation strategies. We began to think about what mathematical mastery orientation looked like in practice as we watched the children in their child-led play. The following four questions helped us to make some significant connections to practice:

1. **What does mathematical mastery orientation mean? Children are:**

- involved, confident, engaged and enjoying learning; 'thinking outside the box' using thinking skills
- problem solvers – able to look at problems in lots of different ways
- confident and motivated, eager to play, explore and find out
- are not afraid to make mistakes; use trial and error, challenging themselves and each other
- confident and resilient; being prepared to 'have a go' and work things out – independent learners who can lead their own learning
- talkers, asking their own questions, explaining, reasoning, reflecting on their thinking and learning (meta-cognition) ("I can show you why – not just tell")
- setting their own plans and goals (self-regulation), focus on process rather than outcome
- able to see links in their experiences and learning; making connections with what they know – seeing and recognising concepts in different situations
- applying what they have been taught (adult-initiated) independently in their child-led play; showing depth of knowledge, sharing and

collaborating with others, e.g. Makhi (Chapter 7), Go Compare (Chapter 6), Love Monster (Chapter 5)

- developing deeper understanding of concepts, knowledge and skills and applying in different contexts – not memorising

2. What does it include?

- child-initiated play and learning with adults knowing when to intervene to enhance, support and extend learning – scaffolding (Chapter 7)
- thinking critically, including critical thinking and problem solving; active learning; the characteristics of effective learning (Appendix 6)
- self-motivation and intrinsic drive from within
- sustained shared thinking
- collaboration, lots of talking (serve and return); independent learning; dispositions, e.g. confidence, curiosity, perseverance, resilience and high well-being
- an accessible, enabling environment with open-ended resources – continuous provision
- time to play uninterrupted and to have the opportunity to save and return
- space to explore and persevere
- first-hand experiences

3. What does it look like in practice? Where will you see it happening?

- *In continuous provision*: Possibilities are everywhere, indoors and outdoors
- *Meaningful contexts*: Mathematics are made *real*, e.g. baking and cooking; role-play/home corners, through children's interests, shopping, art and design, popular culture, home learning, real life problems, games, play and activities
- *Children are engaged and involved*: Involvement levels are high, and sustained shared thinking occurs frequently between children and between children and adults
- *Conversations between children*: Adults skilfully scaffold thinking and learning (co-construction); serve and return conversations take place between children and with adults (see Chapter 2)
- *Child-led play*: Individually or collaboratively, children are creative, resourceful, excited, in a 'state of flow' and deep thinking
- *Children's schematic play*: See Chapter 2

4. What can you do to support mathematical mastery orientation?

- Develop your own understanding of mastery orientation and children's mathematical development
- Ensure children have uninterrupted time to solve problems, develop ideas and talk
- Use possibility questions to broaden and deepen thinking

- Understand when to intervene and when to stand back – observe, wait, listen
- Use playful teaching strategies, e.g. playing alongside children, tuning into what they are doing, saying and thinking. Support and extend the play through co-construction, introducing new language, using possibility questions and modelling a skill, e.g. balancing bricks, role-play (DCSF, 2009b, pp. 14–22; Chilvers, 2015)
- Follow children's interests/ideas; tune into, engage with and teach mathematical concepts through those interests
- Teach in small groups for short period of times and in relevant, meaningful contexts, being aware of the age of the children (see Chapter 5)
- Document children's thinking and learning using narrative learning stories
- Balance adult-initiated/led/directed teaching with child-led play and activities (see Chapter 5)
- Observe children in continuous provision particularly their understanding and embedded learning
- Talk together with colleagues and use your professionally informed judgements about children's development, learning and progress
- Engage with children's parents, family and community

Reflection point

Can you see the connections between what we saw in practice, in the aspects above, and Dweck's theories regarding *growth mindsets* (mastery orientation) and *fixed mindsets* (learned helplessness)?

How do these aspects support children's dispositions and attitudes in mathematical learning and development? (Can you spot the dispositions in the aspects?)

Do these aspects have a wider meaning to *how* children (including babies and toddlers) learn overall?

Nicola Jones and Imogen Lansdale, TFMM partners from Manor Lodge Community Primary and Nursery School, Sheffield, drew together many of these aspects to form the following definition of mathematical mastery and mastery orientation, creating a clear focus on what this means for young children, the adults who work with them and the enabling environment:

> Mastery is having the ability to express mathematical ideas in a variety of contexts through child-initiated play and talk. They can independently apply the skills they have learnt to a new

problem. Children who have mastered a concept will challenge themselves and others in collaborative play. Resources, time and a flexible learning environment are crucial to enable children to practise and hone these skills. Practitioners are 'playful partners', they value play and engage in lots of talk, leading to 'sustained shared thinking'.

As the TFMM initiative progressed, the partners began to look at children's development, learning and progress in different ways, particularly in terms of mathematics. They began to see the mathematical processes like reasoning, problem setting and problem solving, logical thinking, fluency in younger children (see Chapters 2 and 4), as well as in older children, as they led their play in continuous provision. Opportunities for sustained shared thinking in collaborative play and activities showed how children were able to co-construct their own mathematical thinking with one another as well as with an adult, just as Callum and Joey have done in their learning story about numbered footballs. Importantly, through this kind of play and engagement, the adults were able to observe how well the children had fully understood and mastered key mathematical concepts, easily transferring their learning from one context to another and making wider connections to other learning.

We observed some of the key aspects of mastery orientation (Figure 3.3) and what they told us about *how* the children were learning and, importantly the quality of our teaching to support, extend and deepen children's understanding.

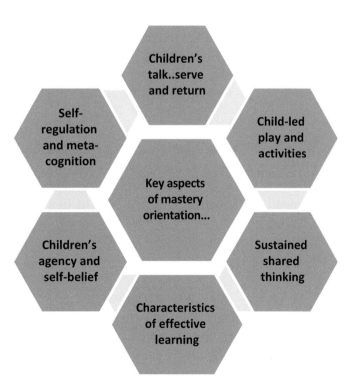

Figure 3.3 Key aspects of mastery orientation

Children's conversational talk – serve and return

Children's conversational talk is like a stream of thought coming straight from their brain, as they think out loud, either as a personal running commentary or in dialogue with other children and adults. It is this type of talk, which often takes place in child-led play, that tells us how much they understand, what they know and what they feel.

It is crucial that adults tune into these conversations and keep them going as this interplay from one to the other, through talk, has a profound impact on brain activity and connecting the neural pathways to build strong foundations for the 'emotional and cognitive skills needed in life', many of which have been discussed in this book. Research at the Centre on the Developing Child at Harvard University (USA) has confirmed the vital place that communication and language development have on young children's development and learning, for example, "The interaction, more than the number of words a child hears, creates measurable changes in the brain and sets the stage for strong literacy skills in school" (www.gse.harvard.edu/news/uk/18/02/brain-changing-power-conversation).

This also applies to the development of 'strong mathematical skills in school' and starts from birth.

These serve and return conversations begin at birth through eye contact and facial expressions, as baby and parents bond. They continue, as babies instinctively know how to communicate (non-verbally through eyes, face and body), as well as verbally (tongue play, gurgling, babbling sounds etc.), stopping and waiting for the adult's 'turn,' then picking up the 'ball' as the game flows from one to the other (see Chapter 2). The more adults engage in this serve and return talk and play, the more children's conversational language is extended, leading to the types of conversation we see Calum and Joey having; and the children in Chapter 2 discussing "Who knows what is zero?" and the class discussion about the Love Monster (Bright, 2012) (Chapter 5).

The best conversations arise from what the children are interested in, particularly in their child-led play. It is up to the adults to observe and tune into this serve and return talk, much of which will develop into opportunities for sustained shared thinking (see the section, "Child-led Play and Activities").

With regard to mathematical language and vocabulary, there is strong research evidence to show that:

> Children learn richer vocabulary in playful learning where the information is meaningful than they do in direct instruction methods devoid of meaningful engagement.
>
> (Ferrara et al., 2011; Fisher et al., 2013)

Child-led play and activities

Children's play, particularly child-led play, tells us what we need to know about mastery orientation in action but only if we take the time to observe and reflect on what we have seen. As adults, we need to know and understand the nature of play, particularly in how it supports the development of children's mindsets, positive dispositions and attitudes. Observing children's play is our window into their mathematical thinking, learning and understanding, as well as lots of other learning.

Through the learning stories, we see how competent and capable children are at following their own paths of thinking usually by being engrossed in something that really 'interested' them and leads them into deep involvement and flow of thinking (Csikszentmihalyi, 1996). We also see how they are taking forward what has been taught, connecting it to their previous learning and understanding and replaying this modified thinking in more complex ways. Which is why it is critical to observe and assess children's progress in their child-led play as this give us the clearest sign that they have truly understood (mastered) a concept and can transfer this skill/knowledge into other contexts (STA, 2019, p. 11).

Younger children's deep interests are clearly visible in their schematic patterns of thinking, frequently mathematical, involving trajectories, balance, cause and effect and a great deal of problem solving (see Chapter 2).

Playing and exploring in the characteristics of effective learning (Appendix 6) effectively outlines the complex dispositions children become engaged in as they play: finding out and exploring, playing with what they know and being willing to 'have a go'. These are all aspects of mastery orientation having their roots deeply anchored in developing a growth mindset particularly through initiating their own activities, seeking challenges and showing a can-do attitude.

Play is also the place where children can think in more imaginative creative and flexible ways. Children find many techniques to represent their ideas and build their autonomy, self-belief and confidence, all processes that are central to mathematical learning.

Moyles (1989) talks about the "Play Spiral" and the ongoing, cyclical process of play as children and adults move between *free play*, *child-led play* and *directed play*, which leads to *mastery* through *practice* and *revision* where children fine-tune their understandings and mastery (pp. 15, 16). It is grounded in Bruner's (in Moyles, 1989) philosophy that "Play is an approach to action, not a form of activity", which we now see in the complex balance between child-led play and adult-initiated/adult-led teaching (Ofsted, 2015) (see Chapter 5).

Sustained shared thinking

Sustained shared thinking (SST) is more likely to happen in play and activities which children have *initiated* and which are based in their *interests*. Whitebread's (2012) extensive research on play, self-regulation and meta-cognition found that SST is 'commonly found in child-initiated, playful activities including group problem-solving' and:

> [w]hat all the high-quality early years regimes, identified by Sylva and Wiltshire (1993), did was to help children develop what they term a 'mastery' orientation to learning and themselves.
>
> (p. 7)

SST involves the same serve and return process, described above, as children and adults (or children and children) keep the conversation going through appropriate serve and returns. Another way of describing this process is cognitive co-construction (Craft, 2010) and particularly relates to the way in which SST:

> builds through children either making their own connections in partnership with each other or with the collaborative support of an adult. Either way the co-construction of learning is formed by connecting what you already know, to new ideas, and transforming this into different and deeper levels of thinking; this is a creative act and involves all the power of critical thinking.
>
> (Chilvers, 2013, p. 49)

We can see how Callum and Joey co-construct their thinking and build firmer understanding as they play; they exchange ideas, batting them back and forth until they come up with a solution that they feel will work. They consider each other's ideas, make links with their previous learning and demonstrate high levels of concentration and perseverance. They check and review what they are doing to ensure that it will work, as they plan, negotiate, make decisions and problem-solve together.

Through their SST, they are clearly displaying many of the characteristics of effective learning and mastery orientation as they work together "in an intellectual way to solve a problem, clarify a concept, evaluate activities, extend a narrative" in which "both parties contribute to the thinking [which] is developed and extended" (Siraj-Blatchford et al., 2002, p. 8).

We see many of the children in the learning stories in this book engaged in SST, but other actions are at play here, all of which contribute to the process of becoming deeply involved in thinking and learning. They include being *involved* in such depth that their ideas, thinking, talk and play *flow* in a seamless stream of actions which have been co-constructed together in very creative ways.

What is involvement?

Laever's (1994; Laevers, Declercq and Thomas, 2010) established work on the Levels of Involvement and Well-being gave early childhood education a universal language to explain what happens when many dispositions come together, as children become engrossed in their play, ideas and interests. He developed a scale from Level 1 to Level 5 with 'signals' or characteristics to observe as children's involvement became deeper,

> Laevers defines the concept of involvement as: "A quality of human activity, characterised by concentration and persistence, a high level of motivation, intense perceptions and experiencing of meaning, a strong flow of energy – a high degree of satisfaction, and based on the exploratory drive and basic development of schemes".
>
> (Dowling, 2005, p. 91)

The 'signals' are dispositions which support the development of mastery orientation such as intrinsic motivation, persistence (stickability), energy, concentration, precision and satisfaction. In practice, our observations of children should be informed by looking for any 'signs' of these dispositions in children's play and activities. For example, in the summary of Numbered Footballs (previously discussed), many of these dispositions have been highlighted. Following Laever's Well-being and Involvement Scale, we would say that the activity is at a Level 5 characterised by the following:

Level 5 – Sustained intense activity

The child/children is/are busy without interruption and completely absorbed in the activity:

- uninterrupted concentration, absorbed by the activity, forgets the time
- very motivated, cannot be distracted
- alert perception, attention to detail, precision
- constantly addresses all his/her capabilities and possibilities
- strong mental activity, imagination and mental capacity in top gear
- gains new and deep level experiences
- enjoys being totally involved

(Laevers et al., 2010, p. 14)

Children who are highly involved operate at the very limits of their capabilities in the zone of proximal development (Vygotsky and Cole, 1978) or sustained shared thinking. For all these reasons, involvement is an excellent indicator for deep-level learning taking place and where the adults can follow the child's lead, tune into their thinking and support as necessary through appropriate playful teaching (see Chapter 7).

Involvement (and well-being) have been included in many early years pedagogies all over the world, including New Zealand where we see 'Being Involved' as one of the Five Domains of Learning Dispositions in the Te Whariki Learning Stories (Figure 3.2) and in the English Early Years Foundation Stage and the characteristics of effective learning (Appendix 6) where it is included in the strand called 'Active Learning'.

The **Active Learning** strand is about children being motivated (Ready, Willing and Able) to learn through *Being involved and concentrating*; persisting by *Keeping on trying* and *Enjoying and achieving what they set out to do*. The Lego Foundation, in their review of children learning through play, identified many of these dispositions, particularly intrinsic motivation and curiosity as "enhancing neural activity" and "supporting activity in brain structures [which] enhances our ability to retain the information that follows" (Liu et al., 2017, p. 8).

What is flow?

Csikszentmihalyi (1996), a Hungarian American psychologist, has written at length about the 'state of flow' in humans whereby children (and adults) become so involved and engrossed in what they are doing that they lose track of time as their ideas flow and extend in a stream of thought. It is a combination of deep concentration, being interested and enjoying an experience. We often see this in children's play, especially collaborative play, as they co-construct their thinking which frequently leads to Involvement Levels 4 and 5 (Laevers et al., 2010). We see this happening in Love Monster (Chapter 5) with the whole class, Makhi (Chapter 7), Daisy in One Is a Snail Ten Is a Crab (Chapter 8) and in Numbered Footballs where:

> Children become deeply involved in something, usually that they have initiated, and they become lost in it, concentrating for long periods and persisting even when the going gets tough. It is at moments like this that children's thinking and learning moves into another dimension and become more meaningful, eventually leading to higher levels of 'mastery' and understanding.
>
> (Chilvers in Moylett (Ed), 2014, p. 77)

There is a connection here with the characteristics of effective learning where children's learning flows between *Playing and Exploring* (engagement) and between *Active Learning* (motivation) and *Creating and Thinking Critically* (thinking) as long as the experiences, support and teaching are at the right level for the child, being neither too difficult or too easy. The skilful adult will ensure that the serve and return nature of children's talking, thinking and learning is maintained through their intrinsic motivation (mastery motivation) and developmental momentum (Redding, Morgan and Harmon, 1988).

Characteristics of effective learning

The three characteristics of effective learning – Playing and Exploring, Active Learning and Creating and Thinking Critically – have been referenced throughout this book and in the children's learning stories. They document the complexity of the dispositions and skills children need to become lifelong learners, building on their developmental momentum in all aspects not just mathematics. Observing children's development through these characteristics gives us a good indication of the depth of their learning and understanding as well as their mastery orientation.

We can see how mastery orientation is woven throughout, including sustained shared thinking, involvement, persistence, motivation, ownership/agency and positive dispositions to becoming a competent and capable thinker and learner. Importantly they promote the development of 'executive functions' which support children to:

- control their attention through concentrating, focusing attention on a task or goal and being able to switch attention
- develop and grow their working memory and engage in flexible thinking, for example "holding information in mind while operating on it" (Whitebread in Moylett, 2014, p. 23), being able to change approach, rethink and accommodate new knowledge and information
- learn inhibitory or effortful control through knowing how to stop an initial, impulsive, automatic response, e.g. taking turns and playing fairly so that everyone can have a 'go'

Executive functions are described by the Centre on the Developing Child (Harvard University) as being like the child's internal 'air traffic control' in the brain, guiding them as they gradually learn to regulate their own thinking and learning and essential life skills (https://developingchild.harvard.edu/guide/a-guide-to-executive-function/). It is these very functions which underpin children's mathematical development and learning, including being able to problem set and problem solve, calling upon all their conceptual knowledge, understanding and reasoning and then applying it in their play in collaboration with others, as we saw with Callum and Joey (this chapter) and with Bailey and his friends in Go Compare (see Chapter 6).

Reflection Point

As you read through this book and the children's learning stories, think about all the references and connections to the characteristics of effective learning (Appendix 6). What connections can you make?

How does Creating and thinking critically, Having their own ideas, Making links and Choosing ways to do things underpin children's mathematical development and learning?

Can you see this in action in the children's learning stories?

Self-regulation and meta-cognition

What is self-regulation?

Figure 3.1 outlines what it means to have a growth mindset and mastery orientation, including *children's intentional thinking*, where children take control of their thinking and learning, actively leading and regulating what they are doing and deciding how to do it. Important life skills. This is cognitive self-regulation which, combined with children's executive functions, become "higher level mental functions" which support children's development and progress and are "associated with long term attainment" (Pascal, Bertram and Rouse, 2019, p. 19).

> Self-regulation comprises a set of *abilities* which enable an individual to be in control of their own cognitive and emotional mental processes.
>
> (Whitebread, 2016, p. 3)

This set of abilities includes children:

- initiating their own ideas and interests
- making their own decisions and choices
- deepening their thinking: **meta-cognition** (see below and Chapters 4 and 5)
- talking, communicating, collaborating
- connecting and transferring their thinking and learning
- knowing, planning what they want to do next and with whom
- being intrinsically motivated and independent

What is meta-cognition?

Meta-cognition occurs when children and adults talk about their thinking in a reflective way. For example, Miss Mercer created Callum and Joey's learning story, Numbered Footballs, and read it with them. They talked together about what they did, explaining their thinking and reasoning and deepening their understanding, becoming aware of themselves as thinkers and reflecting on their learning.

> It is now well established that by far the most significant determinant of children's success as learners is their development of what are termed 'meta-cognitive skills' (i.e. their awareness, knowledge and control of their own mental processes) and positive emotional and motivational dispositions towards themselves as learners.
>
> (Whitebread, in Moylett, 2014, p. 15)

Robson (2010, p. 182) recommends that reflective dialogue with children, like the one just described with Callum and Joey, leads to the "positive development of children's awareness of their own learning and thinking" through:

- talking with children about their thinking
- engaging in thoughtful reflection and social interaction
- joint meaning-making most likely leading to sustained shared thinking
- making children's ideas and intentions visible

(See Chapter 4)

Children's agency and self-belief

Children's *agency* and *self-belief* take us back to the beginning of this chapter and growth or fixed mindsets. Have they developed the dispositions and skills to be mastery orientated learners ("I can do this!") or do they lack the confidence to 'have a go' and get started ("I can't do this!")?

How children see themselves, especially in relation to learning, makes a huge difference to their confidence, resilience and self-belief, particularly with regard to seeing themselves as mathematical thinkers. This can promote the mistaken view that children/adults either 'get maths' or 'they don't' (see Chapter 7). Research has shown that:

> High self-esteem and feelings of self-efficacy are strongly related to educational success, and low self-esteem and what has been termed 'learned helplessness' are equally related to educational difficulty.
> (Whitebread, 2012, p. 8)

Where children can take ownership of their learning, being motivated and confident to 'have a go', 'try things out' and 'make mistakes', their agency and self-belief grow. They can self-regulate their thinking in the ways just described and take responsibility (see Figure 3.2) for themselves – "I can do this, I know how to do this, I will try to do this, I am ready, willing and able". We can see these attitudes in the children's learning stories in this book, as they follow their interests and think independently or collaboratively.

The essential factors in supporting children's agency and self-belief begin with seeing all children as competent and capable and:

- providing them with a warm, secure and enabling environment with strong supportive relationships where children feel that they can 'take risks', 'have a go' and build their confidence and self-belief
- giving them the space to lead their learning, be independent, contribute their own 'funds of knowledge' (Chesworth, 2016) and opportunities to follow the 'flow' of their thinking/ideas in their play and activities
- where they can cognitively challenge themselves or be challenged through adult-led/initiated teaching which supports all children from their own starting points
- with many opportunities to replay and refine their thinking and learning in meaningful contexts where they can make 'personal sense of it, making it one's own' (Carr and Lee, 2012, p. 12) and show their deep understanding and mastery
- time to talk about their thinking and learning to understand and explain their 'mental processes' through meta-cognitive reflections. This is where narrative learning stories play a crucial role in making children's thinking and learning visible to them and others in such a creative way. Learning stories have many purposes including building children's self-belief and agency. In a learning story about Keira taking on a mathematical challenge, Melissa, the adult, wrote:

> Her willingness is even more interesting when we note that the other children in the room backed away from the challenge, but Keira was not influenced by them. She showed that she is the master of her own learning. Keira showed courage, independence and great mathematical skills as she drew her figures. I am interested to see where this work leads her next.
>
> (Carr and Lee, 2012, p. 23)

Summary

This chapter has brought together our findings from the TFMM initiative, particularly the research, reading and theory around how young children's mastery orientation underpins all areas of learning, not just mathematics. Understanding children's mastery orientation is like completing a jigsaw puzzle, bringing all the pieces together and working out how they all connect to clearly show the whole picture.

What helped us to connect all the pieces was to observe the children in their child-led play and look for the signs and characteristics of mastery orientation – the dispositions, concepts and skills. The learning stories show them in their photographs and narrative.

As you observe your children and think about their development and progress, in all areas of learning as well as mathematics, look for the signs of mastery orientation. Starting with the characteristics of effective learning and involvement is a good beginning.

Note

1. SATs (or Standard Assessment Tests) are national tests given to children at school in England.

4 Documenting children's mathematical talking and thinking through observation, learning stories and floor books

KATIE HULME

In this chapter we will consider how we document children's learning and what this reveals to us about their mathematical thinking, talking and learning. Through the following key questions and learning story examples, the chapter will illustrate how children's interests, interactions and misconceptions shape their learning journey and allow them to master mathematical concepts.

Key questions

Why is documentation important, and how can we use it effectively to support mathematical talking, thinking and mastery?

How can children's serve and return interactions support their learning?

How do we address children's misconceptions?

How do we follow children's mathematical interests?

How does children's schematic thinking and learning support their early mathematical development?

Why is documentation important, and how can we use it effectively to support mathematical talking, thinking and mastery?

What is documentation?

The city and preschools of Reggio Emilia (Italy) have transformed the way in which we view observation and documentation with young children, particularly in the way they support and extend children's talking and thinking. Carlina Rinaldi, professor of pedagogy at the University of Modena and Reggio Emilia describes documentation as:

> Visible listening, as the construction of traces (through notes, slides, videos and so on) that not only testify to the children's learning paths and processes, but also make them possible because they are visible.
>
> (Project Zero, 2001, p. 83)

Documentation is an expression of not only *what* children are learning but also *how* they are learning. It captures children's identities as learners, their thoughts, feelings and theories and thus shows how their application of mastery orientation (Chapter 3) underpins their learning. Documentation can be seen not as the *product* but as the *process* of children's thinking, something to be returned to, revisited and reflected on, supporting deeper meta-cognitive understanding.

Documentation through learning stories and floor books

Documentation is central to our practice at Prince Edward Primary School, as we record the process of children's thinking, interests and fascinations. Floor books were introduced as a means of documenting children's thoughts and experiences through using observations and discussions to shape the learning opportunities we offer and help us to plan the direction of learning and next steps.

Floor books are essentially scrapbooks that collate and organise children's thinking, paying close attention to what our children find interesting, meaningful and valuable (see Figure 4.1). They capture the child's voice, their comments, questions and enquiries that inform their learning journey. We record exactly what the children say and the conversations that lead their learning, allowing children to respond and talk through their ideas, as can be seen in the following example:

The children (aged 3.1–4.8) had become fascinated by what our nursery class pet, Gary the Snail, did when the children were not at nursery. One day he went 'missing':

Caitlyn: "I've got an idea! He might be on holiday; we've got to send him a letter."

Mason: "There's slime here. He went out of the door. He's in school! In PE! Ask the grown-ups!"
Evie: "We can draw a picture to show if you can see him."
Corey: "We need a cucumber, it's Gary's favourite, and juicy leaves!"
Kenzie: "We've got to get a jar with leaves, catch him."
Leah: "I'm making a slide. It's a slide he goes up and down there and into his tank."
Grace: "I'm making a trap, when you open the door, we scoop him into the bucket."

The children had very different responses to this provocation and were all highly engaged and involved through their *serve and return* conversational talk. The adult's role was to listen and document (write down) the children's conversation and extend this through play, comments, questions and the provision of resources.

Documenting the child's voice emphasises the importance of talk in mathematical thinking. It is not a focus on the acquisition of mathematical knowledge but rather the mathematical thinking and understanding that underpins this; as such, we really begin to see how children understand and connect new teaching to previous learning.

Learning stories formed the basis of our work in the Talk for Maths Mastery initiative as they allowed us to capture children's thoughts, talk and play and present it in a way that could be shared with and reflected on by the children and their families. As with floor books, there is a focus on the process that children have gone through with the child's voice and photographs to demonstrate this journey.

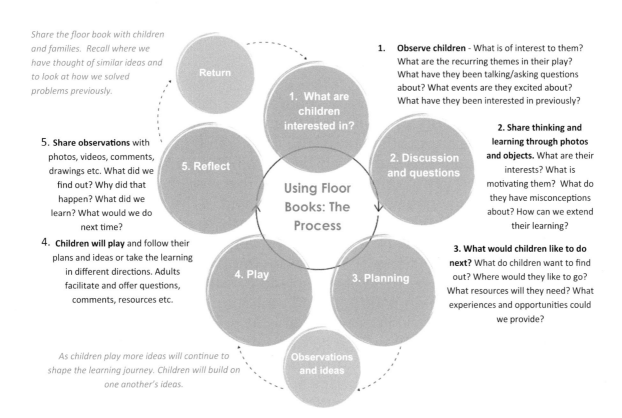

Figure 4.1 Using floor books – the process

The process of using floor books

Floor books are used across the Foundation Stage and the Nurture Group not only to capture learning that has taken place but to plan for future experiences and share ideas and discussions in a cycle of documentation which starts with observation, then evaluation/analysis and planning.

1. What are the children interested in?

The process begins with an idea, it might be something a child has said, an interest that has been observed, an object or an event. For example, we observed lots of tower building. Some children were interested in building the tallest tower whereas other children enjoyed knocking them down, causing some disagreements. We discussed this interest, and the children thought of the best materials for building a tower and the best way to knock it down! This developed into children designing devices and pendulums to knock their towers down, creating many opportunities for problem solving and explorations into shape, height and weight.

2. Discussion and questions

We then consider the many ways children are communicating what is important to them, judging from what they say, observing their schematic play and noting the things they place the most value in. This is shared and discussed, and questions are posed by the children and adults. Objects, photos and videos can be used to support this discussion to enable all children to actively engage and become involved.

Floor book conversations can take many forms; e.g. shorter one-to-one conversation between children and adults may be recorded, as well as small or larger group discussions and ongoing projects. These serve and return conversations are crucial as they lead to sustained shared thinking, stretching and deepening children's talk, thinking and learning. Children lead the conversation, talking about what is important to them. The adult's role is to ensure each child's voice can be heard by being open, listening carefully, clarifying children's comments, asking reflective questions and showing children that their responses are valued. In the Reggio approach, the *listening* is part of deep observation where the adult is actively tuning into what they see, hear and feel the child/children doing and saying and then giving "meaning to the message, and value to the person who is giving it" (Thornton and Brunton, 2005, p. 9). It is called the pedagogy of listening (Project Zero, 2001, p. 81).

3. Planning

As well as these informal serve and return conversations throughout the day, each week we ensure there is the opportunity to meet as a group to share the children's documentation together (using floor books and learning stories). At this point, we will review and reflect on the learning that has taken place and discuss what we would like to do next in preparation for the following week.

As the children in nursery (Foundation 1) follow a mixed pattern of attendance, topics and ideas often intertwine and build on one another. Children take each other's thoughts and questions and use them as inspiration for their own discoveries. One experience paves the way for the next as children have the opportunity to develop their own learning whilst benefitting from the collective, collaborative learning of the group (Project Zero, 2001).

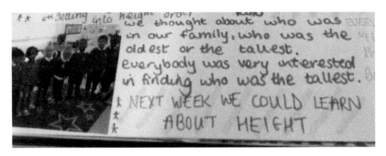

It is in this way that the children's learning journey is organic with one interest leading to another, allowing children to form connections in meaningful, familiar contexts that enable them to make sense of the world around them.

The adult works in partnership with the children as they learn together, co-constructing thinking from current ideas and making important connections, including links between experiences, decision making and the ability to act on and apply previous knowledge and skills. These dispositions and skills are all at the heart of Creating and Thinking Critically and sustained shared thinking (see Chapter 3).

4. Play

The floor book story I Can Jump 4 Metres! is an example of children co-constructing their mathematical ideas through serve and return conversations with adult support that lasted for a single afternoon.

Floor Book Story: I Can Jump 4 Metres!
(Children aged 3 and 4).

One afternoon, a child commented that they could jump 4 metres, then pointed into the air and jumped. We thought about how we could check if that really was 4 metres, and the children quickly went to collect measuring tapes. Realising that it would be quite tricky to jump that high the children wondered if they could jump that far and set up a measuring tape working together to make it a fair test, taking it in turns to jump and with support made name cards to place where they got to. There were many conversations about fairness and measuring.

Lois: "You can only do one jump; two jumps is too many."
Lillie: "You gotta keep your feet still when you land."
Jacob: "I'm going to tell my dad I jumped 125, you didn't even know I could jump 125 Miss Hulme!"

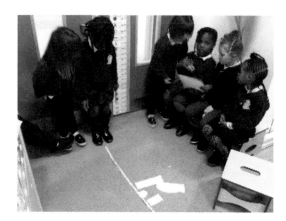

Many children came to join the investigation. They recognised that doing more than one jump, having extra turns or moving your feet changed the distance. We then watched a clip of Olympic long jumpers, and the children realised they wanted a run-up and took their investigation outside.

While this exploration lasted one afternoon, the children still reflect on it and return to the floor book to check if they can beat their personal best!

Seeing mathematical mastery in the documentation?

The concepts of problem solving, fluency and reasoning underpin the teaching of maths mastery (see Chapter 3). In this learning story, we can see how children, through their sustained shared thinking, are able to explore and understand these concepts in their child-led learning.

Problem solving

The children are highly motivated and driven to solve their problem as it is meaningful and set by them; they have ownership and are independently working on this together, competently and confidently self-regulating their learning in a sophisticated way described by Whitebread et al. (2009, p. 41) as "play, particularly pretend or symbolic play, contributes to learning by supporting children's development of meta-cognitive or self-regulatory skills, which are in turn crucial in the development of problem solving and creativity" (see Chapter 3).

First there is the question of how high or far they can jump; then the need to find resources to test this; then learning how to use these resources and create a fair test. At the same time, another child was solving a separate problem of turn-taking and applied their previous knowledge to create a system, asking each child to record their name and numbering them in order. These dispositions and skills are all part of children's mastery orientation and very evident in the characteristics of effective learning (see Chapter 3).

Fluency

Fluency is the ability to effectively recall mathematical concepts and facts. It can be considered in three elements: efficiency, accuracy and flexibility (Russell, 2000). The children choose *efficient* strategies to solve a problem, they use their knowledge of number patterns and relationships *accurately* and they are *flexible* in choosing the best (or multiple) methods to solve a problem.

Rather than memorising a method or an approach to solving a particular problem, children need to understand why they are approaching a problem in that way and when to use a particular strategy. Through play and continuous provision, children are constantly faced with problems that need to be solved, and they must make decisions about how to solve these problems. As Gardner suggests, 'Our view of understanding goes well beyond simple memorisation of facts and concepts to the appropriate deployment of knowledge in new situations' (Project Zero, 2001, p. 26).

Often conceptual fluency within the early years is considered as 'number sense' with children developing a deep understanding of the 'threeness of three' (Woodham and Pennant, 2014). As the children created rules to their play, they showed their understanding of number; the children knew they needed one turn each, and Toochi showed an awareness of number relationships as she managed turn-taking by assigning each child a number, when she got to the final child, she returned to number one.

As the children investigate, they demonstrate skills in counting, ordering, measuring and making comparisons in the main through using mastery-orientated dispositions and skills in their child-initiated play.

Reasoning

When children make their reasoning visible in this way, they demonstrate how they are making sense of mathematical skills and concepts and their level of understanding. For example, as the children negotiate a set of guidelines for the game they are developing, they are calling on all their previous knowledge and experience to create new understandings. Having the time to learn through trial and error is a crucial part of this as they quickly recognise the need for rules and put them in place through their collaborative conversations.

As the adult took a supporting role, it was up to the children to articulate their thinking to their peers. The adult responded to the initial comment of jumping 4 metres by wondering how that could be checked. This prompted the search for measuring tapes. Jacob made a quiet comment about jumping that 'far' rather than 'high'. This might have gone unnoticed, but the adult repeated it back so it was heard by the group, "You think we could jump that *far*, Jacob? Maybe we could . . ." The adult then continued to watch, and when the children faced difficulties such as turn-taking, added comments such as, "I wonder how we could make it *fair*?" to prompt children's thinking and support them in making connections without overpowering or leading the play.

The adult then extended the learning by showing a clip of the Olympic long jumpers, prompting a call for the investigation to be moved outside. The rules then needed to be renegotiated with the addition of a 'run-up' so that the slight variation in activity allowed the children to apply what they had learnt to a slightly different context and make informed changes.

In the learning story As Tall as a Camel, a child's comment about a picture in a book leads to a series of week-long investigations into height and perspective. Children demonstrate similar skills of problem solving and reasoning as they work to make themselves the tallest.

Case Study: As Tall as a Camel
(Children aged 3 and 4)

When reading the story *Lost and Found* by Oliver Jeffers, we turned the page and the character appeared much smaller than the page before as he stood next to a large boat.
 	
   Gracie: "He's shrunk!"
 	
When the adult asked why the boy looked small, the children shared their theories.
 	
   Oliver: "I think he went in the water and it shrunk him."
 	
   Tia: "He's been going big and little he's growing."
 	
   Tori: "I think he's just little and the boat's big."

We took photographs next to small and large items to explore how this changed the perspective of how tall we looked. Tyler and Tia were motivated to take this investigation further. Tyler asked Tia to take a picture of him very close to the camera.
 	
   Tyler: "I'm getting close to look big."
 	
   Tia investigated Tyler's hypothesis. If standing closer makes you look bigger, would further away make you smaller? She directed her friends to test this theory.
 	
   Tia: "Ty, you get right to that door outside and Scarlette you gotta stand this side and take a picture, he's gonna be so small!"

Case Study: As Tall as a Camel (Children aged 3 and 4)	
Other children joined the investigation, and the children were asked, *"How can we make ourselves smaller?"* Gracie commented: "If something's more little we can stand next to it, we will look big." In response, Toochi offered the inverse: "If we stand next to something big we will look small." Tia understood that this would make you appear taller or shorter, but she wanted to really make herself taller. She knew that she could use the height chart on the door to measure herself. The height chart shows animals of comparative heights at 5-centimetre intervals, and the children regularly use this to check how much they have grown (and to measure visitors to our room!).	
Tyler came to show how tall he was and stood on his tiptoes. Tia was keen for all measuring to be done correctly. Tia: "Stand on your foot bottoms, don't be tricky on your tippy toes, get your head straight." Tori: "I want to be as big as a giant, I'm gonna make my shoes a bit bigger." Tia: "I'm gonna make me really, really high!"	
Tori had the idea that making something to stand on, in this case, shoes, would make her taller. Tori went to the workshop to investigate. Tyler liked this idea but preferred to work with wood so went to the workbench and began screwing two flat pieces of wood together. He took them back to the height chart and stood on them to see if he was taller. Tyler: "I've got a wood thing that makes me bigger." Tia questioned his choice of materials. Tia: "You got flat wood; you need big wood."	

Case Study: As Tall as a Camel
(Children aged 3 and 4)

Tori returned with a cardboard box with ribbon attached to fasten it to her feet. As she stood on it, it squashed down slightly.

Tori: "I can stand on it, I'm a bit taller."

Tia: "What about one more stuff?"

Tori: "I'm still a lion, I think I can make it a bit taller."

Tia: "It's coz you're squashing it."

Tori: "What if I put it on the bottom, that won't squash it? I think I need something else that won't squash."

Tori returned with two metal containers and achieved her goal.

Through the week, other children engaged in their own height investigations, e.g. when Asaad's older sister arrived, he predicted how tall she would be then checked against the height chart.

Asaad: "I think you're as tall as a camel, no you're a polar bear. I think dad's as tall as a camel, taller than you."

Photos were shared in our floor book along with the children's comments. As a group, we discussed the investigation and the children were asked a question,

"*How can you make yourself the tallest?*"

Lula: "I would grow up."

Tori had learnt from her experience with different materials: "Get lots of wood, stick it together and stand on it."

Tyler changed his thinking: "Get some wood and . . . put it on your head!"

Gracie built on Tyler's new idea: "I was standing on something on the floor and I put something on my head."

Lillie: "When you get some big cardboard, stick it together, get some more and stand on it, you're as big as a camel!"

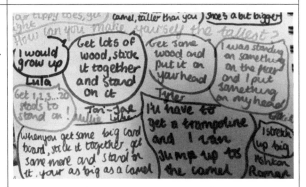

Case Study: As Tall as a Camel
(Children aged 3 and 4)

The camel is the tallest animal on our height chart, even taller than all the adults in the room, so for many children there is a fascination with being as tall as a camel!

The children's investigations continued in their independent learning inside and out over the following weeks and months.

Tyler, Tia and Toochi found crates outside and a pole to measure themselves against writing their names. Tori continued to explore the best materials for shoes and used the stilts outdoors as inspiration for her designs.

When new ideas came, we returned to our floor book to recall, reflect and discuss what we had previously learned. The children could see how tall they had become with their previous investigations and where they could go next (see Figure 4.1: '5. Reflect').

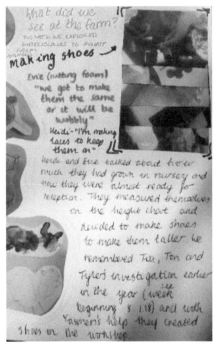

How can children's serve and return interactions support their learning?

In As Tall as a Camel, we observed the role that talk plays in shaping and extending children's thinking. Children present their own theories and ideas while exploring them collaboratively within the context of the group using serve and return conversations to develop their thinking through talking together (see Chapter 3). At ages 3 and 4, the children have not yet grasped all the mathematical language relating to height and length, so instead they interchange words they are familiar with such as 'higher', 'more big' and 'bigger'. While Tia appears to lead the group with theories and ideas, she benefits from her friend's introduction of language such as 'taller'.

The open-ended collaborative nature of the children's investigation allowed everyone to engage in their preferred style of learning. Children could play cooperatively whilst working in a way that motivates them as learners. For example, Tyler was able to take on board Tori's idea of creating something to stand on while working with materials that he felt confident about, achieving the same objective whilst having ownership over his own learning. In the discussion at the end, the children demonstrate how they have listened to and built on one another's ideas, offering them the opportunity to respond in their own way using what Malaguzzi calls the one hundred languages of children (Malaguzzi, 1996).

When we document children's talking, thinking and learning, we value how they are interacting both with one another and with the environment. Through these observations and talk, we can see the process of their thinking as they question, comment and negotiate ideas, and crucially we also see how much they truly understand and have mastered. It also has the following impact on the adults:

> The act of documenting changes teachers' understanding of what goes on in the classroom. It slows them down, encouraging them to reflect on and understand the deeper meaning and value of the learning experiences.
> (Krechevsky and Mardell; Project Zero, 2001, p. 289)

Children are constantly communicating their thinking and interests, and it is up to us to hear, see and feel (listen to) what they are expressing. As such, an enabling environment that provides the time, space and resources to observe and respond to the different ways in which children learn is non-negotiable.

Reflection point

How can we use documentation to capture children's identities as mathematicians?
How can we enable children to set and solve their own problems?
How can we provide opportunities for children's thoughts and ideas to build on one another?

The following learning story Here, There and Everywhere from the nursery floor book and the learning story 'Paths' both capture a short episode of learning that took place during a week.

Floor Book Learning Story: Here, There and Everywhere
Children aged 3–4.5

We observed some of the youngest children (3–3.2) taking an interest in positioning as they began to line up objects around the room.

A previous learning story we called 'Paths' showed the children's interest in creating lines and paths for cars and diggers.

Alongside this the older children (3.5–4.5) started to explore paths on a larger scale using giant Numicon and extending rolls of ribbon down the corridor.

Some of the children wanted to create paths in different directions, and the focus shifted to vertical investigations as the children created a pulley system.

Floor Book Learning Story: Here, There and Everywhere
Children aged 3–4.5

In **'Paths'**, the children discuss making it 'this way'; 'bigger this way' and 'bigger, bigger, BIG'. These children are just three and are clearly demonstrating their early interpretations of size, length and width.

The children's conversations and actions in their play reveal their thought processes. They know what they would like to achieve and use familiar vocabulary to express their ideas. The younger children's emphasis on the word 'BIG' shows that they actually mean more than big, something much larger, but as they don't yet have the vocabulary, they use intonation and actions to make their meaning clear.

Other older children (3.5–4.5) are interested in how to create paths that enable travel. They first made a pathway down the length of the corridor, then devised a pulley system. The children were captivated by the idea of 'big' both in the length of the corridor and the height of the pulley system. Having the space to explore length and height together helped children to develop an understanding of the relationship between the two mathematical concepts.

How language deepens understanding – the role of the adult

In As Tall as a Camel, the children lead the investigations. The adult occasionally offers questions that open up possibilities and stretch children's thinking without setting the agenda for children's play. Craft suggests that this *possibility thinking*:

> [e]ssentially involves a transition in understanding; in other words, the shift from 'What is this?' to exploration 'What can I/we do with this?' Fostering possibility involves enabling children to find and refine problems as well as to solve them.
>
> (2008, p. 1)

We can see how the children are not waiting to be told how to investigate their problem but will turn to one another to share their ideas and will even comment on other children's choices such as Tia's references to Tyler choosing the wrong type of wood or Tori needing more resources. We can see how the children are self-regulating their own learning as they make decisions about resources and they reflect on one another's actions (Whitebread et al., 2009). The children are faced with a problem that they would like to solve. They have not been provided with the resources (directly) or instructed how to solve this problem, so they need to think creatively using their previous knowledge and experiences (see Chapter 3).

It is through talk (dialogue, discussion and discovery) that we can build on children's knowledge and understanding and move learning forward. The floor books enable us to explore children's answers and misconceptions as talk and discussion form the foundation of mathematical understanding (Stevens, 2018).

How talk and play can reveal misconceptions

In children's everyday lives, they are inundated with experiences and information in many ways which they then try to make sense of through forming connections to other information in their brains. From birth, children are meaning makers as they undertake the challenge to make sense of and understand the world around them (Pound, 2006). As children strive to process and make meaning from the information they receive, they can develop misconceptions. Misconceptions are an insight into how children see the world, their thinking and their understanding of mathematical concepts (Cockburn and Littler, 2008).

Children's misconceptions may take many forms, through their play, their talk and the choices they make; for example:

- "I'm the biggest so I'm the oldest"
- "18, 19, tenteen"

- Choosing the tallest container to hold the most liquid despite it being far narrower
- Believing they have more objects when they are spread apart
- When counting children "1, 2, 3, 4, 5", responding "but I'm 3!"

Case study: only big things are heavy (children aged 3 and 4)

In a conversation about which animals, from the story *Dear Zoo*, might be able to be delivered by the postman, one child commented "only big things are heavy". This could be quickly disproved, and often when exploring weight, we will collect small heavy items and large light items ready to address this common misconception.

However, by reflecting on this with the children, we were able to stretch their thinking: maybe only big things are heavy, how could we check? This prompted a discussion followed by a search to find something giant sized to test this idea. Along the way, the children chose different items, and we explored what the words 'big' and 'heavy' meant in relation to each other.

The adults posed possibility questions (Craft, 2008) that extended the line of inquiry or repeated children's responses, e.g. 'Aaron says he is very strong and it's not heavy for him. How do we know if something is heavy?' The children's responses show their reasoning: 'It's easy because there's nothing inside it'! Each response presented is an opportunity to test a new idea.

The children were able to apply what they had previously learned and brought new resources to test their theories. In this way, the children's understanding of 'heavy' and 'light' was not an abstract concept as it was connected with their existing ideas of size and weight. By setting their own problems and testing their own ideas, children made connections with their own learning and understanding. Interestingly, in discussion of the preschools in Reggio Emilia, Thornton and Brunton suggested that children 'discover for themselves much more than they are told' (2005, p. 41).

How do we address children's misconceptions?

Children learn rules and patterns based on their experiences and interactions with the world around them. As children develop their understanding, they may over-apply a rule, for example by thinking that only big things can be heavy or that things have changed size when viewed from further away. In the case study As Tall as a Camel a misconception led to multiple theories and investigations. Through discussion, it also becomes clear that other children shared this misconception. Choosing how to address this can be the difference between children developing a conceptual understanding or simply being corrected. For children to fully understand a concept, they need to not only understand the rule in isolation but also have a deeper understanding that enables them to apply their thinking to new situations.

> Stopping to think about it, most of us find it far easier to develop an understanding of a rule if we are introduced to several examples of it and counter-examples which do not follow the rule.
> (Cockburn and Littler, 2008, p. 14)

To address children's misconceptions, we must first identify where the misconception has come from. This could be lack of experience, over-application of a rule or a misunderstanding of language or a problem.

Brodie.K (2015) describes misconceptions as "ideas that make sense to learners and are reasonable in relation to what they know but are incorrect mathematically". She goes on to suggest, "Misconceptions usually arise when learners take knowledge that is correct in one area of mathematics and apply it in another area where it's no longer correct".

In the first instance, we can help to reduce children's misconceptions by thinking about how we present problems. By offering children real-life problems and the opportunity to apply mathematical knowledge to a variety of situations, we are enabling them to make connections. A rich environment with real-life and open-ended resources allows us to challenge and stretch children's thinking. By giving children the opportunity to

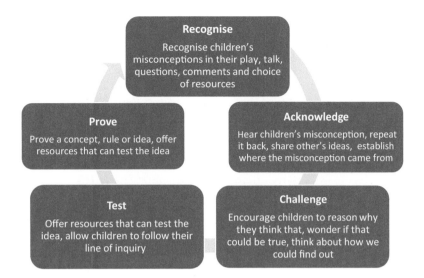

Figure 4.2 Addressing misconceptions

question and explore why a rule or pattern does not apply, they develop skills of problem solving and reasoning. In our teaching we can seek to reduce misconceptions in the early stages by offering resources and problems that challenge rules and show thinking in different ways, but how do we address a misconception once it has already been formed?

The diagram in Figure 4.2 illustrates this process of addressing children's misunderstandings in a supportive way, which does not undermine their confidence and enthusiasm. It is also a model which they can use independently as part of their problem-solving repertoire of skills.

Reflection point

How can we respond to children's misconceptions?
How can we support children to make connections in their learning?
How can we use misconceptions to create opportunities for reasoning?

How do we follow children's mathematical interests?

What is an interest?

When children are fascinated, they often circle and return to a subject of interest. The floor book documents these conversations and allows us to plan activities based entirely upon the child's engagement and involvement.

As subjects are revisited, children strengthen their understanding, each time building on their previous knowledge and beginning to master skills. Children are constantly developing their understanding both of themselves and the world around them. Therefore, when they come to revisit previous learning and experience, it is often at a deeper level of understanding (Bruner, 1960).

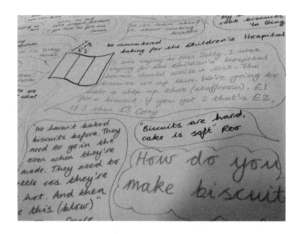

For example, in the Reception class, the children had a particular interest in food that sparked off a variety of learning opportunities such as regular baking and cooking activities where children were able to gain an understanding of measures within different contexts. This supported their play and learning, and they began to contextualise their mathematical skills and knowledge with the additions of scales in the home corner and measuring bowls in the play dough area.

Children were able to follow recipes and began to understand ordinal numbers in meaningful contexts and record their mathematical thinking by writing their own recipes. Each time they returned to the subject, it was at a deeper level, and the children had the opportunity to build on, challenge and extend their ideas. As children approached the activities with a level of familiarity, along with a bank of previous knowledge, they were motivated and confident to take on new challenges having mastered previous learning. In consideration of the resources used to support the teaching of mathematical mastery, the National Centre for Excellence in the Teaching of Mathematics (NCETM) suggests "the focus is on the development of deep structural knowledge and the ability to make connections" (2014).

We need to create an environment that allows children to explore ideas in a variety of contexts over a longer period of time. Documentation then allows us to follow a thread of learning and show how children have understood and applied their knowledge of a concept and, importantly, their mathematical mastery.

How does children's schematic thinking and learning support their early mathematical development?

Children's first interests are innate and frequently displayed by babies and toddlers as schematic patterns of thinking. Atherton and Nutbrown describe schemas as 'Children's choices, and their fastidious inclinations towards objects around them in the learning environment' (2013 p. 4) (see Chapter 2).

Young children's play reveals schemas as repeated patterns of behaviour; for example schemas can include transporting, trajectory, enveloping, enclosing, transforming, connection, rotation and positioning. Within these schema, children show an interest in how things move, respond and fit together. Through this exploration, children begin to learn about cause and effect as they actively engage with objects and make changes to the world around them. As children follow these patterns of behaviour, they begin to build up an understanding of how things work and the way objects move and respond. For example, children with an interest in enclosing may hide or contain objects (and themselves) by finding small spaces or creating walls and boundaries. Through these actions, they develop an understanding of size, shape, space and volume.

As these interests are innate, within children, they provide a rich starting point for early mathematical experiences through their intrinsic, playful explorations; therefore we must look for ways in which we can support and extend children's thinking and learning through their schemas (Atherton and Nutbrown, 2013). In documenting children's learning over prolonged periods, we can identify patterns and repetition in their play that are indicative of a sustained interest. Recognising a schema allows us to extend children's learning in ways they find motivating. We can see this happening in the earlier case study, Here, There and Everywhere where a positioning schema starts to emerge as children line up objects around the classroom.

The following table was developed, as part of the Talk for Maths Mastery initiative, to take a closer, in-depth look at children's schematic thinking and learning from various perspectives starting with the child, then the adult's role, the enabling environment and home learning partnership.

Following Schematic Thinking and Learning
As floor books make the learning process visible, patterns of behaviour begin to emerge showing children's interests at a deeper level, as well as schematic thinking and behaviour. For example, the children in nursery had a prolonged fascination with filling bags and wheelbarrows that showed many of the children to be following a transporting schema, with an interest in moving objects and enclosure.

Child's perspective I like to . . .	repeat and return to play that I find interesting.
	have the opportunity to repeat behaviours to help make connections in my brain.
	fill bags and containers and see how I can move things from one place to another.
Adults' role You can support my mathematical thinking by . . .	allowing me to play out my schema and develop my thinking through activities such as writing and posting letters.
	sharing my actions with me through observations to allow me to reflect on my thinking.
	allowing me to follow my lines of inquiry and test and explore ideas to strengthen my understanding.
	listening to my ideas and encouraging me to find ways to test and explain my thinking. e.g. "How do you know? Why did that happen? What will you do now . . . ?"
Enabling environment and continuous provision To develop and extend my learning I need . . .	resources that enable me to play out my schema such as bags, wheelbarrows, suitcases, wheeled toys, buckets and small objects.
	meaningful activities that stretch my mathematical thinking such as packing bags for adventures.
	provision that is enhanced to allow me to add purpose and direction to my schematic play such as different sized containers, differently coloured objects to transport, items that can be sorted or numbered.
	the freedom to use resources from all areas of continuous provision to test my ideas.
Home Learning Partnership Home learning helps me when . . .	you follow my interest in transporting, e.g. riding on the bus, tram or train.
	you encourage me to help with everyday experiences such as shopping, helping me to pack a bag when we go on visits.
	you recognise and extend my patterns of behaviour with everyday mathematical problems such as collecting items to tidy away.
	we make the most of maths in meaningful contexts such as looking at cause and effect during trips to the park, "I wonder why this side of the seesaw went down? What would happen if . . . ?
	you comment on everyday experiences to give mathematical vocabulary meaning, "Oh this ball is very small I didn't think it would be so heavy!"

Planning for children's interests

When thinking about mastery we looked at how children embed and apply the skills they have learned in different/new contexts. This requires the children to want to take what they have learned into their own play; if it is relevant and meaningful to them, they will pursue their idea independently (see Figure 1.1: '3 Planning').

Throughout the learning stories, we saw the many ways children show their interests and how we can use these to plan for future learning. From individual comments to ongoing schematic learning, children are constantly showing what is important to them. Planning for these interests can mean providing resources, offering comments or questions to explore new possibilities or planning future activities. For example, one Friday afternoon two children in nursery asked if we could make a marble run. *In the moment*, we went to collect tubes, pipes and tape and started the idea. At the end of the day we shared the interest with the group to see what we might need and plan future activities for the following week. The learning continued over the next two weeks from tubes and pipes, to a marble machine, to a conker rollercoaster.

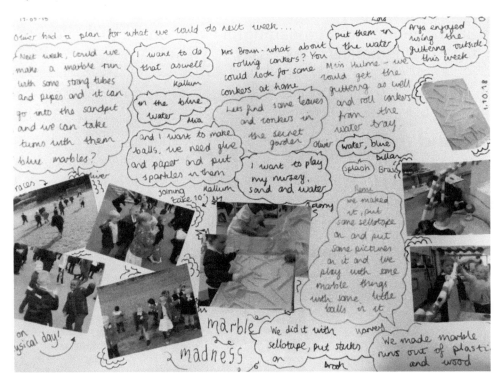

A rich enabling environment with open-ended resources and time, space and flexibility to allow children to explore their own ideas supports mastery orientation. For example:

- Children need the opportunity to solve real-life problems as part of their everyday play offering them the chance to apply their mathematical knowledge

- An emphasis on talk develops children's reasoning as they comment, question, negotiate and articulate their thinking with peers
- mathematical concepts and vocabulary have real meaning as children engage with them as part of their play
- Allowing the children to take the lead, to play and follow through with their ideas and actions empowers them as learners and develops their ability to apply their own knowledge to new situations
- Floor books and learning stories provide children with the opportunity to understand and stretch their mathematical thinking and strengthen their understanding by tapping into what motivates them as learners

---

Reflection point

How do we use children's recurring interests to deepen mathematical learning?

How does revisiting children's recurring interests support them in making connections in their learning?

How can we explore and extend schematic thinking and learning to develop children's early maths?

How can we offer children meaningful experiences that allow them to apply their mathematical thinking?

Mastery and meta-cognition

Being able to return to and reflect on previous learning allows children to develop an awareness of their own thinking (meta-cognition) and deepen their learning, understanding and mastery (see Chapter 3).

As we see children's sustained interests in their play, we can revisit and build on what they have previously learned. Ideas are not repeated but rather extended, developed and deepened, leading to new theories to be explored.

By documenting children's thinking in the floor books and learning stories, we enable children to revisit their learning, committing it to long-term memory. It is this repetition of activities, routines and events which helps children to develop their memory, talk and questioning and encourages children to think flexibly making strong mathematical connections and confidently applying this to new challenges (O'Connor, 2017) – all crucial elements of mastery orientation (see Chapter 3).

Reflection point

How do we encourage children to revisit and reflect on their mathematical learning?

How can we create opportunities for children to represent their thinking in their own way?

How do we actively involve children in making decisions about their own learning?

What is meta-cognition?

Meta-cognition is an awareness and understanding of our own thought processes and being able to think about our thinking. For children to be able to truly master and embed their learning, they need the opportunity to reflect on their thinking. Floor books are invaluable for enabling children to return to their previous learning and reflect on their thinking and experiences. The following table shows how meta-cognition can be supported with regard to mathematics; however, it is an essential cognitive process for all aspects of learning.

Child's perspective I like to . . .	have ownership of our floor book and be able to access it with my friends and family.
	look at, talk about photos of myself, my friends and see my work in our floor book and learning stories.
	contribute to the floor book with drawings, ideas, talk, questions, photos or objects from home.
	be able to return to subjects, themes and issues that I find interesting.
	pose my own questions and create problems based on what is interesting or important to me, e.g. Corey said, "We're going to make a shop up there (staffroom); it's £1 for a biscuit. If you got 2 that's £2, if 3 then £3."

Adults' role You can support my mathematical thinking by . . .	engaging in reflective dialogue and discussion as we talk about my experiences, e.g. "Look at this, do you remember what happened when we wanted to get into teams? Why didn't it work? What do we always have to think about?" making links between my experiences: "I remember when we learnt about food before, can you remember what happened when we . . . ? How do you make biscuits?" paying close attention to and recording what I say to gain an insight into what interests and motivates my learning. posing possibility questions that help to make connections between my experiences and direct my future learning, e.g. "What could we do with this . . . ? What if . . . ?"
Enabling environment and continuous Provision To develop and extend my learning, I need . . .	the floor book to be available for me and my family to share and talk about together, e.g. in the morning when I arrive. opportunities and encouragement to add my own ideas, work and pictures, e.g. my drawing of how we should share my birthday cake. the learning process to be made visual, interactive and meaningful, e.g. with photos of each step of our learning, mark-making and work from home.  to have the time and opportunity to reflect on my previous experiences, e.g. "Do you remember when we tried to do that with . . . what happened? What could we try next time?" the opportunity to revisit learning and experiences, e.g. when we didn't have enough resources for everyone and working out what to do.

Home learning partnership Home learning helps me when . . .	you share and comment on our floor book and learning stories with me.
	you reflect on my learning and experiences with me through photos and memories, e.g. "What happened when we . . . ? Why did that happen? What could we do next time?"
	encouraging me to make decisions about my own learning, e.g. deciding how to share the iPad with my brother or sister so it is fair.
	we make the most of opportunities to apply my skills and interests in real-life contexts, e.g. "Shall we draw a map to Grandma's house? Which way do we go? What do we see along the way?" Or preparing my own lunch, "What will we need? How many do we normally have?"

Summary

The mastery approach to teaching maths has been strongly influenced by South Asian practice which in itself has roots in educational theory. For example, presenting materials in concrete, pictorial and abstract forms can be traced back to Bruner's enactive, iconic and symbolic forms of representation (Bruner, 1966). The aim is to enable children to solve problems effectively by developing their mathematical thinking, language and understanding of concepts (Drury, 2014).

When teaching for mastery, we are asked (Evans, 2017; NCETM, 2014) to consider:

- presenting resources in many forms from the concrete to the pictorial to the abstract
- representing an idea in multiple ways and offering variation to deepen children's understanding
- encouraging reasoning to enable children to explain their understanding
- providing opportunities for problem solving
- developing children's fluency in their ability to recall and apply mathematical concepts

In this chapter we have seen how this can all be undertaken whilst following children's interests and using documentation which, as Rinaldi explains, is the foundation of good practice:

> Teachers who know how to observe, document, and interpret the processes that the children undergo autonomously will realize in this context their greatest potential to learn how to teach.
> (Project Zero, 2001, p. 83)

The pedagogy of Reggio Emilia sees all children as confident, competent and capable. Talk for Maths Mastery comes from this same perspective and the understanding that all young children have the potential of achieving in maths through playing and exploring, practicing and applying concepts over time (Boyd and Ash, 2018).

Finally, there must be relationships and an ethos where children's ideas and interests are valued, wherein the adult works with the children to construct future learning and is excited for where the learning will go next.

5 Building mathematical thinking through whole-class child-led learning

AMY PARKER

In this chapter we share our thinking and practice as we followed the children's lead, listening to their mathematical ideas and how we could use these as a starting point for teaching to deepen learning for the whole class. We posed the following key questions to focus our thinking and understanding.

Key questions

1. What is the place of play in developing mathematical mastery?
2. How do we follow children's interests and build mathematical thinking and mastery?
3. What does mathematical mastery through whole-class, child-led learning look like in practice?

Prince Edward Primary School is in inner-city Sheffield, an area of regeneration with many families who experience high levels of deprivation (over 60% of our children are eligible for Pupil Premium funding). This creates various challenges; however, despite the low levels of attainment on entry, we know our children have the potential to catch up over time and be successful. Taking part in the Talk for Maths Mastery initiative enabled us to work collaboratively with other schools in similar positions, develop our practice and think deeply about how we wanted all our children to experience mathematical learning and teaching.

The Foundation Stage has always had a philosophy of working collaboratively with Nursery (F1), Reception (F2) and Year 1 (Y1) classes (3–6+ years), creating a play-based curriculum which values the true nature of play, acknowledging how fundamental this is to young children's development and learning; recognising when the adults need to step in and guide learning as well as balancing adult-led focused teaching with child-led, initiated play and learning.

1. What is the place of play in developing mathematical mastery?

Following a play-based curriculum gives us an insight into the many ways in which our children approach their learning. Play, as fundamental to young children's development and learning, is a much discussed concept, and although there is wide-ranging evidence (Hirsh-Pasek, 2018; Zosh, 2017; Ofsted, 2015) of its essential role in the Early Years Foundation Stage (EYFS), there is confusion as to what this should look like in practice. The EYFS Statutory Framework (DfE, 2017, p. 1.8) states:

> Play is essential for children's development, building their confidence as they learn to explore, to think about problems, and relate to others. Children learn by leading their own play, and by taking part in play which is guided by adults. There is an on-going judgement to be made by practitioners about the balance between activities led by children, and activities led or guided by adults.
>
> (p. 9)

Ofsted's thematic review in 2015 validated the place of play in supporting how young children learn and develop,

> The significance of play in allowing children to learn and develop across such a broad range of developmental areas has long been understood. Its fundamental value is recognised in the United Nations Convention on the Rights of the Child[1] and the statutory framework for the Early Years Foundation Stage.
>
> (p. 8)

Ofsted (2015) goes on to say:

> Play provides the natural, imaginative and motivating contexts for children to learn about themselves, one another and the world around them. A single moment of sustained play can afford children many developmental experiences at once, covering multiple areas of learning and reinforcing the characteristics of effective learning.
>
> (p. 8)

The Lego Foundation (Liu et al., 2017) highlights how these playful experiences not only allow children to make sense of the world around them now but also prepare them for their future: "Beyond enjoyment, playful experiences have the potential to give children skills they will need in the future that will go beyond facts" (p. 6).

However, this gives adults little guidance as to what a playful approach to learning and teaching should look like in an early years setting/ school. Adding to this is the confusion that often surrounds the balance between adult-led and child-initiated play and what is appropriate. There are many examples of adult-directed activities where the adult has a set idea of the outcome and children are expected to follow this. These are often in the form of beautifully presented counting resources in a dedicated maths area, only for the adult to become frustrated when children do not use them in the way intended. But how does the child know you want them to count and add up how many there are, when they would rather investigate stacking and sorting them? These are both potentially valuable skills and processes in themselves but not what was intended by the adult.

Reflections on practice

As an experienced Reception teacher, I have been through the pain of setting up a beautiful activity, knowing what I wanted the children to do and learn. However, the children had other ideas; after seeing the resources, they did something completely different, ending up in a big, untidy mess.

In **Easter Maths Addition** (see Figure 5.1), the aim was that the children would be able to count out chicks into the cups and then make addition sentences using the chicks and nests. This is not what happened. Everything ended up in a big pile with little addition taking place!

What I learnt from these experiences is that it is much better to observe children's interests, enhance an area and make changes which build on these interests, keeping the children involved but ensuring that it is as open-ended as possible. For example, there was lots of maths happening when we added Conker Fun to provision (see Figure 5.2). The children naturally counted how many conkers fitted in the cylinders, talked about which cylinder had the most and the size of the conkers going into the cylinders. We did not need a specific focus to prompt mathematical talk. Adults were on hand to follow their lead, interact, enhance and extend learning when the children were ready.

It is important to stand back and observe what the children do with resources and remember that, if they are not doing what you intended, it does not mean they are not learning and demonstrating their skills, knowledge and understanding.

Figure 5.1 'Easter Maths Addition'

Figure 5.2 'Conker Fun'

Ofsted in *Teaching and Play in the Early Years: A Balancing Act* (2015) sought to address some of these issues in their helpful definition of teaching, acknowledging the link between play and learning and the many ways this can be applied in practice, saying, "We found no one way of approaching teaching and play" (p. 6).

The Ofsted definition of teaching

> Teaching should not be taken to imply a 'top down' or formal way of working. It is a broad term which covers the many different ways in which adults help young children learn. It includes their interactions with children during planned and child-initiated play and activities: communicating and modelling language, showing, explaining, demonstrating, exploring ideas, encouraging, questioning, recalling, providing a narrative for what they are doing, facilitating and setting challenges. It takes account of the equipment they provide and the attention to the physical environment as well as the structure and routines of the day that establish expectations. Integral to teaching is how practitioners assess what children know, understand and can do as well as take account of their interests and dispositions to learning (characteristics of effective learning), and use this information to plan children's next steps in learning and monitor their progress.
>
> (p. 11)

This definition refers to interactions with children during planned and child-initiated play and activities but does not develop this further or say what the balance should be. Child-initiated learning is often thought of as play where the activity "is wholly decided upon by the child, based on the child's own motivation, and remains under the child's control" (DCFS, 2009b, p. 12). This is true play, rather than playful experiences which may have adult intentions. We talk about this third perspective as an adult-initiated activity rather than adult-led (see Figure 5.3).

There is room for interpretation, and settings/schools need to be clear on their pedagogical philosophies before putting their ideas into practice. The underpinning philosophy of our school is that children learn best when they are happy and motivated through their playful experiences, interactions and interests. We seek to interact with the children and guide their experiences in order to make the most of their fascinations and promote progression in their knowledge and skills. We refer to Fisher's (2013, pp. 148–50) key features of play, which she describes as a *charter* of the essentials of play, and then consider what the children will be able to learn through child-initiated play and where they may need a little or a lot more adult support and teaching.

1. Play has to be the first consideration when planning the environment.
2. Play needs open-ended and adaptable resources.

Adult-led maths

Definition	What does this look like in practice at Prince Edward Primary School in F1, F2 and Y1?			Examples from the Love Monster learning story (with links to characteristics of effective learning and mastery opportunities)
	F1	F2	Y1	
Adult-led activities are those which adults initiate. The activities are not play, and children are not likely to see them as play, but they should be **playful** – open-ended activities presented to children, which have elements of imagination and active exploration that will increase the interest and motivation for children. As well as focused activities with groups of children, adult-led activities can include greeting times, story times, songs and even tidying up. *Playing to Learn* (Chilvers, D. 2012, p. 10).	• Continuous provision is key to the enabling environment with enhancements planned by adults to ensure there is progression of skills and resources • Stories, songs and rhymes are used throughout provision to promote mathematical concepts and skills • Observations are made 'in the moment' by adults during child-led play to assess, plan 'in the moment' and move children's learning forward			• The adult introduced an interesting story which provoked the children's thinking and gave their mathematical learning a purpose in a cross-curricular way (active learning). • The adult modelled the correct mathematical vocabulary, so the children are then able to use it later themselves. • The adult modelled what to do, then provided the correct resources so the children could try it out themselves (counting, calculating, measuring and data handling). • The adult encouraged children to add more information which they might forget by themselves (dates, times). • The adult taught the mathematical skills such as to count 1–1 or sharing objects equally when it has a purpose for the children (active learning).
	• Themes discussed during talk/floor book sessions with the children guide the learning for the week These are recorded in floor books (see Chapter 4) • Learning stories are used to record and reflect on children's learning, allowing them to consider their own learning • Some short carpet sessions with an adult-led outcome, such as learning about the number 3 (what it looks like in different representations and different places)	• Four maths-based carpet sessions a week with a set adult intention, such as learning to say one more than a number. These are linked to the theme or topic where possible • Children complete some follow-up adult-led activities with an adult to support them linked to a key skill learning objective	• Five carpet sessions a week with set adult intention (15–20 minutes) • Children complete one follow-up adult-led activity with an adult to support them each week • Children also complete a follow-up activity set by the adult but completed independently • Challenges are available for the children to complete in provision but are set by the adults	

Figure 5.3 Adult led/adult initiated/child initiated

Adult-initiated maths

Definition	What this looks like in practice at Prince Edward Primary School in F1, F2 and Y1			Examples from the Love Monster learning story (with links to characteristics of effective learning and mastery opportunities)
	F1	F2	Y1	
Adult-initiated activities are those for which the teacher has in mind clear learning intentions but, once the resources are set up and the activity is 'kicked off', the teacher leaves the group to learn independently.

Adult-initiated activities must, by nature, be different from adult-focused activities because they will be left to the children to pursue independently and where children start off their lines of inquiry may not be where they end up.

Moving onto Key Stage One (Fisher, J, 2010, pp. 71–72). | Some activities are set up in provision which the adults have a learning intention for. However, once the children find the resources, they can explore them independently and take their learning in the direction of their choice.

Adults will observe, wait and listen (OWL) before entering interactions with the children. They will consider what the children are *really* interested in and learning taking into account a range of possibilities. These possibilities include schema as well as themes of interests. The resources left in provision are designed to influence the children but are not definitive, and children will never be told they are 'doing it wrong'. | | Adult-initiated activities are more guided in Year 1. They are introduced to the children by an adult and explained. However, the adult then leaves the children to continue the activity independently. When returning to find out what the children have been learning, the adult is sensitive to the fact that the outcome may be different from that which was intended and will discuss this with the children to find out what learning has taken place.

The adult-intended learning outcomes are linked to the maths objective being covered by the whole class that session or week. | The adult helps children organise their thoughts in their play – usually through talk.

The adult recognises the importance of letting children take responsibility for the next steps in their learning and provides opportunities which do not dictate the outcome (mastery).

The adult is aware of what children need to be taught and what they can find out for themselves.

The adult provides the correct resources to support the children's learning and encourage them to use them independently (mastery) (playing and exploring).

The adult enables the children to help solve daily mathematical problems such as, "Are there enough plates for everybody?" (creating and thinking critically).

The adult provides opportunities to follow up the adult-supported activities with child-led activities, such as balances in the water tray, eggs and other ingredients to mix, data handling problems which are about me (mastery) (playing and exploring). |
| | In all year groups adults will observe the children in play before stepping in to ensure the play is purposeful and not just a repetition of low-level skills. The type of resources provided for each age range is important to ensure there is an expected progression through the resources available and not always through adult intervention. Children should be encouraged to challenge themselves.

See child-initiated about how more adult-initiated is introduced through the year groups. | | | |

Figure 5.3 (Continued)

Child-led or child-initiated maths

Definition	What this looks like in practice at Prince Edward Primary School in F1, F2 and Y1			Examples from the Love Monster Learning Story (with links to Characteristics of Effective Learning & mastery opportunities)
	F1	F2	Y1	
Child-initiated activity has many characteristics in common with play, as it is wholly decided upon by the child, based on the child's own motivation, and remains under the child's control. It may involve play of many types, or it may be seen by the child as an activity with a serious purpose to explore a project or express an idea which the child may not see as pure play. It is guided by certain expectations within an early years setting regarding responsible use of space, time and purposes. Playing to Learn (Chilvers, D. 2012, p.9)	• Continuous Provision is key to the enabling environment. Open-ended resources support children to take their learning in which ever direction they choose. They may move away from the class themes to follow their own fascinations and interests. Children may be observed returning to the same types of play again and again • Observations are made by adults and they sensitively enter the play in order to engage in Sustained Shared Thinking with children and move learning forward • Additional resources are added by the adult if requested by the child/ren or as a result of observation			The adult provides an environment where children's ideas are valued and respected The adults respond to children's interests which may lead to covering maths not on the EYFS and Y1 curriculum plans (Creating and thinking critically) There will be more challenging resources which increase the skill level children will need to use them. There will be opportunities to consolidate not simply repeat (Mastery) The adults will give clues/examples/provocations to solve problems, but not do it for the children e.g. "What can we do if there aren't enough buns for everyone in Garnet class?" (Mastery) (Creating and thinking critically) Adults will allow children time to follow their own mathematical ideas and not planning every day for them In Y1, adults will continue to recognise that although children are getting older, they still learn best through play and following their interests. Children are given opportunities to test their own ideas and hypotheses about mathematical problems and challenged to use and apply their mathematical knowledge in different ways (Mastery) There are open-ended continuous provision resources which allow children to explore their own ideas (Mastery) (Creating and thinking critically) Children are in control of their own ideas but share them with friends as they play collaboratively (Mastery)
	• Children engage in child-led play for most of their time in school due to free flow snack and any carpet sessions being at the beginning or end of sessions. There is no 'break time'. This allows children to develop their play without interruption and support the FLOW of their talking and thinking		• There are opportunities for children to engage in play at least once a day as part of their entitled planned time in school. This is not just when they have finished their 'work' • Enhancements (adult-initiated) are much more linked to learning outcomes from planned sessions • The balance is switching to more adult-initiated playful experiences	
	• There are less enhancements (adult-initiated) in provision and more continuous provision which allows children to return to favourites and develop their ideas • There is much more purely child-led learning	• There are a number of planned enhancements (adult-initiated) alongside continuous provision. This increases as the year progresses. • Enhancements consider the key skills needed for Early Learning Goals at the end of the EYFS		

Figure 5.3 (Continued)

3. Play needs the opportunity to flow from one place to the next.
4. Play must be the bedrock of children's learning experiences.
5. Play is not 'as well as', 'instead of', or 'what comes after' work.
6. Play resources and spaces should not be changed too frequently.

In our school, this means that we have an enabling environment in which the children can access resources independently. We make sure as many of these resources are as open-ended as possible so that the children can make them into anything they want. This means they do not have to limit their ideas, and we are not constantly running to the resource cupboard to get something else out, the children have to be creative with what they have got. We encourage children to make links in their learning and use the environment to support this. For example, when the children wanted to make a lists of ingredients (see How to Make a Love Monster Happy learning story below), they were not simply given paper and pencils to record their ideas, they had to think where to find the resources they needed themselves.

Our routines and timetable show the importance of play by allowing children extended periods of time to become absorbed and deeply involved; it is never referred to as what the children do when they have finished learning with an adult. We refer to 'learning time' so the children know they are learning all the time, not just when they are with an adult. We are also careful to make sure there is continuity in our continuous provision; as the word says, it is *continuous* and always there. The children know they can return to it. Enhancements are made within the continuous provision, e.g. putting out the resources to make cards for the Love Monster.

By following the children's interests, which we record in floor books (see Chapter 4), and allowing the children to play for extended periods of time, we are able to keep in mind the dispositions, skills and knowledge that they need to build, while giving the children the freedom to choose the ways in which they want to learn. Thinking more specifically about maths, we agree with Carruthers (2017): "Children do so much more mathematics if given the freedom to engage in their own mathematics" (p. 4). We see the best mathematical skills and understanding when we step back, observe and allow children to take the lead. This was very evident in the Talk for Maths Mastery initiative; as we observed children in continuous provision in their child-led play, the fog began to clear and we could see their deeper levels of engagement, thinking and learning which were way beyond our original expectations.

Maths Is Everywhere

We had given much thought and consideration to the idea that, for children, mathematics is happening everywhere at any moment in time. With this in mind, we devised a reflective observation sheet called 'Maths Is Everywhere' to remind ourselves that maths can happen anywhere and at anytime, not just in a dedicated maths area or during an adult-led carpet session (see Chapter 1 and Appendices 1 and 2).

The more adults observed children's engagement in maths, particularly in everyday child-led play in continuous provision and activities, the more we saw their understanding and how they were making sense and meaning of mathematical concepts. These observations opened our eyes to what the children were really capable of, their deeper levels of thinking and understanding which in turn ensured that our next steps were tuned into the children to maintain their momentum, challenge and progress of learning.

The children often showed us they were much more capable than we gave them credit for during adult-led activities. Observing children in their child-led play was crucial as our window into children's mathematical thinking, learning and understanding (Chilvers, July 2017b), as we saw from the examples in Figure 5.4 observed in continuous provision.

Mathematical skill	What does this look like?	What was the adult role?
Counting objects, properties of shape, size of objects, problem solving	Children are in the deconstructed role play area which has wheels and boxes available among other resources. The children have decided to make a jeep using the materials available. They match the wheels to the corners of the box, problem solving to make sure they create their vehicle.	To be aware of the children's current interests and ensure the materials were available for them to follow this interest. To observe the children's involvement, talk and ideas – taking photographs as the play unfolds.
Time, sequencing events, problem solving	The children know that, if they want a turn on the interactive whiteboard, they should use the sand timer which needs to be turned over; they write their name to wait for their turn.	To set up a turn-taking routine and support the children to use the system independently throughout the school year. To refer to this way of taking turns in other areas of play and activities.
Number recognition, pattern, counting	In the play dough area, there are some buttons and number cards. The children are using the play dough and buttons independently to create whatever they think of. Some children are using the number cards to create their own challenges and use the correct number of buttons on their creation.	To be aware of how open-ended materials like buttons can support mathematical talking and thinking. To add the buttons to extend experiences of patterns, counting, number recognition.

Figure 5.4 Findings from the Maths Is Everywhere observations

2. How do we follow children's interests and build mathematical thinking and mastery?

Allowing children to follow maths, through their own interests, makes it much more purposeful to them, increasing their motivation and determination to set and solve problems. It is this intrinsic motivation we are aiming to create in young children where it arises from within the child and results in their being satisfied with the outcome or process (Stewart, N. 2013).

In terms of mathematical mastery, we want to create children who see themselves as autonomous problem solvers, who make the connection between mathematical skills and knowledge and understand how they relate to real-life situations, contexts and problems. For example, in the Love Monster learning story, we knew that Corey had mastered the concept of halving when he referred to it in context in order to solve the problem of not having enough buns.

By taking Corey's lead and allowing the children to follow the idea through, we were able to support him to explain his thinking and for the children to realise that the idea worked. This is closely aligned to the characteristics of effective learning (Appendix 6), particularly Creating and Thinking Critically which talks about children having their own ideas. These ideas do not need to be groundbreaking; they are unique to that child at that time. By allowing them the time and resources to fully explore this, a sensitive adult can co-construct or scaffold the learning to support and extend the child's thinking (Chilvers, 2013).

In Figure 5.3, we unpicked the concept of child-initiated learning and how the children can take the lead in their learning while still making it purposeful. Often the assumption is that the children will return to low-level play or choose not to challenge themselves. Our children have disproved this myth by extending their thinking and making links between their experiences and their mathematical knowledge in order to solve their own problems and move forward towards a solution. We can clearly see their mathematical mastery (see Chapter 3).

How do we teach?

The How to Make a Love Monster Happy learning story involves the Reception (F2) class and shows how we can create a balance between collaborative, child-led mathematical opportunities and adult-focused teaching for the whole class.

Teaching is through adult-led whole-class sessions, which are 15–20 minutes long, and some smaller follow-up adult-led focus groups alongside child-led play. We plan for extended periods of time when the children are not directed by an adult to allow them to explore their own ideas. In order to do this, we have free flow to the outdoor area and a free flow snack table. This limits the number of 'stoppages' during the sessions, giving children time to concentrate, collaborate and become deeply involved.

Adult-led, whole-class teaching sessions are at the beginning and end of the morning and afternoon. Adults are timetabled so that we can be sure there is always an adult to observe and support the children, engaging and interacting as appropriate while they are in child-led play. The second adult has more of an adult-directed group focus to help us keep the balance between the different types of learning. Sometimes these groups are ability based depending on the nature of the task; however, they are fluid and change as needed. For example, at the beginning of the year, they are much more adult-initiated playful experiences, but by the end of the year there is an adult focus which the children are expected to complete. We share a third adult between the two Reception classrooms, which means we can run outdoors continuously during these sessions.

How many whole-class sessions do we teach?

Since starting to use a floor book approach and encouraging children to talk about and share their ideas to inspire our themes and topics, we decided to set aside two whole-class carpet sessions a week (see Chapter 4). These are usually Monday morning and Friday afternoon to maximise the potential of the sessions. The aims of the Talk Floor Book session are to:

- find out what children already know and address any misconceptions
- find out what children are interested in and explore their ideas further
- consider the key skills the children need to work on and where challenge is needed to ensure progress
- reflect on learning and discuss what has been previously learned using the floor book as a stimulus for dialogue

Sessions for literacy and maths are on the remaining days, leaving four 15- to 20-minute sessions during the week. The aims of the literacy/ maths sessions are to:

- teach key skills in English and maths linked to the themes and topics the children are interested in
- allow the children to follow their ideas through and make links to the bigger picture

How much child-led time is there?

We have planned our timetable to allow as much time for child-led learning as possible. We intentionally do not have a formal break time which allows the morning to flow without any interruptions. The adult-led follow-up activities are usually linked to teaching key skills, such as calculation. We also plan the provision to allow children to demonstrate these skills in their own way and to return to activities they have done before. There is always a practitioner in the environment facilitating and supporting the children as needed 'in the moment'.

We recognise that maths can be taught anywhere, at any time, through the adults being aware of the potential opportunities to teach 'in the moment' and harness children's interests and intrinsic motivation. It is challenging to guarantee spending time with individual children every day, however, by keeping the carpet sessions short (15–20 minutes) all children were involved daily, and both approaches (adult led and child initiated) are combined with the emphasis on child-led play in continuous provision for longer periods. Carruthers and Worthington (2006) talk about the need for a balance between the two, and if children are given too much freedom, they "do not then have the opportunity to see adults modelling mathematics and the learning may not be sufficiently scaffolded" (Bruner, 1971, p. 137 in Carruthers and Worthington, 2006).

3. What does mathematical mastery through whole-class, child-led learning look like in practice?

Love Monster – a whole-class learning story

Our children had shown an interest in Valentine's Day; it was on our class calendar, and they had seen cards and gifts in the shops. An initial group discussion, with the children, established what they already knew and identified what they wanted to learn about Valentine's Day. It is always interesting to ask the children about a subject as they often have totally different perspectives from those of the adults. For example, when we were talking about Zog from the Julia Donaldson (2016) story, the children were much more interested in the animated version, so we became animators. As adults we were much more focused on the book version of the story. The end goal of retelling the story remained the same.

The learning story progressed during the week through a mixture of planned adult-led activities and 'in the moment' planning (Ephgrave, 2012). We are aware that children often develop their ideas in unpredictable ways and that these can appear at any time which is why, although we like to be prepared, we are also open and flexible in changing activities and plans so that the children can explore their own ideas and suggestions. The following is what happened during the week of the Love Monster learning story.

We had a planned literacy focus for our carpet sessions based around the *Love Monster* books (Bright, 2012). The children were going to consider the character of the Love Monster and develop their understanding of him through reading the *Love Monster* stories. The maths carpet sessions were focused on measurement, the Love Monster and creating love potions. We had also planned, with adult support, to make Valentine's Day cards to take home. However, the children had different ideas!

Page 1

We read the first *Love Monster* story at the beginning of the week, and the children's ideas grew. They became genuinely concerned about the well-being of the Love Monster and quickly began to think of ways to cheer him up. It had not occurred to us, either when speaking to the children or while planning the sessions, this is what would become the children's main concern. The children were so interested and inspired we wanted to build on their focus and thinking.

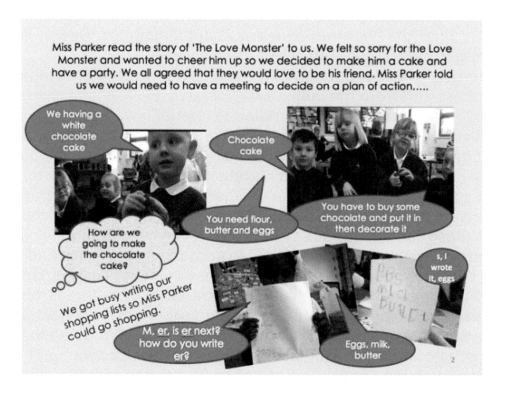

Page 2

We posed a possibility question to the children: "What do you think we should do?" The children were already demonstrating mathematical skills as they saw themselves as active problem solvers who could work out a solution. We can see this in the learning story as the children work out their plan of action; there was lots of discussion about what could happen. A follow-up question from the adult, "How do we make chocolate cake?" helped the children to focus in on their main problem and to reflect on their previous learning. They were full of ideas but needed a little support to direct these ideas towards a shared common goal.

Problem solving is a key disposition and skill in mathematical mastery

Our research throughout the TFMM Initiative highlighted how crucial it is for children to see themselves as the problem setters and problem solvers. For example, in Love Monster, the children decided to work out how to share the cake to make it fair for everybody. They needed to organise their thoughts through serve and return conversations with one another but then also show they could transfer these skills to other contexts around their environment. Their serve and return conversations led them into sustained shared thinking (SST) where they began to think more deeply (see Chapter 3).

What is sustained shared thinking?

Sylva (2015) explains sustained shared thinking as children having "the capacity to work with others in coherent and sustained ways towards a goal or resolution". It can also be described as:

> [a]n episode in which two or more individuals 'work together' in an intellectual way to solve a problem, clarify a concept, evaluate activities, extend a narrative etc. Both parties must contribute to the thinking and it must develop and extend.
>
> (Siraj-Blatchford et al, 2002, p. 8)

Sustained shared thinking is woven into the characteristics of effective learning, especially Creating and Thinking Critically; there are many examples during the Love Monster learning story where this can be seen in action. For example, in pages 6 and 7 of the learning story, children can be seen sharing their ideas together and listening to the suggestions of the adult. The adult is not telling the children the answers or giving her own ideas but reinforcing what the children have said and extending their thinking further for example; "I think that's a great idea, if we cut them in half we have double, that's two times as many".

The enabling environment and continuous provision should support children to frequently engage in this co-constructive process together. The right balance in provision is struck to allow children time to think more deeply, to connect their thinking to previous learning and to maintain their momentum with continued challenge. However, children can return to previous low-level activities in continuous provision if the resources are not extending, challenging and inspiring their mathematical thinking. For example, if early capacity, pouring and filling skills are fully experienced in the Nursery (F1) as they move into Reception (F2), these should be developed further into more complex experiences around volume, measurement and estimation. Opportunities in continuous provision should provide further problem-setting and problem-solving challenges even when an adult is not there. If children are experienced at collaborative serve and return play and talk with one another, this will be a regular part of their child-led play. This is what we found in the TFMM initiative as we documented children's mathematical play and talk in their learning stories.

Creating a maths mastery enabling environment

This comes through good continuous provision where children have plenty of opportunities to play in order to:

- embed new learning so that they can see the links between knowledge and skills and their current experiences
- try out and check their understanding so they can see how their ideas develop across a range of activities and resources
- learn from one another so they can build on their ideas and challenge them to extend their thinking
- return to activities and resources which give them time to explore and experiment without fear of getting it 'wrong' so they can build a growth mindset and see themselves as successful problem solvers
- use open-ended resources so they can take their learning in whichever way they please
- build confidence to approach new learning with self-assurance and self-belief
- develop new ways of thinking so they continue to extend and progress in their learning
- continue to set and solve problems becoming more resilient and not becoming disheartened when faced with an issue or challenge

The **adult's role** in supporting mathematical mastery remains critical, ensuring that they:

- model subtle and complex teaching strategies, e.g. by using playful teaching strategies as they share out the buns equally and teach the skills of division (see Chapter 7)

- tune into the children's interests, such as in the case of the Love Monster in order to maintain their motivation and give the learning a real-life creative context
- have conversations which lead to sustained shared thinking (see the adult's voice in the green thought bubbles throughout the learning story, which show how the adults are extending and challenging the children's thinking through serve and return conversations)
- promote meta-cognition allowing the children to reflect on and see the links between their previous learning and what is happening now
- develop language and vocabulary when discussing events and concepts

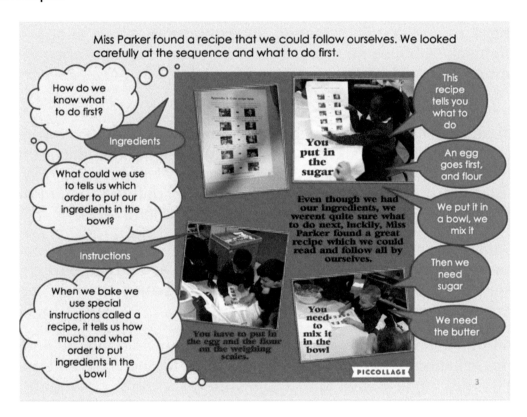

Page 3

Reflection and meta-cognition

As we had made cakes before, we asked the children to reflect on their previous learning about what to do and what we would need. And as the children's ideas throughout the year are recorded in the floor books, we were able to return to this previous learning and encourage children to reflect back and think meta-cognitively about what we had done before and how they could now extend their learning in new challenges (see Chapters 3 and 4).

This process of reflection and meta-cognition involved many aspects of mathematical thinking such as memory and recall. Children had to recall the process of when they had been involved in previous baking experiences. They had to remember what they had done and the mathematical skills they had used, e.g. using a balance scale correctly. Building the children's memory in this way is crucial to their ability to master mathematical skills, understanding and recall in order to apply it to a new context or situation. Giving the children opportunities to do this with meaningful experiences, such as baking a cake for the Love Monster, is essential, as O'Connor (2017) explains:

> Practical first-hand experience is a primary way of reinforcing memory and learning. Having the opportunity to do things for themselves builds neutral pathways and creates memories that inform future learning.
>
> (p. 25)

The adults were also able to reflect on the language the children were using and how the children's talk was supporting their mathematical thinking. The Sustained Shared Thinking and Emotional Wellbeing (SSTEW) scale (Siraj-Blatchford, Kingston and Melhuish, 2015) confirms that, in order to support curiosity and problem solving at an 'excellent' level:

> Staff support children's metacognition by talking aloud to model their thinking and problem-solving processes and support children to plan, undertake and then review activities.
>
> (p. 28)

The children had to not only remember what they had done previously but know it well enough to recall and explain it. By giving children opportunities to do this, while following their own interests and in solving their own problems, their:

> [s]kills of memory and concentration improve, but this is less likely if children are asked to pay attention, concentrate and remember things in tasks that adults have set. Children will best demonstrate these skills in meaningful situations that are relevant to them.
>
> (Dowling, 2013, p. 146)

There was also the development of a sense of time as they began to appreciate that things could not happen immediately and would need to be done in the correct sequence if they were to be successful. As the week went on, the children made lots of preparations for the party, such as posters and invitations, in their own learning time. We kept the maths carpet sessions focused on the initial measurement plans for the week, adapting them as needed to incorporate the plans for the cake but not changing them completely. They were now about measurements for cake baking rather than love potions and supporting the children by teaching them the skills they would need to complete their plans.

The children wrote out their shopping lists having made careful measurements and estimates of what they required. In the Love Monster learning story, adults went to the shop after school without the children. We have since developed our practice and now try to go to the local shops with the children to extend their knowledge and understanding through real-life, contextual experiences. They can then select, check what they are buying, and the costs involved themselves (see Figures 5.5 and 5.6).

Authentic contextual experiences

Going shopping situates children's mathematical thinking, talking and learning in meaningful contexts which the children see as having relevance to their everyday life. Children are much more likely to internalise and remember their learning if it has been personal to them (O'Connor, 2017). In terms of being able to master mathematical skills, the children will be much more capable when recalling their experiences and linking them to new situations. Children making links in this way is a crucial component of the characteristic of effective learning, especially Creating and Thinking Critically (Chilvers, 2013). By making these links in their learning, children are able make sense of their thinking and show they understand it enough to be able to manipulate it fluently in a range of contexts.

We involve parents and carers so they can see how to incorporate maths easily into everyday activities. An important part of the TFMM initiative was the Home Learning Partnership and how parents and carers can support and extend their child's mathematical learning at home in more meaningful, authentic ways such as through cooking and shopping trips. We do this through our class blog (www.onyxclass.wordpress.com) and add learning stories which show parents and carers possible ways to continue and extend the learning at home. Examples of these can be seen in the Love Monster learning story (page 10) and show how situations at home can complement and extend those begun at school and vice versa.

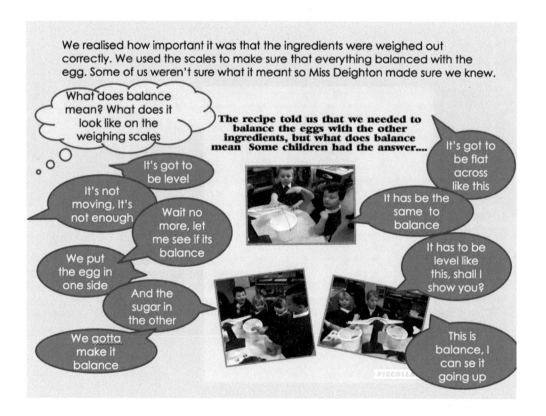

Page 4

In our cake recipe, everything balances with an egg! To ensure the correct quantities, the children add ingredients until the balance scales are equal. Balancing weights and talking about heavy, heaviest, light, lightest, balanced and equal are important mathematical concepts for the children to grasp and key skills when considering the Shape Space and Measure aspect of Mathematics (EYFS, DfE, 2017, pp. 8, 11).

We could see the children were already aware of how the balance worked and how they were applying their previous knowledge. They were able to explain, in detail and depth to one another, how the scale worked and the concept of balance, showing a deeper understanding as they explained this to the other children; only when you fully understand something are you able to explain it properly to someone else. Using carefully formed possibility questions modelled by the adults, they can deepen their thinking and understanding in complex ways which is of far more value than a worksheet or a repetitive exercise set by an adult.

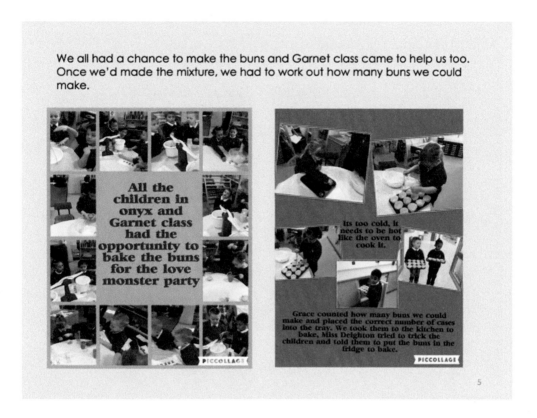

We all had a chance to make the buns and Garnet class came to help us too. Once we'd made the mixture, we had to work out how many buns we could make.

All the children in onyx and Garnet class had the opportunity to bake the buns for the love monster party

Its too cold, it needs to be hot like the oven to cook it.

Grace counted how many buns we could make and placed the correct number of cases into the tray. We took them to the kitchen to bake, Miss Deighton tried to trick the children and told them to put the buns in the fridge to bake.

Page 5

After careful thinking and discussion, the children decided that it would be better to make buns instead of one big cake which added several different, challenging mathematical elements. They chose a different way to do things through their creative and critical thinking.

They now had to:

- share the mixture evenly across all the bun cases (sharing and division)
- count and recount the bun cases to make sure there were enough for everyone (counting)
- practise adding one more each time so there was enough for the Love Monster (early addition)
- find the correct numbers on the cooker for the temperature (number recognition)

- use the clock and a timer and wait 20 minutes counting down the time and watching the numbers change (time)
- share out toppings and estimate if they thought there was enough icing to decorate all the buns (sharing, division and estimation)

The children's mathematical involvement continued to flow through their questions and proposals but there were now too many buns!

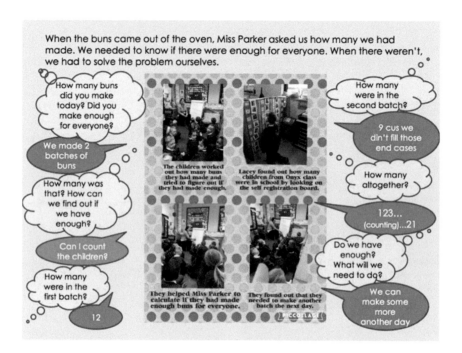

Page 6

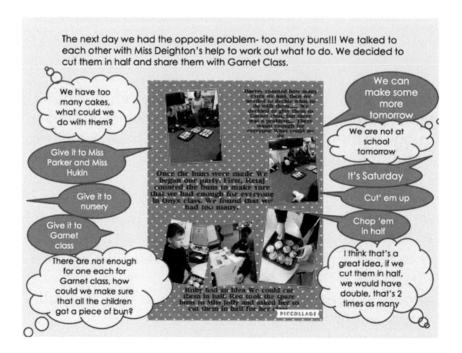

Page 7

Having counted how many there were and comparing this quantity to the number of children in the class, they then had to solve a new problem: what to do with the extra buns? These problems are important to the children and need to be addressed through discussion and mathematical thinking, possibilities included:

- some children wanting another bun and asking the question if that was fair or healthy?
- Reo suggesting letting the other class have one, but then there were not enough. Corey's solution: "We could cut them in half!"

Enabling the children to work through the problem themselves gives them ownership of their learning and encourages them to demonstrate their mastery of mathematical concepts such as suggesting halving as a solution and explaining what they wanted to happen. We could confidently see that the children had mastered this mathematical concept.

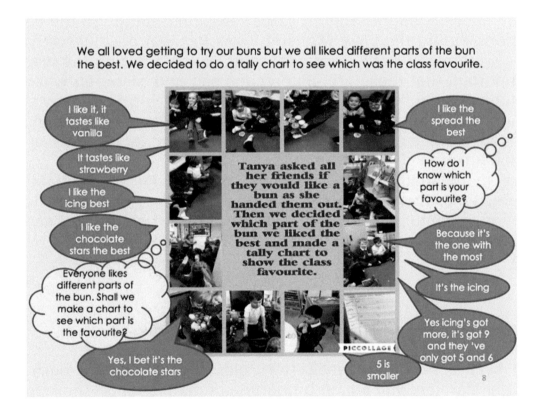

Page 8

The children had their party as planned and shared the buns with the other class. While the children were eating the buns, Lacey commented on her favourite part being the icing, which started a whole new mathematical conversation linked to data handling.

Although, data handling is not specifically on the curriculum planning or referred to in the Early Learning Goals (EYFS, DfE, 2017, p. 11), this is an important concept for the children to have experienced and allows them to show mastery of their number sense when comparing numbers and quantities. Being able to manipulate numbers through data handling shows an advanced level of mathematical thinking which prepares children for later curriculum expectations.

In Year 1 the children will be learning about data handling, but these children were already showing their skills and understanding. If we had taught only what was on the prescribed curriculum, we would have missed this valuable opportunity to extend the children's learning in a meaningful context which they understood and valued.

Reflections on practice

When reflecting on a learning story or period of learning, we consider the concepts taught and what the children have learnt in addition to the specific taught skills in carpet sessions. Although the carpet sessions during the Love Monster week focused on measurement, there were many, many more concepts covered during the week. It is important that these are also recognised and recorded when we are looking at curriculum coverage. It often leads us into new areas of taught learning if we realise that the children have misconceptions or need more support to become fluent in other aspects of the curriculum.

The many mathematical concepts covered included quantities, weight, time, money, number, sharing (division), one more (early addition), counting, estimating, fractions (half/whole), data handling and problem solving.

Reflecting on our mathematical thinking and learning

It had been a successful week. The children had done so much cross-curricular learning with a high proportion of mathematical thinking while they also had the satisfaction of meeting their own goals of cheering up the Love Monster, eating cake and having a party.

We were able to reflect on the mathematical mastery which the children had shown, both that which directly related to the mathematics of number and shape, space and measures and that which built a more holistic view of the children and their learning. The children had covered a wide range of mathematical concepts during the week. We also reflected on the characteristics of effective learning and how the children had shown themselves to be well motivated problem solvers. The children did not particularly know they had been learning mathematics or literacy during the week; they simply saw it as a week of enjoyment in which they met their goals and how they could help the Love Monster. Research (Finch, 2018) shows that this is the way children learn best, when their learning is woven together and is not subject specific (see Chapters 2, 3 and 7).

Analysis of Learning

The children were motivated to continue with the same learning focus for a whole week. Following the children's interests and allowing them to lead their own learning led to high levels of energy and fascination which made the learning much more curricular. The adults in Onyx class provided structure to the learning and ensured the mathematical learning opportunities were exploited. This allowed the maths to be an integral part of the learning while embedding it into the activity.

A number of mathematical concepts were visited by the children. Some of these had been taught before, some were new to the children. They had to measure for a purpose, including explaining what balance meant. There was problem solving involved in the sharing and halving. The children who took the lead in this showed they were working towards the ELG for Number. Tally charts are not specifically on the curriculum but by allowing children to explore the numbers in this way gave them to opportunity to demonstrate mastery of their number knowledge. The children had to use their prior knowledge of number to answer the question posed by the adult.

The children were initiating activities which challenged them. They showed a can-do attitude to their learning and the good relationships with adults meant they knew they were able to take risks and try new things. This learning continued for a whole week while the children tried to cheer the Love Monster up. They even kept going every time there was a problem or they had to change their thinking to accommodate new information. When these problems presented themselves the children chose themselves how to do things and found their own ways to solve problems. They were able to reflect and decide if they had been successful or not.

9

Page 9

The analysis of a learning story is critical to recognising children's learning and development and how this can be further supported and extended. Without this page, it is simply a lovely story about a shared experience the children have had. The reflection and analysis by an adult who knows the children well and makes a professionally informed judgement about the learning that has taken place is needed. With this in place, the learning story becomes a valuable document which can be used to observe and assess both *what* and *how* children have been learning, before planning the next steps to ensure they maintain their learning momentum.

The learning does not stop there either. The Love Monster learning story has been presented again to the children many times so that they can reflect on what they had been doing and why. They can see how maths is an integral part of everyday life and feel how their embedded skills and understanding increases their independence and confidence. Often children will return to one of their stories long after the experience happened, talking about what they did and how their learning has moved on. This happened with Corey and Alfie two Year 1 boys (6+ years) who looked back at their learning in Reception. Recalling what they were doing with the dinosaurs and subtraction, Corey said, "We didn't call it subtraction in Reception, we called it taking away in Reception". Alfie simply replied, "You're making my memory come back".

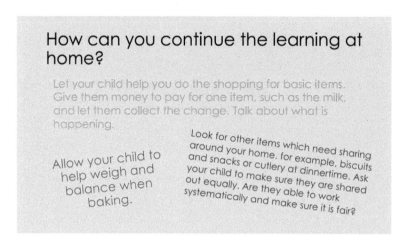

How can you continue the learning at home?

Let your child help you do the shopping for basic items. Give them money to pay for one item, such as the milk, and let them collect the change. Talk about what is happening.

Allow your child to help weigh and balance when baking.

Look for other items which need sharing around your home, for example, biscuits and snacks or cutlery at dinnertime. Ask your child to make sure they are shared out equally. Are they able to work systematically and make sure it is fair?

Page 10

Why whole-class learning stories?

Learning stories are part of an observation and assessment approach used in the New Zealand early years curriculum Te Whariki (Carr and Lee, 2012). As we found on the TFMM initiative, there are several ways learning stories can be presented so that the children's learning is clearly documented as it unfolds, and their voice and thinking are made visible. Chilvers (2018) expresses this when she says:

> Effective teachers and practitioners tune into children's development, language and thinking through their observations and then use this to extend their understanding and learning.
>
> (p. 13)

Learning stories enable us to do this; often they are of individual children or small groups of children; however, in the case of the Love Monster week, we embraced the idea of a whole-class learning story as it seemed to be the best way to document the learning of all the children. We did this for a number of reasons. The whole-class learning story enabled:

- reflection on the week's events and learning
- sharing the week with the children in a format which was accessible to them

- sharing the week with the parents and carers
- the inclusion of all the children and seeing their place in collaborative shared learning
- us to consider the role of each child and how they interacted both with adults and peers
- us to consider the characteristics of effective learning and *how* children were learning
- looking holistically at *what* the children were learning seeing the connections across the curriculum and between the areas of learning
- us to consider the children's progress and possible next steps
- us to consider the provision across our enabling environment and think about whether it had the correct challenge for our cohort (enhancements were made with this in mind)
- a reduced workload for the adults as there was one learning story which included all the children

Summary

During the TFMM initiative, our practice changed considerably. The whole team became much more aware of mathematics happening everywhere and knowing where to see it in our environments. Our interactions with children became much more mastery orientated using sustained shared thinking and open-ended possibility questions to promote Creating and Thinking Critically with the children.

By standing back and allowing ourselves the time to observe, we were able to recognise the children's interests and schema (see Chapter 2) making sure that learning contexts were relevant to them and increasing their motivation to learn. All of this was documented in learning stories which recorded the language of the children and the experiences they had. They were an opportunity to reflect on the quality of learning which had taken place and our respective roles within it. Adults became much more reflective, thinking how they could improve and refine their practice to maintain the momentum of the children's learning. It gave us a window into how the children wanted to learn and what was important to them.

During the TFMM initiative and since then, we have continued to work on the transition to Year 1, ensuring that it is as smooth as possible for our children meeting both their developmental needs and their emotional needs. We continue with a play-based approach into Year 1 and gradually increase adult-directed teaching; however, the emphasis is always on learning through Active Play and Creating and Thinking Critically.

Children continue to have opportunities for child-led learning throughout the year even if the balance does begin to shift towards more adult-led as the children get ready for Year 2. We work closely as a whole-school staff team to ensure there is a shared vision with the children at the centre. By considering the benefits of a play-based curriculum and the role of the adult within it, our children are confident, motivated, independent learners who are able to meet the increasing demands of their curriculum, and we are reassured as 'teachers' that we are meeting the needs of the children through their play (see Chapter 8).

Note

1. *United Nations Convention of the Rights of the Child*, UNICEF; www.unicef. org/crc/.

6 Making their mathematical mark: understanding and supporting children's mathematical mark-making and thinking

DAVID YATES

This chapter explores how children develop their mathematical mark-making through following their interests within an enabling environment and with sensitive, supportive, adults (Bromley, 2006; Anning and Ring, 2004). Children's mathematical mark-making is one of the most powerful ways in which they can demonstrate their mathematical thinking and is an integral part of their mathematical understanding (Worthington and Carruthers, 2006; Worthington and Carruthers, 2011).

Connections are made throughout the chapter to the Talk for Maths Mastery initiative and case studies of children's mathematical development, learning and progression, illustrated through their learning stories:

- Building on early mark-making experiences from birth to 3 – Peyton's mark-making
- mathematical mark-making with 3- to 4-year-olds – Meryam's Shape House and Aadam's Treasure
- mathematical mark-making with 4- to 5-year-olds – Meryam's 3-D Shapes and Aadam and Farhaad's Big Numbers
- mathematical mark-making into Year 1 (5+ years old) – Go Compare

Worthington and Carruthers use the term *mathematical graphics* to describe the mark-making that children engage in as they explore early mathematical thinking:

> Children's mathematical graphics begin in play and support their developing understanding of the standard abstract written symbolism of mathematics.
>
> Children choose to use their own mathematical graphics to represent their mathematical thinking; in a sense they are thinking

on paper. Children, when given the opportunity, will choose to make mathematical marks which can include scribbles, drawing, writing, tallies, invented and standard symbols. Just as in children's early writing, there is also a development in children's early mathematical marks.

(DCSF, 2008c, p. 34)

Mark Making Matters (DCSF, 2008c) acknowledges how young children recognise that they can use their marks as symbols to carry meaning. They then use these marks to make their thinking visible. Dowling (2013) advises against simply viewing drawing and mark-making as a precursor to writing, although there is a link. The most powerful mark-making is used by children to "demonstrate their understandings, to hold thoughts in their mind and to recall events (p. 83)".

Building on early mark-making experiences from birth to 3

The formation of children's mathematical mark-making begins at birth, growing out of early sensory experiences and explorations with a range of media and materials. For the under-threes, this can include noticing and experimenting with a trail of spilt juice, fingerprints in flour, or footprints in mud and puddles. Goddard Blythe (2008) and Gopnik, Meltzoff and Khul (1999) share the now widely accepted view that movement is a child's first form of language and communication. The reflexes that babies develop are the outward reflection of the developing functions of their nervous system. Babies' interest in their hands and fascination with their fingers are developed through early interactions with adults when sharing finger rhymes such as 'Round and Round the Garden', 'Two Little Dickie Birds' or 'Pat-a-Cake' (see Chapter 2). These early embodied experiences (Thom, 2017) help make connections in the brain that children use to strengthen connections within the motor system. Young children's experiences of mark-making develop as they grow. Through playing and exploring, they create, think, feel and interact with adults and one another. For example, sensory experiences, such as finger painting, making hand or footprints, exploring soap flakes, gloop (cornflour and water) or shaving foam, encourage very young children to use their fingers as tools to manipulate media and help to develop early grip, strength and reflex.

It is crucial that children are sensitively supported during the early years to develop a secure understanding of mathematics by having plenty of opportunities to explore practically using physical resources, including natural materials and real-life objects. For example, a question we considered in TFMM was, 'What should a number line look like for a 2-year-old?' (see Chapter 2). For this to be truly meaningful, it should be a physical representation of the everyday *mathematical occurrences* that children can understand and appreciate. For example, when dressing to go outside in the rain, mathematical conversations can be enjoyed by referring to:

- 1 hat
- 2 socks
- 3 buttons on my coat
- 4 wellies for splashing in puddles (2 for a grown-up's feet and 2 for mine)
- 5 fingers on my gloved hand

Adults should provide experiences for the under threes, such as singing number rhymes using fingers to count up and down, counting big and small footsteps, strides or jumps, and counting as they go up and down the stairs, that help children to develop their early mathematical understanding.

Children will engage in early mark-making experiences as they develop gross and fine motor skills, such as using chalk to create a big hopscotch grid on the ground outside or writing the totals on a carefully created tally chart on a clipboard. They will go on to create their own pictures and drawings to demonstrate their understanding and application of mathematics during play.

Children who are encouraged to develop their gross motor skills by mark-making on a small and large scale strengthen early brain connections upon which continued development is built (Chugani, 1998). To provide the firmest foundations and encourage children to engage in these early mathematical experiences, they require a range of resources, including chunky crayons and pencils, chalk, paint and sensory materials to enable them to make marks as they explore the environment indoors and outdoors. The more open-ended the resources, the better, as children can use them for a variety of purposes and reasons. Children also make use of transportable resources, often called 'loose parts', to play, create and make marks in a variety of different ways with infinite possibilities. Natural materials, that are often readily available outside, such as leaves, stones, pebbles, petals, sticks and twigs, can be transported and used to create environmental art that can be as permanent and changeable as children feel necessary.

Continuous provision and the under-threes

Whilst the role of the adult is crucial in the earliest years, the environment and resources are also important. Continuous provision enables the under-threes to demonstrate the characteristics of effective early learning (Early Education, 2012; Department for Education, 2017) and to help them develop independence in their learning and interactions (see Chapter 3). O' Connor (2008) describes continuous provision as "the core of everyday resources that should always be available to children in early years settings". She likens it to the food items on a "regular daily menu" of offerings to the children, with the enhancements being the "specials". All of which offer children opportunities to "be active, confident participants, make choices to create their own learning context, make choices based on their own experiences, have the time and space to wallow in it" (article available online).

Young children need to choose from a range of resources in order to develop their own ideas of mark-making and very early writing in ways which interest them. For example, by making resources such as paintbrushes, water and paint available indoors and outdoors, children can engage in many and varied opportunities to practice and return to fine and gross motor development on a large and small scale.

Having plenty of opportunities to talk and discuss these experiences with adults and peers is crucial to enable children to develop their language for mathematical thinking and reasoning. Opportunities to engage in singing and playing with words and sounds as children develop their phonological awareness enable them to develop their language and vocabulary through a range of experiences. In essence, children need to have someone to talk to and something to talk about in order to develop their mathematical language and shape their mathematical thinking (Pound, 2008).

Continuing learning at home

The importance of establishing a positive relationship with parents/carers became a crucial strand of the TFMM initiative. Creating and following a two-way dialogue, in a reciprocal partnership, is a vital part of the process of maintaining the home learning partnership. In TFMM, we posed the question, 'My home learning helps me when . . .' (see Figure 6.1).

Adults should make strong partnerships with parents to support children's learning and to support parents' understanding of that learning. Much can be gained from encouraging families to use their local environment to recognise and engage with everyday maths in a familiar context. Everyday mathematical opportunities and experiences at home are the most meaningful, appropriate and useful to young children; e.g., using readily available household items such as soap suds (washing up, in the bath), chunky chalk, crayons, pencils, or mud in the garden allow children to mark-make purposefully and at their own pace at home, indoors and outdoors through small and large-scale play.

Children will engage in their own experimentation (where adults can be sensitively supportive rather than directive) to combine different media such as soil or sand and water, splashing in puddles, painting with water, watching the patterns made on the ground by the water coming out of a watering can, as they continue to make sense of the world. They enjoy opportunities to engage in conversational talk and mark-making

TFMM Aspect: mathematical mark-making			
2 years old →	**FS1** →	**FS2** →	**Y1** →
Learning stories			
Peyton's Mark-making	Meryam's Shape House	Meryam's Shapes Aadam; Farhaad's Big Numbers; Aadam's Treasure	Go Compare
Home learning partnership My home learning helps me when …			
we look at mathematical mark-making in the environment and pointing it out, e.g. on buses, number plates, road signs, directions, shop windows, shoe or tyre prints etc.; we talk about which numbers I know by recognising them on buses, doors or number plates and looking at the different shapes or patterns I can see when we are walking in the park.	my family joins in with my mark-making and tell me what they are doing too. When the adults are writing lists or filling in forms, they give me my own paper to join in and make my own marks.	I can use my local environment as an opportunity to recognise and write about numbers, e.g. make a map with me to show how we get from our house to school or the park. We can add numbers and think/ talk about how helpful numbers are in recording information and data.	I can continue exploring the mud in the garden to make my own concoctions and write my recipes for them for others to follow.

Figure 6.1 Home learning partnership

opportunities as early as possible. These serve and return interactions (Harvard University, 2018) provide opportunities for lots of contextual talk, set within the familiar real life of the child's home and local community. Familiar everyday opportunities such as writing shopping lists, notes and letters, using electronic tablets (for short periods of purposeful time), and exploring and acknowledging mark-making and writing in the everyday environment. Buses, number plates, road signs, door numbers, shop windows, shoe and tyre prints, patterns or shapes in the park all offer real-life, contextual opportunities to talk about the abstract numbers, patterns and shapes that build early mathematical skills and concepts.

REAM[1] (Raising Early Achievement in Maths) builds on REAL (Raising Early Achievement in Literacy) focusing on how children acquire early mathematical skills and understanding through everyday interactions. REAM identifies three strands of early maths:

1. **Environmental maths** – packaging and labelling, signs, and the built and natural environments
2. **Everyday maths** – eating, drinking, routines, moving, dressing, playing
3. **Stories, songs and rhymes** – bedtime stories, library visits, nursery rhymes

Children's acquisition of mathematical mastery is dependent on their being able to see and make their own connections between meaningful maths as part of everyday life. As they practice and refine their mathematical mark-making, there should be many opportunities for real-life 'authentic', contextual experiences, especially talking and participating in everyday tasks, e.g. writing shopping lists or notes, helping in the supermarket, making sandwiches and baking cakes. All these everyday experiences make strong connections to maths being everywhere and support the development of mathematical understanding (see Chapter 3).

The developmental progression of mathematical mark-making

The following learning stories from the TFMM initiative demonstrate the mathematical momentum of children's mark-making from their starting points and show the developmental progress that they make from 2 years old to Year 1 (5–6 years).

Peyton – mark-making at 2 years old

Peyton has attended nursery since the age of 26 months. She enjoys engaging in mark-making activities both indoors and outdoors. She shows an interest in things that turn and spends time creating curved lines and circles when she is mark-making.

Peyton's Mark-making

Peyton is busy mark-making. She is using the pencil with good control to draw circular patterns linked to her interest in action rotation schema. The patterns she makes when she is drawing are the beginning of her mathematical mark-making and show how she is making connections between her movements and the marks that she makes on the paper.

She is developing an early mathematical awareness of shapes, space and measures. This kind of mark-making is connected to figurative schema which is a 'static representation of how she sees the world'.

Exemplification (Child's perspective):

I like to learn by:

mark-making with chunky crayons, chalk, paint or mud; often showing my schematic thinking in a figurative form, up, down, around, across

making patterns, drawing and painting – this is the starting point for my mathematical mark making. They are big at first but as I practice they become more refined and meaningful. Often the marks I make show my schematic interests e.g. when I make lots of circular marks and lines, or vertical and horizontal, and dots/spots. This helps me to understand how marks and patterns relate to my later learning about symbols, numbers and recording

repeating play experiences which may show my schematic thinking e.g. when I am mark-making, I might draw lots of lines up, down, around and across. This could be a trajectory or rotational schema which will begin to develop my mathematical awareness of shapes space and measures

Peyton's early experiences show us several key aspects which underpin her mathematical thinking and mark-making:

- **Making connections** – By recognising that the movements she is making with her arm and hand, whilst holding the pencil, are creating the marks on the paper, Peyton is linking her previous mark-making experiences to this one and realises that she can make marks in a range of different ways and with a variety of different media and materials
- **Rotational schema** – Peyton's circular mark-making can be interpreted as the beginnings of a fascination with rotation and the circular. This early schematic interest and exploration will help Peyton as she develops her writing skills as she grows older; curved letter shapes are formed using a rotating, circular movement (see Chapter 2)
- **Figurative schema** – The marks that Peyton makes are a permanent visual *figurative* depiction of her interest in and fascination with rotation. Peyton is at the *sensorimotor level* of schema operation (Piaget in Athey, 2007, p. 131), where she is using her senses, actions and movement to engage in and represent her interest through mark-making (see Chapter 2)

Summary of Learning

Peyton shows **engagement** by finding out and exploring. She uses her senses to explore the world around her and represents this through the open-ended activity of mark-making. She displays **motivation** by being involved and concentrating on her mark-making, and maintains focus as she notices that the movements she makes create the marks on the paper. Peyton displays **thinking** by making links. She is developing ideas of cause and effect as she uses her early figurative schema to make marks on the paper and develop early mathematical thinking, recording and graphical representation.

Next steps

Show a genuine interest in Peyton's mathematical mark-making and use mathematical language to talk about it with her. Point out and describe the 'swirly,' curly' or 'wiggly' patterns in her drawings and mirror these for her as a play partner. Provide a variety of other media and resources to allow Peyton to explore mark-making on a large scale both indoors and outside (e.g. large pieces of paper or a roll of wallpaper, paint brushes and water or wet sand and mud).

This summary of learning links Peyton's mark-making experiences to the characteristics of effective early learning:

- **Playing and Exploring** – Peyton is *showing a particular interest* in rotation and circles through her mark-making. She is *willing to have a go* at her mark-making with the pencil and *shows a 'can-do' attitude* as she confidently coordinates her movements to create the marks on the paper
- **Active Learning** – Peyton is showing motivation as she focuses intently on her mark-making. This deep involvement, where she is *not easily distracted*, shows that Peyton's learning is intrinsically motivated and linked to her interests and fascinations
- **Creating and Thinking Critically** – Peyton is *making links* through her interests. She is *noticing patterns* in this and her previous mark-making experiences and making connections between what she already knows and can do. Peyton has explored mark-making in other forms and has explored rotation in different ways. She is now *making links* between all these different experiences as she continues to make sense of the world around her

As Peyton continues her learning and development journey, her natural curiosity and momentum mean she will return, in many ways, to her interest in mark-making and rotation. This helps to strengthen connections in her brain as her knowledge and understanding of mathematical mark-making progresses.

Learning, Playing and Interacting (DCSF, 2009b) acknowledges children's innate drive to experiment and connect ideas using all their senses, with whatever tools (including mark-making materials) they have, to develop their skills and extend their knowledge of the world around them. Dowling (2013) describes children's creative thinking as a means of generating their own original ideas by re-enacting or representing previous experiences. She extends this idea by referring to the way in which children will visually represent their thoughts and ideas using media such as chalk, paint and pencil when engaged in "the seemingly magical process of making a mark" (p. 83).

It is this early experimentation and enjoyment which, in time, becomes more deliberate and a "product of a systematic investigation, rather than haphazard actions" (Matthews, 1999, p.19). By investigating the effect of movement and marks in this way, children are developing an early awareness of concepts such as shape and spatial awareness. Thom (2018) explains how children's conceptual understanding is developed when they are encouraged to explore and experience using their entire bodies to further their exploration, thinking and questioning (see Chapter 2).

Extending thinking for mark-making

Piaget's (1968) three processes of *assimilation, accommodation* and *equilibrium* are useful in understanding how children's thinking is driven. When thinking occurs, previous, current and new ideas are gathered, arranged and absorbed through *assimilation*. Previous understandings are then changed or modified through the *accommodation* of new thinking. A state of *equilibrium* is reached when children are comfortable with and understand the new thinking. It is within this process that young children are constantly making connections through their experiences as they are introduced to new learning, ideas or concepts, which are often evident in their mathematical mark-making.

Reflection point

What different schema or fascinations have you noticed in the 2-year-olds you work with? How/what could you provide further for them?

How do you use talk to communicate with children and enable them to respond through their mathematical thinking and learning? E.g. have you observed children drawing/mark-making through figurative schema?

Do you model language and vocabulary to help them make sense of their mark-making?

How do you use modelling effectively to explore other possibilities with children whilst sensitively supporting and extending their learning and development?

Mathematical mark-making with 3- to 4-year-olds

As children grow older, they will engage in mark-making experiences with more developed gross and fine motor skills, independently creating drawings and pictures which show their understanding and application of mathematics within the context of their play. As their experience, understanding and confidence grow, they represent their knowledge and thinking in more abstract ways, e.g. creating a representation of how to follow a recipe, writing step-by-step instructions to construct a model using Lego or making the individual pieces of a board game they have devised themselves. These are true indications of their emerging mathematical mastery because they have ownership of them and understand their relevance within the context of their own play and explorations. They are mark-making meaningfully and for a purpose (DCSF, 2008a).

It became evident, through our narrative learning story observations, that mathematical mark-making comes more easily to children within their day-to-day fascinations and is a purposeful way of making their thinking visible (Matthews, 2003; Worthington and Carruthers, 2006). It is certainly necessary to value children's drawings as a precursor to their writing (Anning and Ring, 2004), and when both drawing and writing are used interchangeably, powerful thinking and learning happen. We can see this in-depth thinking in Meryam's, Aadam's and Farhaad's learning stories as well as in the developmental journeys they have made, from Peyton's mark-making to the more complex representations they create. This is a journey into deeper, more complex and connected thinking where they can be described as mastering skills, knowledge and dispositions (see Chapter 3).

The TFMM initiative shows the progression of learning from the child's perspective, using learning stories to show how the mathematical mark-making momentum is maintained (see Figure 6.2).

TFMM aspect: mathematical mark-making				
	2 years old →	**FS1** →	**FS2** →	**Y1**
Learning stories	Peyton's Mark-making	Meryam's Shape House	Meryam's Shapes; Aadam and Farhaad's Big Numbers; Aadam's Treasure	Go Compare
Child's perspective I like to learn by . . .	mark-making with chunky crayons, chalk, paint or mud, often showing my schematic thinking in a figurative form, up, down, around, across. See Peyton busy drawing circular patterns linked to her interest in action rotation schema.	using different mark-making resources, e.g. pens, pencils, paint, crayons, chalk, scissors, sand, mud or spray bottles filled with water or paint. I am becoming more skilled at mark-making and using my own way of recording, though I may not yet fully understand the concepts. See Meryam's Shape House.	creating more complex mathematical patterns/ designs using a mixture of non-standard/ standard marks and graphics which represent my mathematical ideas and thinking (building on figurative schema). See Adam's Treasure.	mark-making independently and skilfully using a range of resources, which makes my thinking, understanding and mastery evident. It shows what I really know and understand. See Go Compare where the children are using string to record their thinking (complex figurative schematic thinking).

Figure 6.2 The child's perspective

As children develop their understanding further, they will begin to make marks which they call numbers and shapes and experiment with joining lines to make shapes of familiar objects. Bruner (1966) acknowledges the shift children make in their thinking and understanding as they learn and develop. He identifies the following three stages of cognitive representation as children move between active and abstract ways of presenting their ideas:

- **Enactive representation** – Children move from physical ways of representing, using their bodies and early schematic mark-making (see Peyton's learning story)
- **Iconic representation** – Children then move to more abstract ways of thinking using mark-making, drawings and paintings (see Meryam's learning stories)
- **Symbolic representation** – Children move into even deeper thought processes through using symbols and more defined marks in their early writing (see Aadam's and Farhaad's learning stories)

As their symbolic representations become more refined, children become more deeply engaged, given enough time, space and resources to allow them to explore their interests in more depth (Meade and Cubey, 2008; Nutbrown, 1999; Dowling, 2013). We can see this in Go Compare where Bailey uses string to explore his interest in comparison and through the way in which he reflects on his own thinking and learning.

Children's mathematical conversations

Children learn by talking and discussing their mark-making with other children (like Meryam, Aadam and Farhaad) and, importantly, with adults who are interested and join in encouraging them to build their talk and confidence further (Chilvers, 2006; 2013). The findings of the Effective Provision of Pre-School Education (EPPE) (Sylva et al., 2004) and the Researching Effective Pedagogy in the Early Years (REPEY) (Siraj-Blatchford et al., 2002) studies suggested that children who were supported to extend and challenge their language and thinking even further, either with one another or with an adult, through 'sustained shared thinking' or serve and return conversations, benefitted from a positive overall impact on their learning and experiences, which in turn leads to mastery (see Chapter 3).

Sensitive adult interactions

When adults join in with children's play and 'tune in' as a play partner, modelling more complex thinking, skills and language, to extend mark-making, children know that they are truly valued and are being sensitively 'listened to' (DCSF, 2009b; Ofsted, 2015). Simple adult acknowledgements, such as eye contact, a smile or gesture can be as effective as taking on the role of the shopkeeper during role play; children recognise when adults are genuinely interested in them and their play.

What adults do to support children's mathematical mark-making is vital in building sensitively upon their developing interests and experiences

- Well informed, skilled, adults observe and respond to children in this context often referred to as a process of 'responsible pedagogy' (STA, 2019, p. 11), also known as professionally informed practice. This involves using knowledge of child development to effectively support each child to learn and develop in the fullest sense
- In addition to their role as an observer is the role of the interactor. This is the way in which adults make suggestions, share thinking, provide resources, play with and alongside children, and create 'provocations' which have a significant, positive impact on children's mathematical understanding, enjoyment and application. Rose and Rogers (2012, pp. 1–2) refer to the 'plural practitioner' to describe the complexity in the role and responsibility of the adult in early years settings. Adults who engage in sustained shared thinking with children, using open rather than closed questions to guide rather than dominate children's learning, support them to make sense of the world
- Adults need to provide mathematical mark-making opportunities that enable children to connect, consolidate and embed their wider mathematical learning and experiences though their play. Children can then show that they have truly mastered and understood what they have been taught and what they have learned. For example, ensuring high-quality, open-ended resources are available within the continuous provision for children to work on their own interests; e.g. they may decide to keep a tally score during a game of skittles or take down meal orders whilst exploring the role play café
- Adults should value children's mathematical mark-making and writing in its many different forms, including regularly accessible, ongoing, large-scale mark-making opportunities such as using large sheets of paper in the construction area where maps and plans can be created (Anning and Ring, 2004). Avoiding mark-making and writing from becoming a formal 'exercise-book only' task enables children to write for their own practical purposes and interests (see Chapter 7)
- By providing lots of contextual opportunities to practise mathematical mark-making in different ways, adults can encourage children to record their own emerging thinking and ideas. By scribing alongside them or using mind-mapping, providing clipboards or whiteboards to create their own tallies or writing their own name on a self-registration system when they come to school, children can perfect their gross motor skills by writing on a large scale, enabling their fine motor skills to become more refined (see Chapter 4)

- As they move into Key Stage 1, children need to be supported by adults who understand and appreciate that their mathematical mark-making is continually developing. They will benefit greatly from any additional time to independently engage with resources in continuous provision to develop their interests and ideas further

Our work on the TFMM initiative shows how the adult can sensitively support the progression of learning and help children maintain their mark-making momentum (see Figure 6.3).

Building on the enabling environment

The environment should enable children to make their own decisions and choices with resources that are provided within continuous provision to encourage and inspire mathematical mark-making. This will support children to independently follow their thinking, ideas and interests, becoming autonomous, self-regulated learners who are less reliant on adults (Bronson, 2002; Whitebread et al., 2007).

There should be many meaningful opportunities to make marks in all areas of provision (e.g. in role play, construction), and not just in an adult-defined mark-making area of provision. The Maths Is Everywhere audit is a useful tool that practitioners can use to support their observations of children. It shows how children are pursuing their own child-led, contextual, mathematical inquiries in all areas of provision (see Chapter 1 and Appendices 1 and 2).

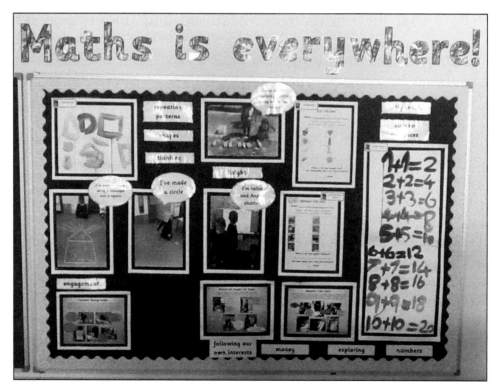

A display created following the use of the 'Maths Is Everywhere audit' in FS2 showing the mathematical learning (including examples of mark-making) evident across all areas of indoor and outdoor provision.

TFMM Aspect: mathematical mark-making

	2 years old	FS1 →	FS2 →	Y1 →
Learning stories	Peyton's Mark-making	Meryam's Shape House	Meryam's Shapes; Aadam and Farhaad's Big Numbers; Aadam's Treasure	Go Compare
Adult's role You can support my mathematical thinking by . . .	observing and documenting the many ways I mark-make, e.g. in mud, finger paint, sand, clay, shaving foam, paint and various mark-making materials. These may represent my schematic patterns of thinking, e.g. trajectories, rotation (circularity). I also use other materials to represent my thinking, e.g. construction materials, loose part materials and open-ended materials often used in heuristic play. This kind of mark-making is connected to **figurative schema** which are 'static representations of how I see the world'. See Peyton's 'LS' and the way Elsie represents her ideas in 'I got all of them'.	being interested in the many ways I mark-make and talk about this with me in engaging 'serve and return' conversations which stretch my thinking. See Meryam's Shape House learning story shows the complex development of her figurative schema and her explanation).	recognising how mathematical mark-making may continue to represent more complex thinking – figurative *schema*; e.g. Adam's Treasure and Meryam's Shapes learning story show how they have represented their mathematical thinking and explained this in conversations with their teachers. The children's explanations show *how* they are thinking and the understanding (mastery) they have of some complex mathematical concepts particularly linked to Creating and Thinking Critically.	understanding that my mathematical mark-making is continually developing. I need time and open-ended opportunities to follow my thinking and use and apply what I already know so I can embed my knowledge and understanding in wider contexts (mastery). See Go Compare, which shows how the children are demonstrating their understanding of measurement and comparison by using string to represent their thinking (complex figurative schematic thinking).

Figure 6.3 The adult's role

TFMM aspect: mathematical mark-making

	2 years old	FS1	FS2	Y1
Learning stories	Peyton's Mark-making	Meryam's Shape House	Meryam's Shapes; Aadam and Farhaad's Big Numbers; Aadam's Treasure	Go Compare
Enabling environment and continuous provision To develop and extend my learning, I need . . .	many varied opportunities to practise making marks using my **gross motor skills** on a large and small scale, e.g. with paintbrushes and paint/water/bubbles on the easel/floor with large pieces of paper, fabric, plastic etc.; to use my whole body to practise mark-making, e.g. printing using my hands and feet/shoes or watching what happens when I jump in a puddle wearing my wellies.	to see mathematical marks in the wider environment, e.g. numbers on doors, number plates, road signs, shop windows, advertising, shopping, petrol stations etc. This is more meaningful to me as they are real-life examples which I can talk about with everyone; mathematical mark-making makes sense to me in these contexts.	a variety of mark-making materials and opportunities which support my mathematical thinking and learning as I am playing and interacting, e.g. in the construction area, role play and home corner and outdoors. This will help to consolidate and embed my wider learning through child-initiated play and lets me show how I have truly mastered and understood what I have been taught. See Aadam and Farhaad's Big Numbers and Aadam's Treasure.	time and opportunities in continuous provision to apply what I have learnt and develop my mathematical mark-making through independent and collaborative play with others; adults who support and extend opportunities for talking and thinking in collaborative ways by providing open-ended resources in continuous provision. It is in these opportunities that I can apply new learning to previous thinking and try things out in meaningful ways as well as reflect on what it all means to me (meta-cognition, self-regulation). It is these processes that will lead to mastery of concepts and skills. See Go Compare.

Figure 6.4 The enabling environment and continuous provision

During the TFMM initiative, it became clear that creating an enabling environment is vital in supporting children to maintain their mark-making momentum (see Figure 6.4).

The influence of the wider environment on mathematical mark-making

Children need opportunities to see mathematical marks in the wider environment with real-life, authentic examples to talk about and relate to their own knowledge and previous experiences. This could mean providing real (empty) food packets and tins containing everyday logos, words, letters and numbers, or leaflets for children to play with in the home corner, introducing them to a builder's design sheet or floor plan for a building in the construction area, or including order forms and price lists in a role play shop (see REAL and REAM, previously discussed).

Maths in 'real-life' contexts

- Opportunities for cooking and baking will enable children to see and talk about numbers and amounts in a meaningful context. Reading the numbers or measurements on a scale or digital dial will enable children to develop further mastery of numbers, amounts, ordinality and cardinality
- Playful engagement with number rhymes using fingers or puppets help children to feel how their fingers and body represent quantity, one-to-one correspondence and order
- Outdoor experiences where children are continually provided with exploratory mark-making opportunities, for example using mud or soil and exciting encounters with snow with adults first observing then providing reciprocal support and interest
- As a result, children will continue to talk about letters, numbers and shapes when out and about as their experience of them widens, and they will enthusiastically represent these in their own mathematical mark-making

Mathematical mark-making at 3–4 years old: Meryam

Meryam has attended nursery (F1) since the age of 38 months. She enjoys engaging in mark-making activities both inside and outdoors. She has begun to show an interest in shapes and enjoys identifying, talking about and representing them in her drawing and mark-making.

Meryam's learning stories show how her mark-making becomes more refined and detailed as she moves into the *iconic* and *symbolic stages* in the representation of her thinking and understanding.

Meryam's Shape House

Meryam is mark-making on a piece of paper. "I'm drawing a house," she says.

As she draws her house, Meryam names all the different features she has included and the shapes she has used to make them.

She draws "a triangle roof," and says, "Look, I've made rectangle windows."

Next, she adds some people to her drawing and says, "The people are made of circles."

Finally, she adds a door to the house, which she describes as, "a big rectangle with a small circle for a handle."

Meryam finishes her drawing with some butterflies and adds her name, in both upper and lowercase letters at the top of the piece of paper.

For example, the way in which Meryam describes the house she is drawing shows how her mark-making has moved into *iconic* representation. She can hold a picture of a house in her mind's eye and recreate that picture in her drawing. Meryam's use of language to describe the shapes she has used and their relative sizes shows how her mathematical mastery is developing. This also suggests a move into *symbolic* representation, as the shapes Meryam has drawn are clearly meaningful symbols that indicate her knowledge and grasp of early geometry and using her own way of recording (see Chapter 2, Figure 2.8).

The evaluation (summary of learning) of Meryam's learning uses the characteristics of effective early learning to show how she is strengthening the connections in her understanding of maths, particularly shape, space and measures, and how she demonstrates the signs of mastery orientation (see Chapter 3).

The next steps show how Meryam's learning could be extended to develop her mathematical interests and understanding. Reflective questions are posed to help adults consider how they might do this.

Summary of Learning

Meryam showed **engagement** by being willing to 'have a go.' She showed a 'can do' attitude by creating her own drawing of a house using her knowledge and understanding of shapes in a meaningful mathematical context. She displayed **motivation** by enjoying achieving what she set out to do and showed her understanding of shapes through figurative schema, as she explained the features of her house as she continually added to her drawing. Meryam displayed **thinking** by choosing ways to do things. She chose to represent her interest in shapes through her mathematical mark-making, through which her mathematical thinking and talk was recorded. She checked how well her mark-making was progressing as she shared her thinking with a grown-up, which helped her to reflect on her own thinking and develop her understanding through meta-cognition.

Next steps

Continue to support and show an interest in Meryam's mathematical mark-making. Provide opportunities for her to explore mathematical mark-making and knowledge of shapes through play in a variety of contexts. How else can Meryam represent her knowledge shapes in meaningful contexts? Could she perhaps use her drawing as a starting point or design for a box model or a 3-D representation of a house built using Legos or Duplos in the Construction area? What other interests and fascinations around shapes does she have or would she like to explore further?

Exemplification (Child's Perspective):

I like to learn by:

experimenting joining lines when I make marks on paper to represent shapes of things I know like a square window, rectangular door or a round face (figurative schema); this may be linked to my schematic interests in trajectories, rotation and connection etc.

by developing and building on my own interests/fascinations and becoming deeply engaged. I need sufficient time to explore my mathematical interests in depth and become focussed and engrossed in what I am doing

Exemplification (adult's role):

You can support my mathematical thinking by:

being interested in the many ways I mark make and talk about this with me in engaging 'serve and return' conversations which stretch my thinking. (Meryam's Learning Story shows the complex development of her figurative schema and her explanation.)

using Learning Stories to record my mathematical talking and thinking and then sharing the 'story' with the group to reflect on our thinking and develop our talking (meta-cognition)

Mathematical mark-making with 4–5 year olds

At this stage, children should have had lots of practical and meaningful experiences with numbers, shapes, space and measures. Consequently, they now deepen their thinking further by creating more complex mathematical patterns, designs and recording in their mark-making. Children will do this by using a mixture of standard and non-standard marks and graphics which represent their developing mathematical thinking (Worthington and Carruthers, 2011) and by engaging in mark-making and writing, using letters and numbers that are becoming more recognisable and in context. We can see this happening in the following learning stories.

Mathematical mark-making at 4–5 years old: Aadam

Aadam attended full day care at the local children's centre nursery from 6 months of age. He moved to the Reception class in primary school at the age of 56 months. Since then, Aadam's interest and enjoyment in representing his own ideas, either through mark-making, talk or modelling and construction, have increased greatly. Aadam spends time communicating his ideas through drawing which he shares with others and talks about in detail.

Aadam's learning story shows how he takes his mathematical interests and fascinations further by assigning complex meaning to his mark-making.

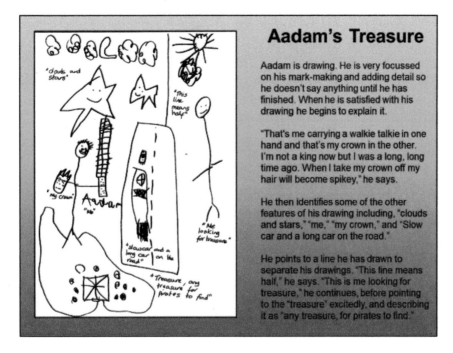

Aadam's Treasure

Aadam is drawing. He is very focussed on his mark-making and adding detail so he doesn't say anything until he has finished. When he is satisfied with his drawing he begins to explain it.

"That's me carrying a walkie talkie in one hand and that's my crown in the other. I'm not a king now but I was a long, long time ago. When I take my crown off my hair will become spikey," he says.

He then identifies some of the other features of his drawing including, "clouds and stars," "me," "my crown," and "Slow car and a long car on the road."

He points to a line he has drawn to separate his drawings. "This line means half," he says. "This is me looking for treasure," he continues, before pointing to the "treasure" excitedly, and describing it as "any treasure, for pirates to find."

Aadam's mark-making includes features of the *iconic* stage of representation, demonstrating his ability to think in the abstract. His drawings also show *symbolic* representation and a move into even deeper thought processes, which is evident in the wide range of symbols and more defined marks that he has used and can clearly explain.

The characteristics of effective early learning demonstrate Aadam's deep understanding and interest in his mathematical mark-making,

- **Playing and Exploring** – Aadam is *willing to 'have a go'* at his mark-making as he provides his own commentary on his drawing. He shows a 'can do' attitude and engages in trial and error as he draws and explains what he has drawn 'in the moment'
- **Active Learning** – Aadam shows *motivation* as he *enjoys achieving what he sets out to do*. He is proud of the drawing he has created and enjoys *meeting the challenge* he sets himself with his mark-making. Aadam appears to be in a state of 'flow' (Csikszentmihalyi, 1996), where the experience of mark-making has become its own reward. He has become totally absorbed in the process, experiencing deep concentration and a feeling of mastery (see Chapter 3)
- **Creating and Thinking Critically** – Aadam's thinking is evident in the way in which he *has his own ideas*. He chooses to represent his thoughts and ideas using drawing and shares his interest in the conversation he has about his drawing with an adult. This helps him deepen his own thinking and understanding through meta-cognition, where he is "thinking about thinking" (Robson, 2006, p. 82)

Aadam's use of language to explain his drawing shows how capable and confident he is of thinking reflectively. His explanation of the symbolism he has used in his drawing, such as the "clouds and stars . . . treasure . . .

walkie-talkie" and the "line [that] means half", makes his thinking visible and shows his conceptual understanding. This is evident in his representation of the "slow car and long car" where he has drawn the slow car smaller in relation to the long car (which travels faster), showing his experimentation with the concepts of size, position, speed and comparison. Throughout this process, he is consolidating his thoughts and ideas, continually building on them, making his own representations, confidently and articulately through his use of talking and drawing. He shows many aspects of mastery orientation (see Chapter 3).

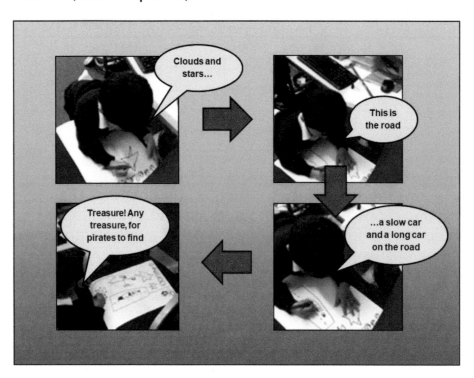

Summary of Learning

Aadam showed **engagement** by finding out and exploring. He engaged in open-ended activity as he chose to represent his thoughts through mark-making. Through his meaningful mathematical artistry he was able to link his imagination (which he represented through mark-making) with narrative (the words he used to ascribe meaning to his drawing). He displayed **motivation** by being involved and concentrating on the detail of his mark-making, and maintained focus as he carefully considered what and how he would represent his ideas. Aadam displayed **thinking** by having his own ideas. He clearly put a lot of thought and effort into his drawing, and created complex mathematical patterns and designs using non-standard marks and graphics to represent his mathematical ideas through figurative schema. Aadam could explain his mark-making afterwards, which shows his deeper understanding of mathematical concepts, such as the line depicting 'half' and his ability to record his thinking imaginatively.

Next steps

Provide further opportunities and a variety of resources to allow Aadam to demonstrate mastery in his mathematical graphics and mark-making through play in a variety of contexts (e.g. on a larger scale outdoors using water, paint, mud, sand, gloop with large paintbrushes, rollers, chalk etc. or perhaps on a smaller scale indoors in the role play area with notebooks and pens or creating a story map or extended narrative using mathematical mark-making). How else can Aadam represent his mastery and knowledge of mathematical concepts? What other interests and fascinations does he have or would he like to explore further?

Boys and mark-making

Mark-making and writing in the early years often raises debate, especially where boys are concerned (Anning and Ring, 2004; Department for Children, Schools and Families, 2008a). During our TFMM action research, we found evidence to counter the generalisation that boys are reluctant mark-makers and writers as we looked for ways in which we could encourage them to access mark-making practically and purposefully within the context of their interests and creative thinking. Our observations and knowledge of their unique developmental journey showed us that boys preferred to write in meaningful relevant contexts, often outside, and related to their interests. We can see this in the learning stories throughout this book.

Reflection point

How are boys in your setting/school engaging in mathematical mark-making?

How do you ensure that boys' interests are recognised and supported in your setting/school?

What meaningful opportunities to mark-make, draw and write on a small and large scale do you offer?

Mathematical mark-making at 4–5 years old: Meryam

Meryam's second learning story, a year later, shows how her interest in shapes has developed much further as she now skilfully represents 3-D shapes in her drawings.

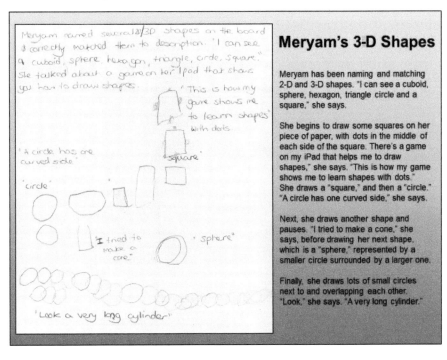

Meryam's 3-D Shapes

Meryam has been naming and matching 2-D and 3-D shapes. "I can see a cuboid, sphere, hexagon, triangle circle and a square," she says.

She begins to draw some squares on her piece of paper, with dots in the middle of each side of the square. There's a game on my iPad that helps me to draw shapes," she says. "This is how my game shows me to learn shapes with dots." She draws a "square," and then a "circle." "A circle has one curved side," she says.

Next, she draws another shape and pauses. "I tried to make a cone," she says, before drawing her next shape, which is a "sphere," represented by a smaller circle surrounded by a larger one.

Finally, she draws lots of small circles next to and overlapping each other. "Look," she says. "A very long cylinder."

The characteristics of effective early learning show Meryam's further fascination with shapes and the way in which she confidently undertakes the challenge of representing them in her mark-making. In particular, her explanation of the symbolism she has used in her mark-making, such as the dots, which are like those in the shape game she plays, help her to make sense of her own thinking. This is even more evident in the representations of the "sphere" and the "very long cylinder" which show her *testing her ideas* of how she can create accurate images of those shapes.

Meryam's next steps show how her thinking and understanding can be extended in different ways in collaboration with the adults who know her well.

Summary of Learning

Meryam showed **engagement** by playing with what she knows as she represented her own experience and knowledge of 3-D shapes. She engaged in meaningful mathematical exploration as she followed her interest in shapes and developed a deeper level of thinking, which enabled her to explain her mathematical thinking, reasoning and mastery. She displayed **motivation** by paying attention to details in her mark-making, such as the dots on the iPad shapes, and her perceptive representation of the long cylinder and the sphere. Meryam displayed **thinking** by making links as she developed her understanding and thinking around shapes further. Her figurative, schematic, mark-making has become more detailed as she confidently and competently shares her ideas with adults.

Next steps

Continue to support and show an interest in Meryam's mathematical mark-making. Provide opportunities for her to explore mathematical mark-making and knowledge of shapes through play in a variety of contexts (e.g. on a larger scale using water, paint, mud, sand, gloop with large paintbrushes, rollers, chalk etc. or perhaps on a smaller scale indoors in the role play area with notebooks and pens or creating plans for buildings in the construction area). How else can Meryam represent her knowledge shapes in meaningful contexts? What other interests and fascinations around shapes does she have or would she like to explore further?

Meryam is continuing to use figurative schema to represent her more complex thinking as she makes connections between two-dimensional and three-dimensional representations of shapes in her drawings. Her figurative schema are now more complex and becoming consolidated concepts (see Chapter 2, Figure 2.8). She demonstrates her ability to represent symbolically as she now moves into a more conceptual understanding of shape and size, laying the foundations of understanding much more complex concepts, such as mass, capacity and volume.

Exemplification (adult's Role):

You can support my mathematical thinking by:

recognising, understanding and appreciating the **mastery** I am showing in my child-initiated play and activities. The characteristics of effective early learning (*EYFS, 2017*) highlight dispositions to look out for when I am engaged, motivated and thinking critically, e.g. problem setting and problem solving, finding new ways to do things

recognising how mathematical mark-making may continue to represent more complex thinking - (*figurative schema*) e.g. 'Meryam's Shapes' learning story shows how she has represented her mathematical thinking and explained this in conversations with her teacher. Children's explanations show how they are thinking and the understanding (mastery) they have of some complex mathematical concepts particularly linked to creating and thinking critically.

Mathematical mark-making at 4–5 years old: Aadam and Farhaad

Aadam's learning story Big Numbers shows him sharing his ideas with a friend as their mathematical thoughts about big numbers grow through their talking and sustained shared thinking (Siraj-Blatchford et al., 2002).

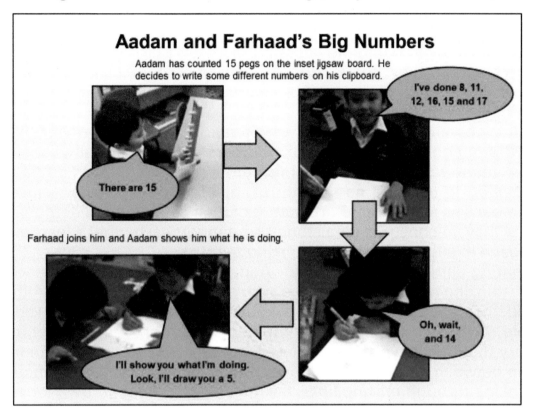

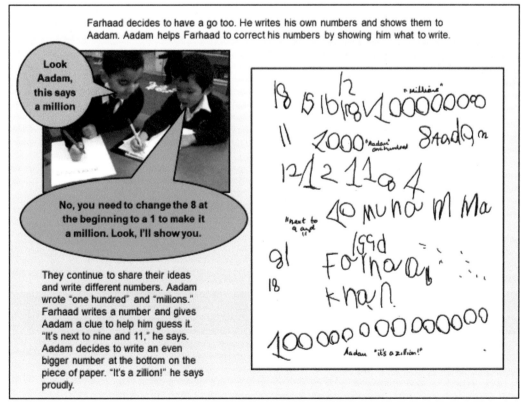

The characteristics of effective early learning show how the boys deepen their thinking further by pursuing their interest together (co-construction). Their thinking and understanding are now much more complex:

- **Playing and Exploring** – Aadam and Farhaad enjoy *finding out and exploring* as they *share their interest* in numbers, which goes beyond the expectation of 20. They engage in meaningful mathematical exploration in a context that they created themselves. Through their talk and conversation, they *show curiosity*, set ambitious challenges for each other and share their ideas of big numbers together. Their play has purpose, flow and excitement

- **Active Learning** – The boys show motivation by *being involved and concentrating* on the detail of their numbers. Aadam carefully considered how many zeros some of his big numbers needed, and Farhaad *paid attention to detail* as he thought of the clue to help Aadam guess his number. The serve and return nature of their conversation demonstrates how they co-construct ideas together, support each other's learning and engage in sustained, shared thinking together

- **Creating and Thinking Critically** – Aadam and Farhaad extend each other's thinking together in the serve and return aspect of their talk. Although Aadam appears to be a 'more knowledgeable other' (Vygotsky and Cole, 1978), this results in their mathematical mark-making becoming a story that they have co-constructed, in a two-way exchange of information between each other. It shows how they have both deepened their thinking through *making links*, talking and *sharing their own ideas*, and resulted in the conversation becoming an episode of sustained, shared thinking which supports mastery orientation

---

Summary of Learning

Aadam and Farhaad showed **engagement** by finding out and exploring as they shared their interest in numbers. They engaged in meaningful mathematical exploration in a context that they created themselves. They set challenges for each other and shared their ideas of 'big numbers' together. They displayed **motivation** by being involved and concentrating on the detail of their numbers. Aadam carefully considered how many zeros some of his big numbers needed and Farhaad concentrated as he thought of the clue to help Aadam guess his number. The boys displayed **thinking** by making links with their own and each other's knowledge of numbers as they engaged in collaborative mathematical mark-making. They drew on what they knew about zeros making 'bigger numbers' as they experimented with their mark-making and ideas of the huge range of numbers and infinite possibilities.

Next steps

Provide further opportunities to allow Aadam and Farhaad to explore mathematical mark-making through play in a variety of contexts (e.g. on a larger scale outdoors using water, paint, mud, sand, gloop with large paintbrushes, rollers, chalk etc. or perhaps on a smaller scale indoors in the role play area with notebooks and pens, or creating plans for building or measuring in the construction area). How else can Aadam and Farhaad represent their knowledge of big numbers? What other interests and fascinations around numbers do they have or would they like to explore further?

Reflection point

In what varied ways do you ensure that there are meaningful opportunities for children to engage in mathematical mark-making in all areas of provision, both indoors and outside?

How often do you observe and notice mathematical mark-making and engage sensitively with children to extend and deepen their thinking and understanding?

Is this recognised as mastery orientation?

How do you encourage children to celebrate and share their efforts with adults, peers and parents?

Mathematical mark-making into Year 1 (5+ years old)

As children move into school (Key Stage 1), their transition is strengthened when they can continue to access familiar, high-quality continuous provision within their environment and maintain the momentum of their previous learning (Fisher, 2010; Ephgrave, 2017).

Children need to continue to build on their existing knowledge and skills by having opportunities to engage in skilful, independent mark-making. This makes it possible for them to continue to show what they really know: their deeper understanding, thinking and mastery. For example, encouraging informal, meaningful opportunities to write number sentences and when labelling amounts as part of role play during continuous provision or building on some adult-led, focused teaching on money, amounts, addition or subtraction (Fisher, 2010; Ephgrave, 2017) (see Chapter 8).

When talking about standard and non-standard shapes, space and measures and using them in their own investigations, children can engage in complex problem setting and problem solving. It is here that they can then invent creative ways of recording their thinking and learning. They may make predictions or compare results. They could be practising their skills of addition, division, multiplication to keep a record of a score during a game or when sharing out resources in a group of friends. The children in the learning story Go Compare interacted collaboratively to share their thinking and understanding when they compared the lengths of their Superworms. They recorded their comparisons by arranging the worms next to one another and ordering them by length.

Fisher (2010, p. 134) explains how continuous provision supports children's transition into Key Stage 1 and helps them to maintain (their own) learning momentum:

> Continuous provision in Year 1 looks pretty much the same as it does in the Foundation Stage (it is the increased challenge

that children bring to using the resources, the increased mastery of play itself and the increase in challenge from the adults that support the play that differentiates it appropriately for older learners).

Older children build on these interests and fascinations when they engage with new provocations, challenging themselves, through their play, to explore more deeply. This self-initiated play provides rich opportunities for sustained shared thinking (Siraj-Blatchford et al., 2002) with time for adults and children to talk, think, reflect and discuss together. As a result, children make suggestions, use 'possibility thinking' (Craft, 2002, p. 91) and apply newly understood language and concepts independently. They have opportunities to concentrate upon tasks that they have grown themselves, which they can return to and develop further at a later stage.

By supporting children in this way to consolidate their now more mature schematic thinking, they continue to develop their ever increasing awareness of mathematical concepts, such as length, distance and time. By having numerous opportunities in continuous provision to apply and embed new learning to current thinking, children will be naturally supported to refine and reapply their ongoing mastery and creativity into their investigations by recording and mark-making in even more interesting, complex and abstract ways. We can see this whole process unfolding in Go Compare.

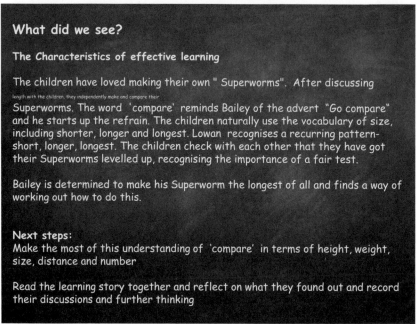

Bailey's reflections on his mathematical thinking show how he is an autonomous, independent and self-regulated learner. He has made many connections in his thinking and learning by engaging in abstract mathematical representations with string and applying this to the concept of comparison. The early schematic playful mark-making we saw in Peyton at 2 years old has now developed into a greater, deeper, more abstract understanding of mathematical concepts shown by Bailey at nearly 6 years old.

Bailey's thinking demonstrates many aspects of mastery orientation. He sees his self-chosen task of comparison as a **challenge**, being a **problem** that he **set** to **solve** himself. He **believes in himself** and his own **efforts**. His actions and thoughts all show mathematical mastery at a high level. Bailey is certainly showing "**embedded learning** and **secure development** without the need for overt adult support" (STA, 2019, p. 12). He **understands** and has **mastered** what he has learnt. Ultimately, he can **apply** his understanding of the complex concepts within shape, space and measures to his current thinking and interests and **enjoy** being mathematical (see Chapter 3).

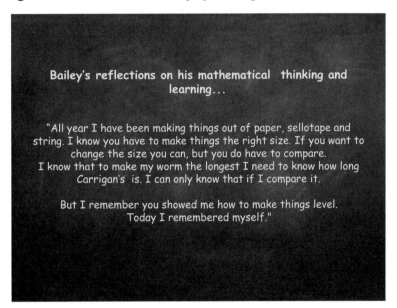

Bailey's reflections on his mathematical thinking and learning...

"All year I have been making things out of paper, sellotape and string. I know you have to make things the right size. If you want to change the size you can, but you do have to compare.
I know that to make my worm the longest I need to know how long Carrigan's is. I can only know that if I compare it.

But I remember you showed me how to make things level.
Today I remembered myself."

Reflection point

How do you ensure that the daily routine or timetable is flexible enough to allow children to remain autonomous, self-regulated and independent learners whilst having opportunities for whole group discussions or short 'adult-led' teaching sessions?

How does practice remain developmentally appropriate and allow children to continue to learn in an enabling environment which includes continuous provision?

How are the children supported to apply their learning independently by following their own interests and engage in serve and return conversations with peers and adults?

Summary

In this chapter we have seen how building children's mastery orientation requires firm foundations to be in place with opportunities for them to become well practised and observed by the adults around them. Bailey, who is confident in his learning and a competent, capable mathematician, is a good example of this. Meryam's fascination with shapes shows how children develop their understanding of complex mathematical concepts by exploring her thinking through the development of schema. Aadam and Farhaad's playfulness with numbers and Aadam's representation of his treasure map demonstrate how mastery orientation supports children in refining and understanding their own symbolic representation. Peyton's early mark-making reminds us of the direction of travel from birth upwards, building on firm foundations to maintain and effectively support children's mathematical momentum by enabling them to follow their own paths of thinking.

These children are becoming skilled, confident mathematicians by building on their development and maintaining their mathematical, mark-making momentum so that they experience a smooth, seamless transition as they move from one key stage into another.

Note

1. The National Children's Bureau (NCB, 2014) has more information about how REAM developed from REAL on the dedicated website at www.ncb.org.uk/what-we-do/our-priorities/early-years/projects-programmes/real-approach-maths.

7 How do adults support children's mathematical talk, thinking and mastery?

KATH PRIESTLEY

This chapter focuses on raising the confidence, self-awareness and mathematical understanding of all the adults who engage with young children in their earliest experiences of maths. Posing a key question, Kath Priestley shares her experiences of working with children from 2 to 6 years old and how to build solid foundations of mathematical thinking, learning and mastery.

What do young children need to support their mathematical thinking and learning?

A report by the independent charity National Numeracy (2017, p. 14) highlighted government statistics which suggested that "17 million adults, 49% of the working-age population of England, have the numeracy level that we expect of primary school children". Some of the reasons identified in the report included adults' lack of confidence about maths, a dislike or 'fear' of maths and a belief that maths is a 'can or can't do' subject rather than one that people can become better at given the right support and effort.

The report also highlighted how the culture within the UK of saying "I'm no good at maths" is socially acceptable and how damaging this can be in terms of negative attitudes being passed on to very young children. The report states that negative attitudes are the foremost barrier to making the country numerate: "Removing them, getting rid of mistaken beliefs and the widespread 'rubbish at maths' tag is fundamental to change" (p. 22).

Included within these statistics are adults who work with our youngest children. Haylock and Cockburn's (2008) research also found that adult's attitudes to maths reveal that many have feelings of panic and anxiety when faced with an unfamiliar mathematical task and that they are often unsure about the basic mathematical knowledge underpinning the teaching of particular concepts to children.

As an early years consultant, I frequently came across adults who admitted that they "hated maths". Many felt that they were "no good at maths" and "could never understand maths at school". Some adults would say that as soon as they were asked to look at "anything to do with numbers", their minds would go blank.

Whilst working in a children's centre with children from birth to 4 years of age, one of our key priorities as a staff team was to look at why, according to our assessments, children's progress and 'attainment' in maths were lower than in all the other areas of learning. Looking into this as a team raised everyone's awareness of several interesting issues:

- levels of confidence in mathematics
- confidence about assessing children's mathematical understanding
- ability to identify maths when it was taking place in child-initiated play situations and everyday routines
- varying levels of knowledge about child development, particularly in relation to mathematical thinking
- maths, as an area of learning, featuring the least often in their observations of children. The following are some of the comments made by the adults in this case study

I am not sure personally that maths is the area where I'm least confident, but it is the area that I find most difficult to monitor/assess/record. Because it is difficult to see happening, it becomes a really difficult area to assess.

It's the language that you use with the children. They actually don't understand it, so you are not getting the responses, or the evidence to prove that they understand about things like biggest, smallest, fullest, emptiest, quantities, estimating, calculating – you know, so I feel that's why the children find it a difficult area.

I think it's a confidence thing. Personally, I think maths is so easy to think of as the issue you had at school and that can very easily impact on even the maths with a 2, 3 and 4 year olds and perhaps that's a barrier. We need to just get over that because I think – and I include myself – there are those that have a real fear of maths.

But actually, at this level, at 2, 3 and 4 year olds there needn't be a fear because even if you really, really have struggled with maths personally, I possibly still do, there is such a difference at the level that we are actually talking about. We really can do it! But it is all about changing those attitudes, changing those fears and just growing everybody's confidence about what maths is.

Do any of these comments sound familiar?

Over ten years ago, the Williams Review (DCSF, 2008a) highlighted the importance of adults' knowledge in maths and, crucially, the impact that a lack of knowledge and understanding in the subject can have on children's learning and development. It also highlighted the 'significant impact' that parental attitudes towards maths can have on children's cognitive development and numeracy skills and the "widely accepted 'can't do' attitude to mathematics in England" (p. 71).

Williams said that "attitudinal change" was needed in order that parents and adults working with children do not pass on this "pervasive negativity" to their children. Sadly, the issues raised during this case study are still all too familiar and highlight the need to change this 'I can't' attitude towards maths to an 'I can' attitude.

My maths story

I never found maths easy at school and always felt it was one of my weakest subjects. I remember the humiliation of being made to stand on a chair in class, at primary school, for not being able to chant back the correct answer to a times table question fired at me by the teacher. What he had hoped to achieve by this, goodness knows, other than my humiliation and further lack of confidence and 'fear' of maths. As I moved through the secondary school system and towards GCSE exams, my anxieties about maths became worse. I would spend half of most lessons trying to look and sound as if I understood what was being taught and copying from the person next to me rather than face the humiliation of getting something wrong or being made to look stupid. I passed my GCSE, but I know that this was due to relentless revision based on *memorising* processes and formulas for achieving the correct answer to mathematical questions rather to any underlying *understanding* of how and why. The relief was huge when the exam was over that I would never have to study maths again or think about any sort of maths.

So why am I writing a chapter in a book about maths mastery?

Over the last 35 years, I have taught in primary schools, mainly in Reception. I have been an early years Phase Leader in a large primary school, a children's centre teacher, a local authority early years consultant, and a lecturer in early childhood studies. Throughout this time, I have been fascinated by the way that children develop their mathematical thinking and use it to make sense of the world. I was determined that children should not have to feel anxiety or 'fear' about maths and have taken a great interest in how adults can support them to do this. I still don't consider myself to be an expert at maths, but I do understand how to support young children's learning and development, including mathematical development, and how to ensure that they develop the qualities they need to be able to approach maths with a 'can do' attitude (see Chapter 3).

The Talk for Maths Mastery initiative looked at mathematical development from four perspectives:

1. the children's ("I like to learn by . . .")
2. the role of the adult ("You can support my mathematical thinking by . . .")
3. the enabling environment and continuous provision ("To develop and extend my learning, I need . . .")
4. the home learning partnership ("My home learning helps me when . . .")

This chapter will focus on the perspective of the adult role and the key skills they need to be able to recognise, support and extend children's mathematical thinking and learning.

The role of the adult: "My mathematical thinking is supported by . . ."

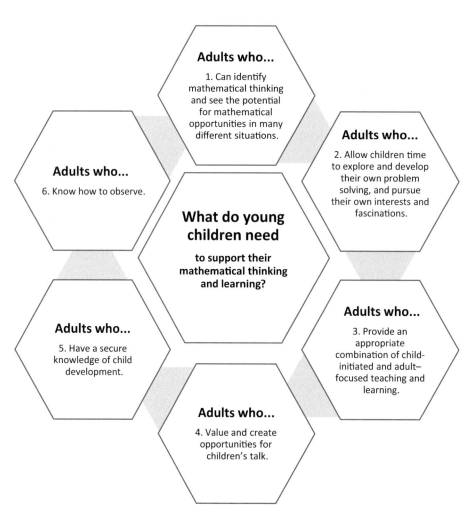

Figure 7.1 Role of the adult: "My mathematical thinking is supported by . . ."

1. Adults who can identify children's mathematical thinking and see the potential for mathematical opportunities in many different situations

Maths is all around us, and, as adults, we are continually involved in some form of mathematical thinking throughout our daily lives. This can be something obviously mathematical, for example, calculating how many litres of petrol we will need to get from one place to another or working out whether we have been given the correct change in a shop. Many of our daily routines that we do almost without thinking involve some form of mathematical skill or knowledge, without which the outcome would be very different; e.g. understanding calculation and estimation, time, speed, sequencing, quantity and capacity are all needed in order for us to get out of bed in the morning, dress, make a cup of tea, travel to work and arrive at a particular time. People are sometimes surprised by the amount of maths that they actually use each day without thinking. They are also surprised that what they are doing can be classed as maths.

Reflection point

Think about the different kinds of mathematical thinking you have done so far today.
How much of your day was mathematical?
What did it involve?

Adults who work with young children need to both recognise when children are using maths or thinking mathematically as well as the potential for maths in all sorts of situations. It is important to remember that children are always learning more than one thing at a time. Children's learning is not linear; they don't compartmentalise what they are thinking or learning into neat boxes, and there is always overlap among the areas of learning. Rather than following a straight developmental trajectory (Figure 7.2), it is entwined and interwoven (Figure 7.3).

Rinaldi (2006) explains this metaphor further:

> Learning is a process of constructing meaning while knowledge, in the words of Reggio's co-founder Loris Malaguzzi, is like 'a tangle of spaghetti' with no beginning, middle or end, but always shooting off in new directions.
>
> (p. 7)

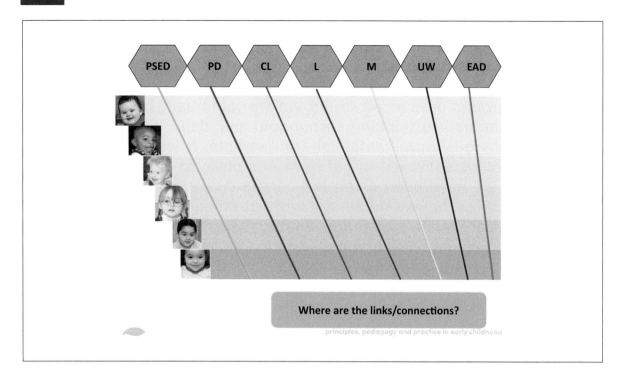

Figure 7.2 How do young children learn? In a straight developmental trajectory?

Source: National Strategies Slides 2009

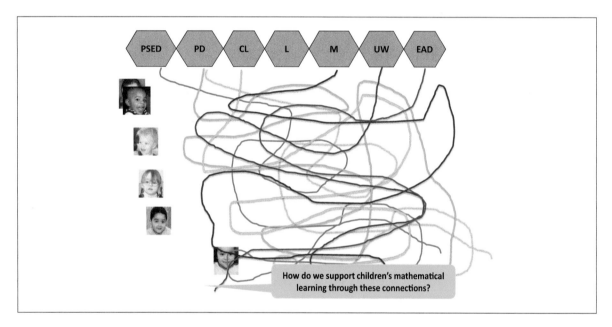

Figure 7.3 How do young children learn? In an entwined and interwoven way?

Source: National Strategies Slides 2009

It is important to remember:

- Some maths is obvious and easy to see; e.g. a child counting out objects, ordering numerals or using and naming shapes, particularly in adult-initiated tasks. It can also be quite obvious in certain play situations and daily routines. However, some of the most interesting, revealing and valuable instances of mathematical thinking take place when children are involved in their self-initiated play or activities of their own choosing. This is often when and where children reveal the depth of their understanding (mastery orientation) or, indeed, their misconceptions or lack of understanding

- Makhi's learning story, in this chapter, reveals the extent of his mathematical mastery in his self-initiated activity. He clearly demonstrates **what he knows** and crucially **understands** in terms of his mathematical knowledge about:
  - shape
  - size
  - length
  - comparison
  - properties of shape
- Most importantly, this narrative observation reveals Makhi's level of mastery orientation as he demonstrates all the characteristics of *Creating and Thinking Critically* (crucial for the development of mastery), as well as most of the dispositions within *playing and exploring and active learning* (see Chapter 3 and Appendix 6)
- Maths does not only happen in a classroom or during adult-focused activities; maths is much broader than this and happens all the time in many ways and forms. It can be happening in the most routine, unexpected moments; the role of the skilled adult is to be able to identify, through observation, these moments of mathematical thinking taking place and to know how to react and respond
- When a planned activity is not specifically 'maths' focused, that need not stop a child from using and developing their mathematical thinking. A PE lesson, junk modelling, den building outdoors, or a child quietly looking at tadpoles in a pond can all provide many opportunities for mathematical talking and thinking. Adults need to be able to tune into and recognise the many kinds of mathematical thinking that children are doing and consider what the best way of extending it may be
- Some of the adults at the beginning of this chapter said they found maths was 'difficult to assess because it was difficult to see'. If the adults approach observation only with a preconceived idea and a narrow tick list of statements about what maths they are hoping to see, e.g., a child identifying or forming numbers correctly or adding or subtracting two amounts or naming simple shapes, they may well find it difficult to recognise more complex mathematical learning such as problem solving or making connections. mathematical development and learning are much broader/deeper than a tick list of statements. The skill of the adult is in identifying the maths occurring through observing the child and knowing just when and how to intervene (or not) in order to support, challenge, address misconceptions or move thinking forwards
- The Early Years Foundation Stage (DfE, 2017, p. 9), section 1.8, clearly states that most of the children's learning must come from "planned,

purposeful play and through a mix of adult-led and child-initiated activity". It states, "Play is essential for children's development, building their confidence as they learn to explore, to think about problems, and relate to others" (see Chapter 5)

- Observing children in their play will provide adults with the best opportunities to see the development, application and understanding of children's mathematical thinking and understanding. This could be through schematic learning (see Chapter 2), an individual's interest in a topic or theme (e.g. dinosaurs, trains), through an activity or within a group or class project (see Chapter 5). However, it does not have to be something so obvious, often children's attention and interest can be caught throughout the day by the things that they see, hear or experience around them

- These times can't be planned for, but they can be responded to by skilled adults who are 'tuned' into the signs, recognise mathematical thinking taking place and have the skills needed to move the child's learning on. These 'teachable moments' are perhaps the things that can be most easily missed in a busy classroom environment or setting but can offer the most wonderful opportunities to extend mathematical talking and thinking. mathematical thinking can be revealed in a comment, a question, a gesture or an interaction with another child. It can be through sustained activity or conversation or in a fleeting moment (Chilvers, 2015)

Reflection point

Consider this snapshot of conversation that took place in a reception class

Four children were sitting together drawing in a self-chosen task.

Sofia: "There are 6 classes in school, Year 1, Year 2, Year 3, Year 4, Year 5 and Year 6 so we must be zero".
Amelia: "We're not zero, we're reception".
Sofia: "Well, we're not called zero but reception doesn't have a number so we can say zero cos Year 1's are older than us. Actually, that makes 7 classes!"

What does this conversation reveal about Sofia's and Amelia's understanding of numbers?

Spontaneous mathematical learning goes on all the time, in different ways for different children, and there are endless opportunities for seeing maths within child-initiated play and everyday activities. In their own explorations, children will be covering many aspects of mathematical learning in some form or another.

Examples of this can clearly be seen happening in the learning story Numbered Footballs (see Chapter 3) as the boys:

- talk about what they are doing, share their ideas and work collaboratively
- are absorbed in their play and are intrinsically motivated
- use mathematical language to develop and deepen their understanding of concepts
- set and solve problems
- choose new ways to do things
- make links in their learning, e.g. to previous learning, their knowledge of football

The skilful adult needs to be able to identify the mathematical learning that is taking place and what the child needs to support it.

2. Adults who allow children time to explore, develop and revisit their own problem solving and pursue their own interests and fascinations

One of the key findings of the Williams Review (DCSF, 2008a) was that, although the "EYFS provides guidance on developing mathematical understanding through play, opportunities in this area seem to be missed. Opportunities for problem solving, reasoning, critical thinking and reflection are vital if children are to make the most of their emergent understanding of mathematics" (p. 7).

If the adults who work with young children are to be able to see mathematical talking and thinking taking place, children must be given the right kind of learning environment and opportunities for mathematical talking and thinking to happen. The learning environment must offer a range of stimulating open-ended materials, outdoors and indoors, which children can use and combine in their own way to meet their own purposes.

Children need play opportunities to develop their social interactions, to negotiate relationships with other children and adults and to explore and develop their own problem solving and interests.

Through play, children learn to:

- interact with and relate to other people
- experience the world using all their senses and movement
- communicate their ideas and thinking to others through actions, sounds and talk
- hear and take account of other people's ideas
- represent their experiences, ideas and thinking in different ways, e.g. through movement, talk, model making, music, pictures, role play
- develop positive dispositions and a 'can do' attitude (growth mindset)
- make links in their learning

- try out and test ideas
- take risks
- learn from mistakes
- rehearse and practise new skills in a variety of situations
- develop self-esteem, self-worth, confidence, independence
- think critically and problem solve
- follow and extend their own interests

(DCSF, 2009a, p. 11)

One of the challenges increasingly faced by adults who work with young children today, is the top-down pressure being placed on early years to conform to timetables, planning formats and ways of working that are often inappropriate for very young children. If we consider the preceding points about identifying and extending children's mathematical thinking through their child-initiated play and individual interests, it becomes difficult to justify:

- the use of maths schemes which advocate whole-class teaching of the same concept in timetabled daily sessions and the filling in of worksheets/workbooks
- planning in advance what children are going to learn and the rate at which they are going to learn it
- being asked to focus for a short time on a particular area of maths and then not revisit it for a long time when it is ever present within children's daily routines and play
- telling children to only focus on numbers up to ten or 20 and not to go beyond when in children's mathematical minds, it is the really huge numbers that fascinate them!
- predominantly focusing on number and missing out on the much wider view of mathematical development and learning

If children are fascinated by something else or are making more relevant and interesting connections in their own child-initiated play, this is what will be at the forefront of their minds, not an adult's planned agenda or 'learning objective'. Children may well be able to answer questions and fill in worksheets correctly in order to achieve what has been asked of them, but the learning that they take from the experience will often just be at 'surface level' to satisfy what an adult has asked them to do.

Adults need to be flexible and responsive to children's ideas, and sometimes this will mean that any predefined planning has to be dropped in order to follow the flow of the children's thinking. Relentlessly following a maths scheme may not 'value' the mathematical capabilities that children already have when they join a setting and actually serve to 'shut down' children's enthusiasm, motivation and interest in mathematical play and explorations.

Children need to be given time to really 'master' their understanding of different concepts. Having the time and provision in which they can practise, revise, test out and become deeply engaged in their explorations in order to make sense of their learning and truly 'master', assimilate and understand each new concept. Having the freedom to move in and out of their play throughout the day and the rest of the week, revisiting, consolidating, adapting and assimilating their thinking as they do so. This cannot be rushed and will take different amounts of time for each child (see Chapters 2 and 3).

Reflection point

Imagine you are being taught a new skill or concept as an adult. For example, how to work out a percentage, multiply fractions, use a new computer program, use a sewing machine or even learning to drive.

How would you approach this? What would you need? How would you feel?

Would everyone need the same amount of time?

Most of us would need a mix of instruction/teacher input and time and space to 'have a go' for ourselves. We would need the opportunity to be able to:

- practise as often as we needed
- check back with the 'teacher' to have our questions answered
- try things out until it made sense to us
- apply it to what we already know and make links in our learning
- be allowed to make mistakes and re-adjust our thinking
- receive encouragement and praise for our efforts
- become confident enough to do it for ourselves
- enjoy what we are doing and become deeply involved

Would our needs be so very different to those of young children?

In Makhi's learning story (see below), the adult-initiated activity on cylinders and making cylindrical shapes had clearly piqued his interest, and he wanted to follow that interest through in his own play. The enabling environment provided resources for him to choose from and, importantly, the time for him to follow through his interest at his own pace, in his own way, which supported Makhi to become deeply involved in his learning. Makhi needed access to all the opportunities and support listed for the adults above.

Makhi's exploration and creativity demonstrate how deep levels of understanding and 'mastery' can be achieved when the right kinds of opportunities, provision and adult-focused teaching are provided. "Rehearsing skills in similar tasks or new contexts helps children to build mastery, to enjoy their own expertise, and to consolidate what they can do" (DCSF, 2009b, p. 9).

Makhi transforms a cutlery box....

Makhi found a box in the workshop that had previously had cutlery in it. It had a moulded plastic tray that had held the different pieces of cutlery.

Completely independently he had the idea of rolling up paper to make cylinders to fit in each of the spaces.

He showed great perseverance, not asking for any help, just remaining focussed throughout and trying out different ways of doing things if one way didn't work.

He studied the box carefully in order to make the cylinders the right length and depth to fit. He used his measuring skills to measure the size of the hollow and work out what size piece of paper he needed to start with before rolling it up and adjusting it to make it the correct length and diameter.

He showed high levels of concentration, motivation and involvement. Also his manual dexterity in making the cylinders and using tools and materials.

He worked methodically, working out which spaces he was going to fill next and selecting pieces of paper.

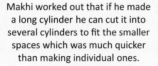

Makhi worked out that if he made a long cylinder he can cut it into several cylinders to fit the smaller spaces which was much quicker than making individual ones.

What did we see?

Makhi was really proud of his achievement and shared it with the rest of the class.

He chose to do this after various activities we had been doing to learn about length and measuring. One of the activities had been to make a Russian doll by rolling up three pieces of paper of different lengths to fit inside one another.

This clearly shows Makhi applying his learning, knowledge and understanding of length, measuring, size, capacity and cutting and joining skills to an activity of his own choosing.

Further possibilities for Makhi?

Provide more opportunities for Makhi to apply his skills and use different open-ended materials to experiment with and develop his design ideas.

Read this learning story together and talk about his ideas and thinking.

Send the learning story home. Does Makhi make things at home?

3. Adults who provide an appropriate combination of child-initiated and adult-focused teaching and learning to get the balance right

The previous points have considered the adult's role in recognising and extending mathematical learning within children's self-chosen play and individual interests; however, it is important to remember that the adult also has a role in supporting and extending children's mathematical learning within well planned and appropriate adult-led activities.

Knowing what an appropriate balance of the two should look like can be a challenge for the adults who must be able to judge and respond to what children need. This includes following children's interests and deciding when, what and how much adult input or focused activities are needed to support and extend their learning and to teach new concepts, skills and knowledge:

> Effective early years practitioners will organise the time, space and activities in the daily routine to reflect the overall combination which best supports children's well-being and learning.
>
> (DCSF, 2009b, p. 4)

Short sessions of carefully planned adult-focused activities support the teaching of specific skills, introducing new concepts and thinking and building on small-group or whole-class interests. However, adults need to consider carefully how these sessions are delivered. When planning 'appropriate' adult-focused activities practitioners need to:

- tune into what the children already know and can do
- know what their current fascinations are
- know what will motivate and engage them

Adult-focused activities are not play as the child knows it, but they should still be 'playful' (DCSF, 2009b, p. 14), even those with a specific learning objective in mind; playful learning and teaching are crucial.

What is playful learning and playful teaching? What does it look like, and what is the adult's role?

For adults to be playful teachers, they need to be operating within an environment that provides children with opportunities to be playful learners. As discussed earlier, children need to be in an environment that provides opportunities for open-ended play and exploration with a range of interesting resources. They need to have opportunities to work collaboratively and problem solve, make choices and mistakes and be given the time and space to rehearse new skills. They need to be able to express their own ideas and follow what interests them.

'Playful teachers' are those who are able to see the potential for children's learning in a particular moment or activity and know how to intervene in a 'playful' way which will not interrupt the child's involvement whilst extending their thinking and learning. Within an enabling environment, this can be done throughout the day and within a range of situations (see Chapters 4, 5 and 6).

Example 1

In the run-up to Christmas, we had a Post Office themed role play area in the classroom. The children enjoyed making and writing cards for one another and 'posting' them in the post box. Someone would put on the post outfit, empty the box and deliver the cards to the children. The children enjoyed this for a few days, but then most of them lost interest.

What really piqued their interest was when they found some parcels in the post bag wrapped up in Christmas wrapping paper with name labels stuck on them! These were handed out and unwrapped after a lot of guessing about what might be inside and whether there would be one for everyone. This generated a huge amount of talk and excitement about what everyone had received, and the adult skilfully used and modelled mathematical vocabulary around size, shape, weight, length and comparison. She then provided wrapping paper, Sellotape, string, ribbon and sticky labels.

The children became deeply involved and engaged in wrapping and giving parcels to one another. When we ran out of wrapping paper, children and parents brought in paper from home, such was their interest. This example of 'playful teaching' was led by the adult's knowledge of the children's interest and 'allowed' to take place for as long as the interest lasted. Sensitive and 'playful' teaching enabled the children to extend their learning in a 'playful way' about different mathematical concepts. They were able to measure, estimate, predict how much paper was needed, whether they had a long enough piece of string or needed more, how heavy or light things were, what kinds of shapes were the most difficult to wrap and how many presents everyone would have. They problem solved, worked collaboratively and even made checklists of who had received a gift.

Playful teaching is not about finding out what a child is interested in and then 'theming' everything else around that interest. Just because a child shows an interest in parcels, for example, it does not mean that they will be interested in counting how many presents there are on a worksheet or in identifying a particular shaped present on a sheet and colouring it in. This may hold a brief interest for those children who enjoy 'colouring in', but it will rarely be extending their learning about shape, size, weight, capacity, problem solving or collaborative working like the preceding example.

Real-life events and routines throughout the day can also be used to extend children's mathematical learning in a playful and engaging way as a lot of these routines involve some form of counting, checking, sequencing or other mathematical concepts.

Example 2

The children had the choice between having a cooked school meal or bringing their own packed lunch. Our morning routine involved the children taking a Duplo brick from a basket when they came in to represent their lunchtime choice that day: red for a school meal and yellow for packed lunch. They placed it on one of two towers and watched with interest to see which tower was the 'tallest' or had 'the most' bricks in it that day.

It was a visual, concrete way of showing how many children were having what and provided lots of opportunities for accurate counting, adding, subtracting, finding the difference, using the vocabulary of comparison, more than, less than, most, least etc. This became so embedded within the daily routine that, by the end of the year, most children were able to confidently 'read' the information from the 'block graph' and answer a range of questions, using and applying the correct mathematical vocabulary. This activity had clearly been initiated by the adult, but it also led to children taking their learning from it into their own 'playful learning' along the same theme.

Thomas decided to create his own representation of the dinner and packed lunch graph. He first went around the class and asked children what they were having that day and made two lists of names (Figure 7.4a). He then drew a visual representation of his findings and wrote the amounts next to his drawings of a 'lunchbox' or 'school meal' represented by a plate with a knife and fork (Figure 7.4b).

This was done completely independently by Thomas from start to finish. It took him a long time, but he was driven to complete it through his own interest and motivation. This was only made possible by the fact that the environment, the timetable and adults who knew and understood the value of 'playful teaching and learning' were all in place.

He asked the adult to help him check the calculation for the cooked dinners as there were so many but then confidently wrote '15'.

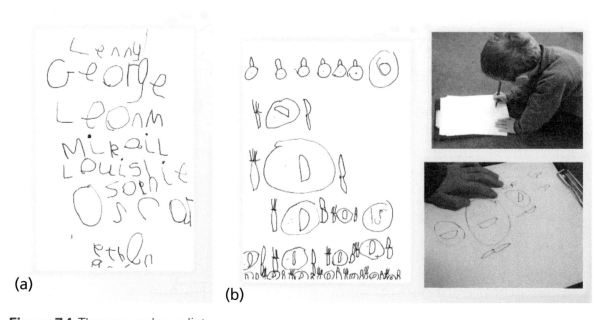

(a)   (b)

Figure 7.4 Thomas makes a list

Reflection point

Consider the role that the adults play in extending children's mathematical thinking in the learning story How to Make a Love Monster Happy (Chapter 5).

What kinds of strategies do the adults use?

Can you see examples of **playful teaching** which tune into the children's interests and:

- use them as a starting point
- give the learning a real life, meaningful and creative context
- extend and challenge the children's thinking through serve and return conversations
- encourage conversations which lead to sustained shared thinking (SST) (see Chapter 3)
- promote meta-cognition, allowing the children to see the links between their previous learning and what is happening now (see Chapters 3 and 4)
- develop mathematical language and vocabulary

What impact do you think these sorts of interactions have on mastery orientation?

Knowing just when and how to interact with children to extend their learning is a crucial skill and one that develops with experience and by watching adults who are already skilled in this. It is not always easy to 'teach' as some of the interactions that experienced adults have with children to extend their thinking can be extremely subtle. For example, the interactions can happen within:

- a brief moment
- the exchange of a look, facial expression
- an affirmation
- a question posed or answered
- a suggestion
- a particular word used, introduced, explained, reinforced
- the recap of a child's thinking
- the use of a provocation

Because of the subtlety of their nature, these interactions, often intuitive for the skilled adult, can easily go unnoticed to the untrained eye and ear. Noticing and tuning into these subtle interactions and strategies is a skill to be learned. Adults new to working with young children need time to observe and tune into the subtle interactions of a more experienced practitioner. They should also have time to analyse and reflect on what they have seen or heard and the impact it has had.

The same should apply to those adults, including the head teachers, leaders and managers required to make professionally informed judgements about the quality of teaching and learning happening with young children. The many strategies that experienced adults use intuitively, day to day and moment by moment, to develop young children's thinking are often less obvious but extremely powerful and demand a huge amount of skill.

4. Adults who value and create opportunities for children's talk

So why *talk* for maths mastery? Why is talk so important for extending children's mathematical learning and understanding?

Reflection point

How much 'mathematical' talking and thinking takes place in your setting/school?

- What types of activity does it take place within the most? Child initiated or adult focused?
- Where and when does it take place?
- Who asks the most 'mathematical' questions? Is it the adults or the children?

Do you consciously look at how you can create meaningful opportunities for 'mathematical' talk? (See Chapter 1 and Appendix 2.)

Through talk, children can:

- share their ideas
- listen to and consider other's ideas
- take in new information
- make their understanding visible – think out loud
- think about their own thinking (meta-cognition)
- talk through their problem setting and problem solving
- develop, use and understand new mathematical vocabulary
- make sense of new concepts

Adults need to ensure that children have the opportunities to engage confidently in the kinds of talk which enables children to do all of the above.

This kind of talk, often referred to as 'serve and return conversations' (Harvard University Centre on the Developing Child, 2018), supports mastery orientation through the development of children's critical thinking and deeper levels of involvement and learning (see Chapters 2 and 3).

Extending children's talk through possibility thinking and questions

To effectively extend children's talk and mathematical learning, adults need to ensure that their interactions are timely, meaningful and appropriate. A skilled adult will observe, tune into the learning that is taking place and decide, often intuitively, on how best to intervene to move language and learning on. This means avoiding the use of 'closed' questions such as "How many have you got? . . . Can you count them for me? . . . What shape is this?" Such questions do nothing other than make the child feel as if they are being tested, do not move thinking on and often interrupt the flow of the children's play, closing learning down.

A more effective approach is to ask thought-provoking possibility questions such as:

> "I wonder how many you are going to need?"
> "I wonder what would happen if . . . ?"
> "What do you think . . . ?

These types of questions enable children to respond with their own thoughts and ideas and generate further talking, thinking and problem solving. The adult 'working' alongside the child as a 'play partner' follows the child's lead and responds to their emerging needs and interests in the moment. Craft (2010) identifies the importance of posing and responding to questions in what she terms 'possibility thinking'. She describes possibility thinking as a process that allows us to develop ideas and thinking through careful questioning, self-expression, imagining, collaborative view sharing and taking risks.

In the example of Numbered Footballs (Chapter 3) we see the adult Miss Mercer posing 'possibility' questions:

> "I wonder how many you have made . . . ?"
> "Oh no, what are you going to do now then?"
> "Hmmm. I wonder if it will have a 10 and then a 4 like the number 11 is a 10 and a 1. How could you check?"

It is this skilful interplay between the adults and the children that leads to sustained shared thinking and deepens mastery orientation (see the section on "Observe, wait and listen (OWL)").

Introduce new mathematical vocabulary and reinforce it throughout the day in different situations

Repetition in meaningful contexts supports language learning and children's 'mastery' of new mathematical vocabulary and terminology. For example:

> "You were the first to finish, I wonder who will be second?"
> "Are you sitting *in-between* Sophie and Asad?"
> "Can you put your plate *next to/under* . . . ?"
> "Oh, look if we use a cylinder, it means it will be able to roll."
> "Do you think we need to use something that is flat or curved?"
> "Is that okay, or do you need something heavier?"

Young children love words, especially complicated mathematical words for numbers – e.g. one hundred million, thousands, a trillion – and sometimes use words that we may feel are too complex or difficult for them. However, they have a fascination for new and unusual words for things which interest and motivate them to learn, which in turn means they understand and remember them. Think about the 2- to 3-year-olds you know who can remember and use the names of different dinosaurs correctly or know all the names of characters in a favourite television programme or story (see Chapters 2 and 3).

Reflection point

Look at the following examples of children's talk.
In what way are they significant?
What do they reveal about the children's thinking and mathematical knowledge?

Max: "I'm the tallest in our class."
Eden: "You're the tallest but you've got the shortest name. M-a-x that's only 3!"
Beth: "We've got a bottle of play foam on the side of the bath at our house, and it's a cylinder with a triangle top. Well . . . it's not a triangle. It's a bit like a cone without a point at the top. What do you call that kind of shape?"

How would you support and extend this talk through being a play partner and using possibility questions?

Harry (5.6 years) expressed a great interest in words and an insightful mathematical ability to remember the order and names of all the stations the train from Sheffield passed through on the way to Bedford. This was a journey he did regularly to visit relatives. His interest was so deep that he often drew detailed pictures of the journey and mapped out each station they passed on the way.

His drawings show how he can remember and visualise the numbers on the platforms, the alphabetical order of the coaches and the names of the different train companies including Thames Link and Virgin (see Figures 7.5 and 7.6).

He drew meticulously detailed maps of places and buildings he was familiar with in Sheffield which were all geographically correct (see Figures 7.7 and 7.8). At 5.5 years old, Harry's mathematical mastery was evident in his

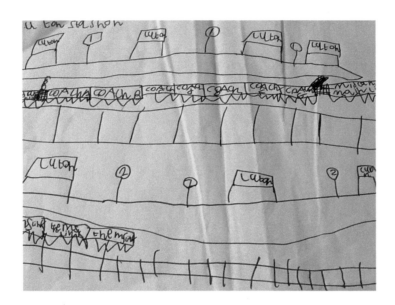

Figure 7.5 Harry's drawing of Luton station

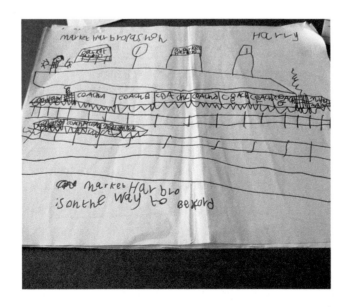

Figure 7.6 Harry's drawing of Market Harborough station

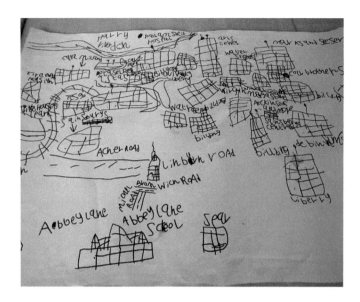

Figure 7.7 Harry's map of his route from home to school

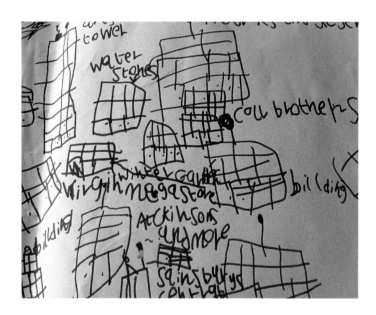

Figure 7.8 Harry's drawing of buildings he knew in Sheffield city centre

use of spoken language, in his vocabulary and in his drawings, as well as his ability to think in complex abstract form to create maps. Harry's abilities were revealed to us as he followed his own interests and fascinations which he explored and developed through his child-initiated learning.

These fascinating drawings, initiated by Harry, also involved conversations with a skilled and interested adult who tuned into and knew how to use his interest in train journeys as a vehicle to support, encourage and extend mathematical thinking and learning.

Adults need to allow children the time and support to follow what interests them or they may miss and even underestimate children's capabilities, their depth of thinking, understanding, knowledge and learning.

Observe, wait and listen (OWL)

Adults may find it hard not to jump in and speak 'for' the child. This happens for various reasons; e.g. if a child has limited language, adults may feel that they are giving support by doing the talking for them or even hurry them along. What the adult needs to do is to reduce their own language and use strategies to encourage children to interact more and build up the number of words that children are able to use for themselves. This can be done through:

- Modelling the correct use of vocabulary and sentence structure; e.g. the child says, "I goed park", and the adult models, "You went to the park?"
- Building on what the child says – adding one or two more words to extend their vocabulary; e.g. the child says, "I got train", and the adult says, "Yes you've got a big, blue train"
- Commenting on what the child is doing and what is happening
- This is a non-directive approach and can be used to engage children who struggle with communication. It involves observing or playing alongside children and commenting on their actions, e.g. "Sophie's pouring the water". The adult doesn't ask questions or give instructions but allows the children to take the lead and encourages them to interact with their peers non-verbally

At other times, adults need to observe, wait and listen (OWL) as they watch and then decide whether and when to join children in their play. Adults sometimes invite themselves into children's play without having taken a moment to stand back first, to observe what is happening and to think:

- At what stage is the play?
- Who is involved?
- What learning is taking place?

In their busy roles, adults can all too easily misunderstand the play that is happening, take it over with their own agenda, lose the children's engagement and ultimately close it down. Standing back, reflecting and quickly making an informed judgement is a highly skilled, professionally informed decision.

5. Adults who have a secure knowledge of child development and how children learn

Underpinning all the complexities, skills and elements of the adult role is the fundamental need for a secure knowledge of children's development and *how* they learn (see Chapters 2 and 3).

Above all else, a secure knowledge of the development that a child moves through, from birth, and the ways in which a child learns about the world and the people around them, is essential to becoming a skilled adult. This knowledge will impact on the adult's interactions, communication styles and responses; the strategies they use with children; the types of resources and materials; and the different experiences and activities that they provide.

Knowing the difference between HOW *children learn and* WHAT *children learn (see Chapter 3)*

The characteristics of effective learning (Appendix 6) describe *how* children think and learn. These are the characteristics and dispositions that adults should be looking to develop in children for them to become confident and capable lifelong learners

What children learn is connected to subject knowledge (the areas of learning) in this case mathematics.

In the introduction to this chapter, I referred to the view that many adults lack confidence in their own mathematical ability. Whilst adults working with children do not need degree-level maths, it makes sense that they do have enough subject knowledge to know about progression, to identify misconceptions, and to be able to introduce and use mathematical vocabulary correctly to ensure that children are building on their understanding.

Subject knowledge is important for knowing where children are in their mathematical development and what stage they need to move on to next in their understanding. Adults need to be able to identify the small steps in understanding that a child has made or, equally, to be able to identify and address children's misunderstandings.

With a secure knowledge of child development, the adult will understand each individual child's level of development, needs and interests and how to move their thinking on. If children are moved too quickly through these stages before they are ready, it can lead to confusion, misunderstanding and ultimately a lack of confidence and self-belief about maths.

One of the most effective ways for adults to deepen and further their knowledge of child development and to learn how best to intervene, interact, and extend children's thinking is through observing children. Knowing how, what and when to observe, why we observe and understanding what we see are the most crucial skills adults need in order to develop their knowledge about individual children's learning and development.

6. Adults who know how to observe

The six points from Figure 7.1 have all focused on the adult's role in recognising, supporting and extending children's development and learning. However, these are by no means separate, step-by-step processes; it is the skill of the adult to weave them all together as they engage with the children they teach. One of the key aspects of the adults' role is the way in which they can see and understand children's development and learning; how they interpret what they see and hear children doing and saying; and how they recognise the connections they are making and their progress, all through their informed reflections and evaluations (see Figure 7.9).

Observation is part of the cycle of teaching, learning and assessment, as well as a statutory duty of the Early Years Foundation Stage in England (DfE, 2017, p. 13);

> Assessment plays an important part in helping parents, carers and practitioners to recognise children's progress, understand their needs, and to plan activities and support. Ongoing assessment (also known as formative assessment) is an integral part of the learning and development process.
>
> It involves practitioners observing children to understand their level of achievement, interests and learning styles, and to then shape learning experiences for each child reflecting those observations. In their interactions with children, practitioners should respond to their own day-to-day observations about children's progress and observations that parents and carers share.

As the adult tunes into children's development, language and thinking through their observations, they can use this to extend their understanding

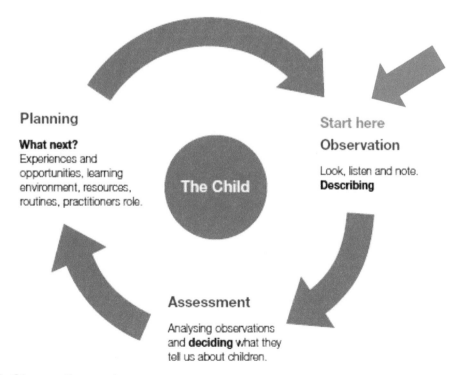

Figure 7.9 Observation cycle

Source: Early Education, 2012

and learning. It is a fundamental part of the adult's role and a significant professional skill.

> Knowing when to observe and describing what we see (verbally and in documentation) and then interpreting what we have seen is a professional skill which is fundamental to teaching and learning. Just as doctors need to diagnose their patients, adults who work with young children need to look at the evidence and make decisions about how to support children's development. Observing children is one of the best ways to fine tune your knowledge of child development and how they think and learn.
>
> (Chilvers, 2019, p. 7)

Through observation . . .

Adults find out about children's . . .	Adults can . . .
Needs interests what they already know and can do *how* they approach learning (characteristics of effective learning) *what* they need to learn next (areas of learning, knowledge, skills) what they enjoy where they need support how they interact how they behave or react to different situations life and learning at home levels of engagement and involvement levels of well-being confidence empathy self-regulation what motivates them to learn likes and dislikes schematic patterns of play and thinking mastery orientation (see Chapter 3)	gain a holistic view of the child. see thinking and learning taking place. hear and see serve and return conversations. identify 'mathematical' learning. decide how and when to intervene. decide which strategy or approach to use. decide next steps for the child, group, class. assess whether a child's needs are being met. follow the child's lead. find out about their interests. clarify misunderstandings. support in situations the child may find difficult. support with interactions, conflicts and self-regulation. share information with parents and other practitioners. provide resources and opportunities for challenge. be there 'in the moment' with the children and move their thinking on. share their moments of quiet reflection and contemplation.

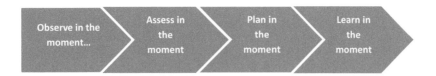

Figure 7.10 Process of observing in the moment

Observation is a professionally informed skill without which we miss the complexities of children's mathematical thinking, learning and mastery orientation.

Observing in the moment happens many times during the day, as you engage with children, though you may not be aware that you are doing it! You will be intuitively 'observing in the moment' and making informed decisions about how to support and extend children's development and learning. This is experienced observation at a skilled professional level; it is hard to teach effectively without it. It develops with experience, practice and a good knowledge of child development which forms part of teachers' and practitioner's observation tool kits (Chilvers, 2019, p. 29) (see Figure 7.10).

Planning in the moment has become an integral part of the vocabulary of good observation and assessment. Developed by Anna Ephgrave (2015), it is at the heart of exemplary professional practice. Anna describes it as follows:

> We do not plan ahead, rather we remain "in the moment" with the children as they explore and learn. We observe carefully and enhance the learning whenever we spot a "teachable moment". Our observations, interactions and the outcomes are recorded afterwards.
>
> (https://eyfsmatters.wordpress.com/2015/04/16/anna-ephgrave-guest-blog-in-the-moment/)

Opportunities for extending learning and supporting children's needs in the most appropriate way can be misjudged and, in the worst case, be entirely inappropriate. For example, look at the picture in Figure 7.11. What do you see?

This picture in the figure was drawn by Billy, aged 4, a child who never usually chose to draw. It happened while I was busy working with a group of children at the other side of the room. I felt unable to leave what I was doing with the group and break away to fully observe Billy drawing.

I managed to quickly take some photographs and intended talking to Billy as soon as I could. His drawing looked amazing – some sort of boat with a mast and sails?

Later in the day, I talked to Billy about his 'boat' he told me that it wasn't a boat, he had been drawing "ten". When at last I understood, I realised with astonishment that he had drawn a representation of his mathematical thinking showing how to split the number ten in different ways, a concept

Figure 7.11 Billy

we had been focusing on in class using tens frames. I had no idea that he had such a good understanding of this concept as he was always quite difficult to engage in any form of adult-focused number activity. This insight into Billy's level of mathematical development and understanding could so easily have been missed.

As adults, we must try and resist the temptation to impose our own assumptions and interpretations on what children 'appear' to be thinking or intending as they explore and represent their mathematical ideas through their play and child-led activities. We must take the time to *look carefully* and analyse what we see, including the context in which it has taken place. The way in which we record what we observe can vary from spontaneous snapshots, Post-it notes, photos and videos to just a 'mental note' or longer planned observations and learning stories, as in the case of the Talk for Maths Mastery initiative.

Working with young children, we are constantly observing what children think, do and say. Not all of this can or needs to be recorded. What is more important is that we analyse this wealth of information and use it to plan a child's next steps and move thinking along. This is a process that a skilled adult may do intuitively, in the moment, or take more time to reflect on, share with colleagues and feed into planning to meet the child's developing needs.

Summary

The role of the adult in supporting children's development is highly skilled, complex and crucial to children's overall development, learning and well-being. Having teased out some of the key skills required to support children's mathematical development and learning, it is important to remember that they are all inextricably linked, woven together and interdependent.

What is clear is that the professional skills of the adult are multi-layered and interwoven in the same way that children's thinking, and learning are interconnected and by no means linear. As children's knowledge, skills and dispositions constantly move back and forth, making the connections between previous and new learning, they gradually become assimilated and mastered with the help of the informed adults who have supported them in this amazing process.

> Stand aside for a while and leave room for learning, observe carefully what children do, and then, if you have understood well, perhaps teaching will be different from before.
>
> (Loris Malaguzzi (in Edwards, Gandini and Forman, 1998, p. 57)

8 Maintaining children's mathematical momentum into Year 1 – a case study*

NATALIE REILLY AND DAVID YATES

In this chapter, Natalie Reilly, Senior Assistant Head and Phase 1 Leader (EYFS and KS1) at Fordbridge Community Primary School in Solihull, Birmingham, explains how they were inspired to take the TFMM approach into their Year 1 classes, to maintain the children's momentum of learning, particularly between the end of the Reception year (FS2–EYFS) and into Year 1 (Key Stage 1–National Curriculum), a critical transition point.

Following the school's participation in another Talk for Maths Mastery initiative, the Phase 1 team worked together to create a developmentally consistent approach to maths starting from the children's centre with under-twos and progressing into Foundation 1 (Nursery), then Foundation 2 (Reception) and into Year 1. This was all underpinned by the following important principles and key questions, explained by Natalie:

1. Having a strong overall vision
2. Implementing the vision into Year 1
3. What were the challenges?
4. What about the role of the adult in Year 1?
5. How are children's interests followed?
6. Continuing continuous provision
7. Partnership between home and school

Previous chapters have shown how, when the momentum of children's mathematical thinking and learning is maintained and built upon from birth to 3, into Nursery (Foundation Stage 1–FS1) and on to the Reception year (Foundation Stage 2–FS2), children are supported to be competent and capable mathematicians, building their mastery and deepening understanding (see Figure 8.1).

* With thanks to Natalie Reilly, Senior Assistant Head and Phase 1 Leader; Dawn Scrimshaw and Jayne Weaver, Year 1 Teaching Assistants; Claire Green and Hayley Tufft, Reception teachers from Fordbridge Community Primary School, for sharing their experience thinking, philosophy and practice.

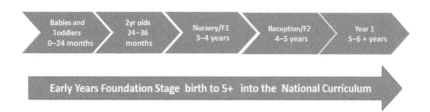

Figure 8.1 Maintaining children's learning momentum

However, children need to experience a smooth and appropriate transition particularly as they 'cross the bridge' from Reception into Year 1. This is a critical part of ensuring that children's development and learning in mathematics and in other areas continue with as little disconnection as possible, rather like relay runners smoothly transferring the baton to their partner. Transition also needs to ensure that children continue to see themselves as competent, capable and secure learners. Fisher (2010) also recognises the need for sensitivity:

> Child development tells us that children's learning needs in Year 1 are broadly similar to those children in the Reception year and that children should not go from being seen as a 'unique child' (DCSF, 2008d) to a 'Year 1' in one small step down the corridor.
>
> (p. 18)

1. Having a strong overall vision

Having a strong, clear and informed vision, combined with experienced leadership to take it forward and working across the age ranges, from the under-2s to 6- and 7-year-olds, as part of the whole-school shared pedagogy were fundamental. The team felt that the issue for their children in Y1 was being constrained by having the opportunity to learn only in an adult-directed, formal way and the perception that it must be formal for it to be learning:

> We went too formal in Y1 then discussed it with the Head Teacher and decided to change.

Being able to see the whole journey of the child, including considering the characteristics of effective learning (Appendix 6), was important, as well as continuing the philosophy and practice of Talk for Maths Mastery into Key Stage 1 by drawing on the knowledge and expertise of the Reception class team. An integral part of this was to support the Y1 team to develop their understanding of how young children learn.

Commenting on the overall vision for teaching and learning at Fordbridge, the team said:

> Our whole school shared pedagogy has enabled us to develop a curriculum that is balanced between child-initiated learning and

the opportunity to acquire new knowledge through more direct teaching. In Phase One we place children's well-being at the forefront of all learning experiences. Through the characteristics of effective learning we endeavor to promote a resilient, challenging and independent learning culture which reflects the uniqueness of the early years curriculum.

Terms such as the *independent learner* are now used, and staff consider how "children are taking their own learning forward". The team have been able to reflect on how "this looks different as children progress further on in the school".

The children in Phase 1 now experience a seamless mathematical journey that enables them to know, understand and practice mathematical concepts in a concrete way, so that they make connections in their daily lives, relating their learning, and applying the knowledge and skills to everyday problems. Our aim was for children to develop their resilience in tackling mathematical problems and adopting a 'can do' attitude to maths in general. Previously, children were less likely to attempt mathematical activities independently.

We also wanted the children to enjoy maths, to know that it is okay to make mistakes and to link their mathematical achievements with the characteristics of learning, well-being and involvement levels (see Chapter 3).

Prior to the TFMM initiative, Year 1 was formal with little opportunity for child-initiated maths and the children lacked resilience, perseverance and confidence. They only had the opportunity to practise and develop their mathematical skills and understanding in the morning and in a formal way. After completing the Maths Is Everywhere observation sheet (see Chapter 1 and Appendices 1 and 2), we realised that continuous provision enabled the children to practise and consolidate their learning independently and in meaningful contexts which they were used to doing in the Foundation Stage. Continuous and enhanced provision approaches to teaching and learning in Year 1 have evolved over a long period of time but have made a significant impact on children's independent and collaborative learning, as Daisy and Tristan show in their learning story.

One is a snail ten is a crab

Daisy and Tristan (6yrs)

Each term we plan a maths week in phase one. We begin by introducing the book one is a snail ten is a crab as a starting point for their new learning - repeated addition and times table. In the continuous provision activities were set up so the children could access them independently and adapt where necessary.

Daisy was using the concrete resources to make her own equations. By observing the children we can see how they approached their child-initiated activity. For example Daisy was talking through this to herself. Possibility questions are asked to gain more knowledge of her thought processes and how she was solving her own problems.

The Learning Story shows a good picture of the individual child's levels and next steps. When completing the evaluation we can assess what the children have learned and understood. We refer to the characteristics of effective learning and the Leuven scales to underpin our professionally informed judgements and understand how children are learning and their possible next steps/future planning.

Daisy use the resources from the story to complete the repeated addition and multiplication equations. She went to the people and put one each in a bowl.

Daisy used the cubes and numicon to help her count. She also wrote out the equation.

> Can I make one? It's nine.

> Nine what Daisy?

> Nine groups of 2

> Oh, so what equation are you going to do?

Daisy then put the one crab in each bowl. Tristan came over to see what Daisy was doing. She continued to make other equation of ten using the numicon shapes of eight and two.

Tristan helped her to count to 80. Then he helped her to write the correct numerals for her repeated addition.

> It's eight, where's my paper?

> What will you count in now Daisy?

> Tens – 10, 20,30, err....

> It's an 8 and a 0.

> Maybe Tristan can help you count in tens Daisy?

Daisy then wanted to do fives. She picked up the dogs and the snails. She decided to do arrays – new learning from today's lesson. Daisy counted in ones and then we counted together in fives. She continued to make other equations of five using the dogs and the snails.

Tristan wanted to make the characters from the book with the transient art. He picked a number from the pack. He made an insect with it. He then used the picture cards and post its to make the equation.

> Wow Daisy, can you show me how work out the answer.

> Shall we try to count in fives together?

> It's 5 Five times five

> 1,2,3,4,5 6,7,8,9,10, 11,12,13,14,15

> I'm gonna make six

Evaluation

Daisy showed great interest in the maths activities today. Recently she has become more confident with her maths work and has moved up a group. She persisted to complete all of the activities for working with five, two, and tens times tables even though she struggled to know the tables fully. She used previous learning to try out different approaches to find the answers. She showed resilience and was able to accept help from another child when it was offered. She was proud of her work and allowed me to take pictures of it.

Leuven Scale: High

Daisy shows obvious signs of satisfaction (as listed under level 5). However, these signals are not constantly present with the same intensity.

Characteristics of effective learning	Next steps
• <u>Being involved and concentrating</u> • Maintaining focus on their activity for a period of time • Not easily distracted. • <u>Keeping on trying</u> • Persisting with activity when challenges occur • <u>Creating and Thinking</u> • Having their own ideas • Thinking of ideas • Finding ways to solve problems	• Help children to become aware of their own goals, make plans, and to review their own progress and successes. Describe what you see them trying to do, and encourage children to talk about their own processes and successes • Be specific when you praise, especially noting effort such as how the child concentrates, tries different approaches, persists, solves problems, and has new ideas • Encourage children to learn together and from each other • To use more pictorial work such as arrays • To practise these times tables verbally

KPI's Counts, reads and writes numbers to one hundred in numerals; counts in multiples of twos, fives and tens.

The team created opportunities to focus on the importance and enjoyment of maths throughout the school and shared this with families by documenting and celebrating children's learning and understanding using narrative learning story observations.

2. Implementing the vision into Year 1

Aligning the new vision of teaching and learning with the previous one required some thought by the team. Figure 8.2 shows the journey of progression towards implementing Talk for Maths Mastery in Year 1 and the reflections of the team on the way in which mathematics teaching and learning were experienced by the children at Fordbridge.

The team found that implementing a less formal approach to teaching and learning has helped the children become more independent, autonomous thinkers and learners. Fisher (2010) also advocates this pedagogical approach in Year 1 classrooms as part of the seamless transition from the Early Years Foundation Stage into Key Stage 1.

The key to the success of the approach is being able to reflect on the learning potential and capabilities of all the children in the classroom. Fisher (2010) notes that the skill of the adult is to be able to give equal attention and recognition to the independent learning taking place, as well as the adult-initiated learning that they have been supporting. Most importantly, she states, "Independent learning must not be abandoned learning" (p. 88). This may be a challenge to those working within the National Curriculum KS1, but it is worthy of careful reflection when considering the effectiveness of such an approach as previously described.

Before implementing Talk for Maths Mastery in Year 1	After implementing Talk for Maths Mastery in Year 1
Children experienced mathematics through a daily formal whole-class lesson.	– Children participate in a maths lesson, which is supported with resources in continuous provision that are related to previous learning. – Children have an in-focus task, which is a short independent task that should take no more than 5 minutes to complete to check on previous learning. – There is some direct class teaching, where the teacher supports the whole class on the carpet with relevant resources and PowerPoint slides. The teacher and teaching assistant (TA) then work with small groups to complete activities. – Post-teaching is delivered as misconceptions arise. – All children in the class receive some direct teaching over the session in small groups for a very short period of time, which enables adults to differentiate teaching and provide support for children at different levels of development and understanding.
Mathematics was focused on formally for an hour every day.	– Following the 1-hour adult-focused teaching session, children can practise and consolidate previous learning in continuous provision (see the learning story One Is a Snail Ten Is a Crab) – Adults are present to support sensitively in response to each child's needs. – The focus may be on reinforcing number formation or posing challenges for children who are now number experts. – During the afternoon, children can access the continuous and enhanced provision independently where they can use maths-focused and other resources to deepen and master their understanding. This also helps them make links with the other areas of learning.
Maths intervention took place outside of the maths lesson.	– Mathematics post-teaching and intervention now happen in the lesson when and where required; e.g. whilst the teacher is delivering a plenary, the TA sensitively works with children to support their learning and check their understanding. – When they are more confident to join in independently, they then join the rest of class.

Figure 8.2 Implementing the vision

Before implementing Talk for Maths Mastery in Year 1	After implementing Talk for Maths Mastery in Year 1
Tracking children's progress was difficult as adults sometimes would not see all children within the lesson.	– All children work with the teacher or TA in the lesson in a group situation. This enables staff to address misconceptions or challenge the more expert mathematicians. – This enables them to develop mastery and deepens their knowledge and application of learning using their own interests and contexts. – Subsequent understanding is developed and embedded within continuous provision and not always in the lesson. – The knowledge is delivered by the teacher during the lesson, but deeper understanding comes when children apply their learning when they are pursuing their own interests through child-initiated learning. For example, the use and application of numbers up to 20 may be modelled by the adult, but children will often use higher numbers related to their own knowledge and fascinations when they are learning independently (see the learning story One Is a Snail Ten Is a Crab).
Misconceptions were not addressed through post-teaching.	– Post-teaching happens within the lesson and enables the children to fully understand their learning as the teacher and TA know the children well. – Adults pose questions skilfully for the children to answer. If the children demonstrate skills, confidence and reasoning when they answer these questions, they usually demonstrate a sound understanding of the teaching and learning they have experienced. – If necessary, adults provide further sensitively guided practice using concrete or pictorial methods to develop children's understanding and application.
Children did not appear to show resilience regarding maths due to a perceived fear of failure.	– Children are resilient and persevere with challenging tasks. – Learning stories demonstrate evidence of children's perseverance, resilience and challenge, e.g. Trevor in Let's Build a House and Daisy in One Is a Snail Ten Is a Crab.

Figure 8.2 (Continued)

Before implementing Talk for Maths Mastery in Year 1	After implementing Talk for Maths Mastery in Year 1
Children did not have opportunities to consolidate their skills to enable them to deepen their understanding and develop mastery of new and revisited concepts. The environment was resourced without continuous provision.	Continuous provision now supports Talk for Maths Mastery by promoting deeper understanding of maths skills and concepts through opportunities to: • revise and rehearse new skills • consolidate and embed concepts and skills through independent learning • engage in sustained thinking time (leading to sustained shared thinking) • revisit skills, concepts or interests when they need or wish to • have a choice of a wide range of resources with no limits or requirements of how they should be used • access open-ended resources, e.g. loose parts or transient art • enable children to select and use 'less obvious' resources to represent mathematical understanding, e.g. Tristan in One Is a Snail and Trevor in Let's Build a House • self-regulate their thinking and learning through regular use of continuous and enhanced provision in both the indoor and the outdoor environments
Staff were less enthusiastic about teaching maths and supporting children with mathematical learning and understanding. Maths lessons were hard to manage.	– Staff are enthusiastic and confident about teaching maths. The small-group maths teaching within the lesson means that behaviour is easier to manage, providing more time for adults to support or challenge where necessary. – The teacher and TA 'check in' with all children during the lesson. This enables TAs to develop, extend, support, and engage as a play partner at the appropriate level in continuous and enhanced provision.
Children were uninspired by maths; there was a lack of 'can do' attitudes. Maths resources were rarely used by the children.	– Children now enjoy engaging in maths and can see the links with other areas of learning. This has been achieved with the development of the continuous and enhanced provision both indoors and outdoors, which means children can practise, develop and extend their understanding and master the concepts during self-directed learning.

Figure 8.2 (Continued)

Before implementing Talk for Maths Mastery in Year 1	After implementing Talk for Maths Mastery in Year 1
	– Children will have a go and display a can-do attitude – Play partnering by adults is essential here, requiring the adult to stand back and observe and know when to intervene or pose questions. – Children also invite adults into their play. – Adults know when to interact or when they are in danger of interfering in children's play (see Chapter 7).
Children were reluctant to access maths resources outside of the daily maths lesson, and there were no connections with everyday life or meaningful contexts.	– Children independently access everything all the time and are enthusiastic to share their learning with the adults and other children. – Maths concepts are related to children's own experiences and provide them with contextual opportunities to practise and develop their understanding and mastery.
Resources were only 'maths resources', children found these were limited and did not deepen their understanding.	– The children use all open-ended resources from around the environment to develop and deepen their understanding of maths. – They self-regulate their learning, feel empowered and enabled – they are confident.
Year 1 teachers took little notice of what the children had previously learned, starting from the Year 1 curriculum, as opposed to continuing the learning journey from the EYFS and letting children master/deepen their understanding and maintain their momentum.	– Year 1 staff communicate all the time with Reception staff and are well informed of where the children are and where they have come from. – The children's starting points in Year 1 follow on from where they left off in Reception. This means the momentum of learning is maintained and not started from scratch at the beginning of the year. – The concrete, pictorial, abstract approach and shared terminology have enabled this to be successful.
Maths weekly, short-term planning meant that children were exposed to different concepts, e.g. capacity, number, shape, measure, but there was no opportunity to deepen and master skills, and if a child was absent, they missed the learning.	– The TFMM approach embeds and consolidates concepts. – The children know that they can use the CPA approach in whichever way they need to. – *Blocking* the teaching of concepts and skills, e.g. measurement into a week, half term or term, means that if children are absent, they can easily catch up. The resources are available in the continuous provision to enable them to have opportunities to practise and replay new experiences as well as previous experiences.

Figure 8.2 (Continued)

Before implementing Talk for Maths Mastery in Year 1	After implementing Talk for Maths Mastery in Year 1
Observations of maths were often superficial snapshots and did not show the depth of thinking and learning or the process.	– Maths learning stories have developed observation techniques and enhanced the staff's understanding of what the children know and their next steps. – The children now have more opportunities to really deepen their understanding and use the terminology of maths in everyday conversations with one another and the adults and through reflecting on their learning stories. – The team created opportunities to focus on the importance and enjoyment of maths throughout the school and shared this with families by documenting and celebrating children's learning and understanding, using narrative learning story observations.

Figure 8.2 (Continued)

3. What were the challenges?

Realising the vision of TFMM was not without its initial and ongoing challenges, including understanding the vision and the reasons behind its implementation. Reviewing or refining practice often means changing the mindset of staff and building a secure understanding of child development and how children learn, especially as observations showed that children were not retaining prior knowledge as maths lessons were limited to the hour of teaching.

The Senior Leadership team's reservations about the change, including fine-tuning planning, linked to the characteristics of effective learning and resourcing the environment, were all overcome by a positive trial-and-error research approach and a strong sense of purpose, reasoning and research evidence. The end-of-year outcomes were extremely positive in the Early Years Foundation Stage Profile (EYFSP) and for the Y1 children (an 8% increase in secure/working at expected levels). During the TFMM initiative, children made considerable progress each year; e.g. the Good Level of Development (GLD)[1] in the area of Number increased by 5–10%; in Shape, Space and Measure, the increase was 6–11% in Speaking, the increase was 4–20%; and in Understanding 7–20%.

The biggest challenge faced by the staff team was the need to change the lesson structure across the unit, in collaboration with the Maths and Foundation Stage Leaders. As a result, the team now have a shared vision of the way maths is developing across the phase and are on the journey together.

Narrative learning stories were introduced as a way of documenting and recording children's mathematical thinking, talk and understanding, which enabled staff to really notice how children were learning and experiencing maths, including when becoming play partners with adults. This process helped the staff team to develop their skills of play partnering by allowing themselves time to observe, wait and listen, intervening when necessary and, at the right time, supporting children to think more deeply about their own learning instead of letting it be taken over by adults or waiting for adults to give them 'answers' (see Chapter 7 on the role of the adult).

The team now use the characteristics of effective learning as their starting points for teaching, learning and observation rather than the areas of learning. This supports children to become more independent learners and gives adults so much more information about children's dispositions for learning, including their levels of involvement (Laevers, 1994) (see Chapter 3).

Reflecting on the changes to practice by the mathematics coordinator led to the following feedback:

- Children think critically, problem solve and reason as to why they chose that particular method to complete the questions. They develop their own ideas and make connections to their learning
- Children have developed independence. They aren't afraid to tackle a problem. They have gained resilience to explain why they got the problem wrong and are confidently able to unpick the question and explain their reasoning

As children moved from Y1, the Y2 teacher commented that children's mathematical vocabulary was well embedded along with basic skills and greater depth of understanding. The momentum of their learning was maintained through the interaction between the adult's and the developmentally consistent approach across the key stages.

4. What about the role of the adult in Year 1?

To teach, support and extend children's mathematical learning and understanding in Year 1, the team describe the role of the adult as a 'facilitator,' which includes:

- Adults being aware of and teaching using all learning styles ensuring that there are many opportunities for independent, hands-on learning. The CPA approach (concrete, pictorial, abstract) activities can be practical e.g. sorting activities, using ICT, recording using a range of materials in creative ways such as learning stories
- Adults observing children's learning in the maths lesson and intervening to support/extend where appropriate being aware of the children who will need to keep practising a skill and/or consolidate it; then following up in the continuous provision through play

- Adults are skilled at identifying and seizing 'teachable moments' to ensure learning and experiences are immediate 'in the moment' and tailored to each child's individual needs. Teaching and learning is within the context of children's play and activities
- Adults discuss children's progress each day, so they are aware of any 'pickups' which need to be planned for the next lesson. This also applies to children who need to extend and deepen (master) their thinking and skills in different ways
- The enabling environment is well resourced, and children follow their own lines of inquiry, particularly engaging in problem setting and problem solving. Adults sensitively support children using open-ended questions, adapting the Elklan approach (www.elklan.co.uk), which supports the development of children's speech, language and communication skills, to Talk for Maths Mastery
  Level 1 – Making sure they understand naming
  Level 2 – Describing – Who and what?
  Level 3 – Retelling – What they have done and how they did it
  Level 4 – Justifying – Explain why something cannot be done
- Referencing the "Maths – No problem!" scheme ensures that we are more aware of consistently using the correct mathematical vocabulary and that the children follow this closely. For example, the team report children proudly announcing, "Look, I've done these *equations*"
- Adults engage in serve and return interactions to encourage children to clarify and justify their thinking, tuning into the child's level of language development. Discussion and conversation include reasoning, provocations and possibility questions to extend children's thinking and to develop their mastery. For example:

  "Is 13 a bigger number than 14?"
  "No, it isn't, 14 is bigger"
  "How can you prove it?"

  "I think 2 + 3 is the same as 3 + 2"
  "How can you show that?"

- A weekly working wall in the classroom documents new learning to provide the children with opportunities to see different ways of approaching problems. Vocabulary such as, "concrete, pictorial and abstract" is used with children and supported with examples to develop understanding further. A vocabulary display is added to each week
- Adults ensure that all children's needs are met through shared planning, which is guided by the maths lead, with regular meetings to check that provision and questioning is at the right developmental level and whether it needs adapting. Children's thinking, learning and understanding are documented, shared and discussed in timely learning story observations (see One Is a Snail Ten Is a Crab and Let's Build a House)
- The senior leadership team gather at regular staff meetings and updates and undertake observations and learning walks to monitor the quality of the mathematics provision and teaching for their children

5. How are children's interests followed?

Continuing to follow children's mathematical interests from Reception into KS1 is essential to maintain the momentum of learning and enable vital connections to be made, especially in the transition period. Figure 8.3 from the TFMM Exemplification (Chilvers, 2017a) shows the link between F2 and Y1 and the transition of learning to continue this approach in Y1, building on children's interests and using this to teach mathematical concepts and skills. It shows the momentum of the children's learning as they follow their interests as a class in the Love Monster learning story and how this can be taken forward in Y1 (see Chapter 5).

The TFMM exemplification (Chilvers, 2017a) noted how, in Go Compare (Chapter 6), Bailey and his friends showed themselves as mature, self-regulated learners, as they decided to follow their interest and explore comparison independently with their Superworms, needing minimal adult direction or involvement to do this. They were self-motivated, curious and excited to engage in their own child-led research and thinking; this was cognitive self-regulation in action (see Chapter 3). Children who have been supported to develop such proactive attitudes to learning will continue to benefit from adults who continue to recognise, support and build on these dispositions in Year 1.

At Fordbridge, the children in Y1 continue to follow their own interests, ideas and fascinations in maths as they have done throughout the EYFS. The team found, from their observations and learning stories, that children were learning more from their independent play as they were more focused, inquisitive and involved when following their own ideas. By being able to follow their own interests and represent their thinking and learning through the things that are most meaningful to them, we saw the connections they made, their deep understanding and mastery. For example, in the autumn term, Teon was interested in buses and bus routes, creating a detailed map using the cars and construction resources to plan and represent the map of the route of the Number 45 bus going to Northfield.

TFMM Aspect: Following Children's Interests		
	F2 →————→	**Y1**
	How to Make a Love Monster Happy	
Related learning stories	Wall-E 'None the Number'	'Calculation Whizzes'
Child's perspective I like to learn by . . .	– talking about things I am interested in then following a line of inquiry based on my questions and ideas such as in None the Number where we used talk to explore the concept of whether none is a number – Creating and Thinking Critically, sustained shared thinking. – using maths as part of my everyday life, e.g. comparing heights with my friends; using ordinal numbers to decide who is the winner of a race – Active Learning, Creating and Thinking Critically. I am building a bank of skills and knowing when to apply different mathematical concepts, e.g. in Wall-E the children talk about 2-D and 3-D shapes. – following a group interest to create a collaborative learning story with lots of opportunities for shared sustained thinking such as in Wall-E where we engaged in complex mathematical talk around shape properties as we explored how to create a robot using loose parts.	– confidently applying my mathematical knowledge in everyday routines and activities, e.g. calculating who is here and who is absent, dinners etc.; keeping score in PE and team games – Active Learning, Creating and Thinking Critically. – engaging in mathematical discussions where I talk about my ideas and test them out, e.g. working out how everyone in class can have a cake when there are not enough – "chop them in half" in the learning story How to Make a Love Monster Happy – Creating and Thinking Critically. – having the opportunity and time in my play to plan and make a decision about how I will approach a task, e.g. by using an ordered approach when finding all the number bonds to 10, starting with 1 to 9. See the learning story 'Calculation Whizzes' – Active Learning, Creating and Thinking Critically. – using my bank of knowledge and experiences to choose when to use different strategies, e.g. finding the difference in the number of children who are school dinners and who are packed lunch – Active Learning, Creating and Thinking Critically.

Figure 8.3 Building on mathematical thinking through child-led interests from FS2 into Y1

| **Adult's role**
You can support my mathematical thinking by . . . | – giving me the time, space and opportunity to explore my own ideas about maths in play and solve problems myself – How to Make a Love Monster Happy, Playing and Exploring, Active learning, Creating and Thinking Critically.
– giving me clues and asking open-ended questions, to make me think, which help me to solve problems rather than solving them for me – Active Learning, Creating and Thinking Critically.
– looking for patterns and themes in your observations of my learning (learning stories) which allow the next steps to be fully developed and met in appropriate and meaningful ways.
– encouraging me to set my own next steps and targets in maths. Learning stories help to set next steps and maintain the momentum of learning – Creating and Thinking Critically. | – having time to develop mathematical interests in depth as a collaborative task which may not link directly to the curriculum and current plans. If we do this together with your support, we can develop our language and thinking, e.g. how can you get the balloons back into the net? See learning story 'Balloon Escape' – Sustained Shared Thinking, Creating and Thinking Critically.
– teaching different strategies to solve problems in a range of different ways, e.g. how to make sure there are enough cakes for everyone. See learning story How to Make A Love Monster Happy.
– encouraging me to record my thinking, problem solving and reasoning in my own way and giving me time to explain my understanding. Asking possibility questions to extend my thinking and mathematical language, e.g. "How do you know? Why did it work out? Can you prove it?" See 'Calculation Whizzes', recording own problems and using a number line to solve them – Creating and Thinking Critically.
– celebrating my independent learning in the same way as adult-directed by displaying my work in the classroom and sharing with other children and adults. |
| **Enabling environment and continuous provision**
To develop and extend my learning I need . . . | – a range of creative thought-provoking resources in continuous provision, which make me think and talk, including having time and space to expand my ideas, try things out and work in collaboration with others – Playing and Exploring, Active Learning, Creating and Thinking Critically. | – resources that reflect everyday maths so I can apply my skills and knowledge in meaningful contexts, e.g. by having a self-serve play dough area I can apply my measuring skills in baking activities at school and home – Active Learning. |

Figure 8.3 (Continued)

– open-ended resources which allow me to plan and direct my own learning using what I already know and can do to try out in new and inventive ways, e.g. having blank game boards for me to create my own games or pipes and tubes in the water tray to allow me to explore ideas critically – Creating and Thinking Critically. – songs and stories that teach me mathematical concepts and how they apply to real life e.g. How Many Legs? Active Learning, Playing and Exploring.	– interesting open-ended resources in continuous provision which enable me to make the most of the mathematical possibilities they present and allow me to master the skills I have learnt, e.g. money, clocks, songs, stories, junk modelling – Active Learning, Creating and Thinking Critically. – complex stories that offer more challenging mathematical skills such as calculation, e.g. One Is a Snail Ten Is a Crab and provoke creative mathematical dialogues leading to – sustained shared thinking.
Home learning My home learning helps me when . . . – you talk to me about things that I like and use my interests to motivate me, e.g. football on the TV at home led to conversations about goals, teams and who had won – Active Learning, Creating and Thinking Critically – you encourage me to be more independent and solve problems, e.g. working out how to make my shapes balance when building my models, such as my robot in Wall-E – Active Learning, Creating and Thinking Critically. – you send photographs to the class email to share special events and interests which show how I have continued my learning at home – floor books (see Chapter 4).	– you encourage me to explain my ideas and mathematical thinking, e.g. when making buns, do we have enough? What will we need to do? See How to Make A Love Monster Happy – Active Learning, Creating and Thinking Critically. – I can be independent in my mathematical thinking and take responsibility for solving problems (self-regulation), e.g. right change for the bus, how long until . . . etc. – Active Learning, Creating and Thinking Critically. – you are involved in what I am doing, talking and playing alongside and reflecting on my learning with me, e.g. reading through my learning stories together or the class blog. – we share my class blog/learning stories, and we talk together about what I have been learning and my interests and read learning stories and continue this at home.

Figure 8.3 (Continued)

Opportunities are also provided for children to experiment with new and exciting resources. Most importantly, even when the learning focus may be on number within the classroom, the children are still exposed to other maths concepts, such as shape, measures or capacity. This helps them to widen their mathematical knowledge and interests independently and ensures that they are learning all the time. Whilst child-led play should continue, in order to maintain the momentum of learning, it is important that children are sensitively encouraged and supported by adults, through what they say and in the resources they provide or the possibility questions they ask, to engage in play at a more complex level.

6. Continuing continuous provision

Going forward with continuous provision in Year 1 to support and extend children's learning in mathematics and in other areas was identified by the senior leadership team as one of the key priorities on the school development plan. It was described as being "fundamental to young children's learning and a right for the children in our school," because "experiences matter":

> We have been able to keep the continuous provision going throughout the year due to the support of the Senor Leadership Team. This is the vision of the Phase leader, Year 1 staff and EYFS staff and is a continuous development. A senior member from the EYFS Full Day Care came and watched the children in the hub and remarked on the difference from previous years and how great it was to see how the children were learning.

Regular team meetings with the EYFS staff ensure that we are moving the children forward, maintaining their momentum and that they are not repeating previous learning, although children are using their prior learning and knowledge to further challenge themselves and each other. A recent development for the Y1 team is the addition of a 'working wall' which includes role play, construction and small world showing the children's progression from full day care to Year 1.

Both Fisher (2010) and Ephgrave (2017) advocate the benefits of bringing continuous provision into Year 1 classrooms. Fisher considers the use of tables and chairs as "controlling mechanism[s]" whereby children are safely and securely seated in their own space to allow teachers to feel more secure and in control of the learning taking place (2010, pp. 115–116). She points out that when children are engaged in provision that interests and motivates them to learn, they are less likely to require "control". Ephgrave (2017, p. 16) supports this view by acknowledging that it soon becomes apparent when the environment is suited to the needs, interests and learning styles of the children as unwanted behaviour is less likely to be an issue.

Continuous provision also supports children's 'mastery orientation' (see Chapter 3) by allowing them to follow their own interests in play and to pursue their own lines of challenge and inquiry. Fisher (2010, p. 132) sums up the rationale for using continuous provision in Year 1 classrooms to allow the momentum of learning to be maintained:

> Sometimes children need the new and provoking [resources], sometimes the familiar and repetitious. Effective Key Stage 1 environments should have both.

The management of the resources within continuous provision in Year 1, as in EYFS settings, should be sensitively considered; for children to learn and engage effectively, there should be a balance between the new and the familiar in order for children to be continually motivated to learn and progress at their own developmental level and with a sufficient level of challenge.

7. Partnership between home and school

The home learning partnership with families continues to be important in maintaining children's mathematical momentum into Key Stage 1. Parents can effectively support learning by continuing to recognise that, although children are growing older, they still learn best though play and that enabling them to continue to follow their interests helps them to see and experience the rich everyday mathematical experiences and opportunities all around them. Maths scrapbooks are used as a link between home and school, making a connection between 'school' learning and 'home' learning through as many real-life mathematical experiences as possible and following children's interests.

The Early Years Foundation Stage meets the National Curriculum

Ephgrave (2017, pp. 120–122) notes the concerns raised by teachers surrounding the issue of every child accessing all the subjects of the National Curriculum when following a play-based approach to learning. She acknowledges the need for staff to know their children well, monitor their learning and experiences, notice 'gaps' in learning and modify the environment or attract children to pursue learning experiences that will 'fill the gap'. She suggests that adults who support play-based learning are more likely to know the 'whole child' and notice the characteristics of learning that each child demonstrates and therefore know how best to support and teach them further,

When working in a more child-led way, the children are constantly demonstrating their knowledge and understanding without the need for testing. The adults spend their time interacting with children, constantly observing and interpreting what their observations tell them. The best education is one that teaches children *how to learn*. We are trying to teach our children in Year One how to learn, but we are doing this through whatever interests them, recognising that they are all unique, interested in different things and equipped with different approaches to learning.

(pp. 120–121)

Through their learning story observations, the team at Fordbridge have demonstrated that their approach to mathematics teaching and learning is the same. They have found that the interests the children have a desire to pursue result in their innate engagement in provision that supports those interests. This means that the children will challenge and push *their own* thinking and learning further than if the learning and teaching is always insisted upon by the adult. They will have mastery mindsets (see Figure 3.1).

For example, in the learning story One Is a Snail Ten Is a Crab, both Daisy and Tristan followed their interests. Daisy wanted to independently explore equations and became highly involved in her play with concrete materials, using Numicon and then recording her equations. Tristan, after helping Daisy with her equations, decided to make some of his own using various materials including picture cards and sticky notes to make his insect equation creation!

Daisy is confidently and independently showing her understanding of numbers to "Count, read and write numbers to 100 in numerals; count in multiples of twos, fives and tens"; "Identify and represent numbers using objects and pictorial representations"; and "Solve one-step problems involving multiplication, by calculating the answer using concrete objects, pictorial representations and arrays" (DfE, 2013, pp. 6, 8). She knows that, when she needs help after trying and persisting, she can rely on the adults and other children to help her. She also showed a high level of involvement in her self-chosen learning activity and most of the characteristics of effective learning, particularly in Creating and Thinking Critically, where she was:

[f]inding and solving problems; Finding new ways to do things; Developing ideas of grouping and sequences; Planning, making decisions about how to approach the task, solve a problem and reach her goal; Checking how well her strategies were going and changing them when needed and Reviewing how well her approach worked.

(Appendix 6)

In the following learning story, Let's Build a House, the children demonstrated their ability within the Y1 statutory requirements of measurement (National Curriculum, DfE, 2013, p. 9) by following their interest, exploring and comparing measurements after reading 'The Three Little Pigs' story. Some 'provocations' and 'possibility questions' to challenge and support children's independent learning in continuous provision were added:

> The 3 pigs all live in the brick house, but they have no furniture.
> What could you use to help them?
> Can you make it the right size? How will you know?
> I wonder if the pigs will fit on the furniture? How can we check?

This provides the children with an opportunity to put all their knowledge and understanding into action, as they collaborate and talk together, their ideas flow into sustained shared thinking, and we see how they call upon their prior knowledge and mastery orientation to deepen their mathematical mastery,

> Mastery learners are fascinated by the journey itself. They are more interested in the process of learning than in any external goal or reward, embracing new challenges and delighting in finding innovative solutions for overcoming them. Failures and mistakes are viewed as opportunities for critical thinking, problem-solving and creativity, to be valued rather than feared (with) time to stake stock, analyse and find new possibilities.
>
> (Jaeckle in Bruce, 2006, p. 7)

Let's Build a House

Year 1 children aged 6

Continuous Provision was set up in the hub with access to a range of resources and materials. The children were set various activities one of which was to make some furniture for the doll's house.

Two of the children decided to make beds;

Jorgie understood that the base of her bed was not going to be big enough so adapted what she was doing. She measured the inside of the house with a tape measure to ensure the bed fitted. When she measured she did not start from the end of the tape measure. They used mathematical vocabulary that they had been taught in their previous maths lesson *short and longest*.

Trevor chose to make the top of the house into 2 rooms. He used wooden bricks that were too big, this would not allow him to close the roof without the wall falling over. He attempted to do this several times before the Mrs Weaver asked *"Is there something you could change so that you can close the roof?"* We asked the question because Trevor was continuing to do the same thing and was frustrated. After asking this possibility question he soon realised what he needed to do and changed the size of the wooden bricks at the front, this enabled him to close the roof.

The activity was child-led with minimal support from the adult. Just a few key questions were asked so they could complete what they were trying to achieve. The children did not always use the tape measure correctly because they had not yet been taught this skill, further sessions would be needed to support them to understand that when you measure you do not start in the middle of the tape measure.

We observe the children through the characteristics of effective learning so we can see how the children are learning. Trevor really showed a can-do attitude and was willing to have a go **Playing and Exploring – engagement**. An evaluation is written to document and understand what the children had learned, plan their next steps and consider what needs adapting within the learning environment to further support and extend their mathematical development.

Let's Build a House

The children were in the hub where the dolls house had no furniture in it. They were set a task to see if they could build an extension or furniture for it. There was a wide range of resources they could use to build and to measure.

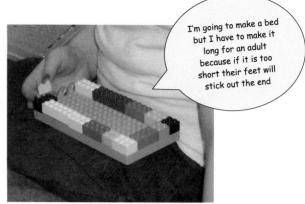

> I'm going to make a bed but I have to make it long for an adult because if it is too short their feet will stick out the end

Jorgie changed the size of the Lego base she used so it was bigger/longer than the first one that she had picked.

> How are you going to make sure it fits in?

> I can measure my bed to see if it fits in. I'll use the tape measure.

Leighton and Jorgie then put their beds together to see who's was longer. They said that Jorgies bed was longer.

Trevor joined Leighton and they used the tape measure to measure the length of the house. They decided that the house was 60 cm long.

Trevor built a wall to make two rooms in the roof of the house. He then tried shutting the roof, but the bricks kept falling over. After asking him what he could do to solve this problem, he realised that the two front bricks were too tall for it to close

> Is there something you could change so that you can close the roof?

> I'm going to use the smaller bricks at the front so the roof can shut.

As soon as Trevor changed the size of the bricks, he was able to close the roof

Summary
All children worked together really well on this task. They were keen to use resources they had never used before. They were all willing to have a go. Trevor persisted with the activity even when his wall had fallen down several times. He remained motivated until he had completed what he had set out to do.
Mathematical vocabulary was used from prior learning.

Characteristics of effective learning

Playing and Exploring (engagement)
Being willing to 'have a go'
Initiating activities.
Seeking challenge.
Showing a 'can do' attitude.
Taking a risk, engaging in new experiences, and learning by trial and error.

Active Learning (motivation)
Maintaining focus, concentrating, not distracted
Paying attention to detail
Showing an 'I can' attitude, okay with mistakes and asking for help
Enjoying the challenge of the activity and the process
Setting their own goals and showing satisfaction

Creating and Thinking Critically (thinking)
Choosing ways to do things
Planning, making decisions about how to approach a task, solve a problem and reach a goal.
Checking how well their activities are going
Changing strategy as needed.
Reviewing how well the approach worked.

Next Steps
Ensure the children can use the tape measure or ruler correctly, starting at 0 and not in the middle

Encourage children to record their measurements and to continue to use correct mathematical vocabulary

Year 1 KPI
Compares, describes and solves practical problems for:
Lengths and heights; e.g. long/short, longer/shorter, tall/short, double/half

In the learning story, we see the interplay between the children and the adult as they exchange ideas, try things out and ask great questions. For example, Mrs Weaver asks, "Is there something you could change so that you can close the roof?" and explains why she has done this. She also describes her detailed understanding of the children's thinking processes and development. Her informed experience and knowledge show how the children's mathematical learning is a complex weaving together of several key aspects:

- continuous provision
- time for independent and collaborative play
- time to talk, think and experiment
- sensitive adults who observe, analyse and support children's learning, either in the moment or through using reflective learning stories

The analysis of Jorgie and Trevor's learning shows the richness of their mastery mindsets as well as their mathematical understanding where they "[c]ompare, describe and solve practical problems for – lengths and heights (for example, long/short, longer/shorter, tall/short, double/half)" and "[m]easure and begin to record lengths and heights" (DfE, 2013, p. 9) as well as showing a high level of involvement in their self-chosen learning activity, displaying each of the characteristics of effective learning.

Summary

This chapter has shown how crucial it is to maintain children's mathematical momentum as they make transitions between year groups and key stages. A strong, pedagogically informed shared vision is the key factor, combined with seeing the child's learning as a balance between child-led play/activities and adult-directed teaching, as well as providing high-quality continuous provision and time for children to self-regulate independently to practice, develop and embed their mathematical skills in meaningful contexts. The children's learning stories show us how effective this is in sustaining mastery orientation not just for maths but for all areas of learning:

> There should not be a significant change in children's experiences between reception class and Year 1 – both sets of teachers should work together to ensure that children's experiences in reception class prepare the ground for their move to Year 1, and their time in Year 1 builds on the successful principles and approach encapsulated in the EYFS. In other words, schools need to be ready for children and children need to be ready for school. If this does not happen transition is harder for children than it needs to be.
>
> (Tickell, 2011, pp. 35, 36)

Note

1. Children will have reached a GLD at the end of the EYFS if they achieve "at least the expected level in the early learning goals in the prime areas of learning (personal, social and emotional development; physical development; and communication and language) and in the specific areas of mathematics and literacy".

Final thoughts

Looking back at the children's learning stories and the many ways in which they are deeply involved in their mathematical play, activities, conversations and self-research, we see how confident, motivated and inspired they are to keep going. The enjoyment of the task is clear to see; even if it requires some hard thinking or physical energy, they keep on trying, looking for further ideas to solve problems and find solutions, rarely accepting setbacks or defeat. The Bob the Builder effect of 'Yes, I can' is obvious. These children are mathematical and have shown mastery in their confidence, persistence and embedded understanding as they engage in child-led play.

For these children their mathematical experiences have empowered them to develop a positive mindset and self-belief, with supportive adults who have carefully observed, reflected on and understood their developmental momentum. The adults have then taught well, tuning into the child's thinking, seeing where support and bespoke next steps are needed and then putting them in place through using appropriate teaching strategies. We can see how well the adults have taught by how well the children show their mastery in child-led play and continuous provision. Mastery happens through this combination of factors, and children's development and learning are on a positive trajectory. Our aim must be to make sure that this trajectory continues for all children and that they maintain their love of mathematics throughout life.

This is a challenging aim and one that requires firm foundations on which to build. This book has explored many of these foundational prerequisites for young children based on research, theory and practice of how children learn and develop. The most powerful of these being the voices of the children themselves:

> All year I have been making things out of paper, Sellotape and string. I know you have to make things the right size. If you want to change the size you can, but you do have to compare. I know that to make my worm the longest I need to know how long Carrigan's is. I can only know that if I compare it. But I remember you showed me how to make things level. Today I remembered myself.

Bailey's reflections on his mathematical understanding in Go Compare (Chapter 6).

Appendices

Appendix 1

Name of practitioner: Setting: Date:

Spend 10 minutes and have a look around the setting and the outdoor environment.

Where can you see maths happening? What sort of maths is it?
About the characteristics of effective learning, e.g. problem solving, reasoning, ideas etc.? About number, shape, space and measures? Serve and return conversations? Anything else?
Turnover/get more paper if you need to!

What can you see? What are the children doing?	Where is it happening?	What type of maths is it?

Appendix 2

Name of practitioner: Setting: Date:

 Maths <u>talk</u> is everywhere!

Spend 10 minutes and have a look around the setting and the outdoor environment.

Where can you *hear maths talk* happening? What sort of *maths talk* is it? *About the characteristics of effective learning, e.g. problem solving, reasoning, ideas etc.? About number, shape, space and measures? Serve and return conversations? Anything else?*
Remember children communicate what they are thinking in other ways not just through talk – can you see this?
Turnover/get more paper if you need to!

What can you hear? What are the children saying?	Where is it happening?	What type of maths is it?

Appendix 3

Learning environment audit: developing indoor and outdoor learning environments to support mathematics

Providing a wide and diverse range of high-quality learning experiences both indoors and outdoors which support mathematics is vital.

	In place	Area for development	Comments and next steps
The overall environment: indoor • Is the setting bright, well organised and inviting to walk into? • Are the resources and working areas clearly labelled – with words, pictures or real objects where appropriate? (Don't go mad here with labelling). • Do the resources reflect all families and cultures? • Are there authentic opportunities for mathematics embedded across the setting? E.g. self-registration, snack time, across continuous provision? • Is there a number line which reflects children's interests displayed at child height – with picture clues where appropriate?			

	In place	Area for development	Comments and next steps
- Do displays include typed and handwritten numerals, by both adults and children? - Do the displays celebrate children's achievements in mathematics *and* support children's future learning? - Are there interactive displays/investigation areas which promote children's exploration of mathematics? - Are numbers written in other languages and scripts? - Is mathematical vocabulary identified and displayed as prompts for adults? - Are mathematical opportunities/questions identified throughout the learning environment? - Are there regular opportunities for cooking and baking indoors and outdoors? - Are there opportunities for imaginative play on a large and small scale with open-ended creative materials? E.g. small and large cardboard boxes, thick and thin tape, lengths of fabric, tubes and cylinders etc. **Mathematics Workshop/zone/reference area** - Are there story and information texts which support numbers, counting, calculating and shapes, space and measures? - Is there a height chart showing standard and/or non-standard measures? - Is there a meaningful number line with picture clues at child height? - Are resources organised so that children can access them independently?			

	In place	Area for development	Comments and next steps
• Is there a wide range of natural resources? E.g. pebbles, fir cones, shells, open-ended materials for pattern making?			
• Is there a wide range of commercially produced resources to support exploration of number and calculating?			
• Is there a wide range of commercially produced resources to support exploration of shape, space and measures?			
• Can children access games independently? E.g. lotto, snap, dominoes, track games. Can they make their own games?			
• Are there 'collections' of things for children to investigate, sort and sequence? E.g. boxes, buttons, socks, coins, beads, keys?			
• Are there collections of objects from core number rhymes, in different materials, sizes, colours? E.g. ducks, frogs, elephants?			
• Is there a display which draws attention to numerals in the environment/everyday life?			
• Can children display their early attempts at recording independently?			
• Is there a washing line at child height so that children can peg numerals in the correct order?			
Other areas of provision • Are high-profile resources that support mathematics in all areas of provision/learning zones?			

	In place	Area for development	Comments and next steps
• Are children encouraged to use resources from the maths workshop/area to support their learning in other areas of provision?			
• Are there opportunities for children to match 3-D objects to 2-D silhouettes in storage? E.g. water play, sand play?			
• Are there books/cards with words of number songs and rhymes in the music and sound making area? With number props? E.g. 'Five Little Speckled Frogs', 'Ten in the Bed'?			
• Are there empty boxes and packaging, reclaimed materials, materials to encourage exploration of pattern in the creative workshop?			
• Are books which support maths high profile in the book area? With story props?			
• Are numerals explicit in small-world, imaginative play? E.g. road signs?			
• Are there practical, hands-on opportunities to explore shape, space and measures? E.g. sand, water, play dough clay?			
• Does the large block area/small construction area have visual images of things children can construct, photos of children's constructions and a range of construction equipment, including reclaimed materials?			
• Do the role play/home corner areas exploit mathematics? E.g. note pads, directories, matching sets of cups, complete sets of cutlery, different sized dolls, bedding and clothes, recipe books and cards, weighing scales, measuring spoons etc.?			
• Is there a wide range of resources to engage in mathematical mark-making? E.g. clipboards, tally charts, forms, various sizes of paper and envelopes, paper with grids on them, registers, tiny/small paper folded books and large books etc.?			

	In place	Area for development	Comments and next steps
The outdoor learning environment • Does the outdoor environment complement and extend the indoor environment? • Is the area well organised, inviting and challenging? • Are there opportunities for children to be physical on a large scale? E.g. big maths outdoors? • Are there opportunities for children to be messy on a large scale? • Are there opportunities for children to explore maths through movement? E.g. obstacle courses, den making, travelling games, tracks, construction on a large scale? • Can children access resources and return them independently? • Is there a washing line at child height so that children can peg numerals in the correct order or socks/T-shirts to make repeating patterns? • Are there opportunities to explore drawing shapes, patterns or numerals on a large scale? E.g. chalking on floors, large-scale chalkboards, easels, 'painting' with water and decorators' brushes? • Is there a number line and height chart which is added to by the children and changed occasionally? • Are there small resources and 'targets' to support scoring? E.g. basketball hoop, beanbags, quoits, skittles, knock down cans? • Are there resources to support the use of tallies or scoring?			

Appendix 4

Action plan

Next steps – actions . . .	Who will lead this? Who else will be involved?	When will you start? How long will it take?	What resources will you need? E.g. people, time	How will you know if it has been successful?	How will you know if it has made a difference?

Appendix 5

101 uses of learning stories

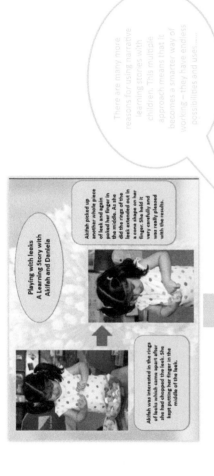

Playing with leeks
A Learning Story with Akifah and Daniela

Akifah was interested in the rings of leeks which came apart after she had chopped the leek. She kept putting her finger in the middle of the leek.

Akifah picked up another whole piece of leek and again poked her finger in the middle. As she did the rings of the leek extended out in a cone shape on her finger. She hold it very carefully and was really pleased with the results.

There are many more reasons for using narrative learning stories with children. This multiple approach means that it becomes a smarter way of working – they have endless possibilities and uses......

- An observation, to record and celebrate children's ideas, thinking, progress
- To share with parents/carers – connection between home and setting/school
- A story book . . . first reading book to support the development of early literacy
- Displays for children and parents
- Pedagogical documentation
- To raise self-esteem, well-being and confidence

- To show planning and what may happen next
- To illustrate imaginative play and language development
- A respectful way of recognising and acknowledging what children think, say and do
- To acknowledge, document and understand child-led play and activities
- Seeing children's creative and critical thinking and being inspired by what they already know and can do

- To share with the children; re-proposing the observation to reflect
- To support and develop memory skills, meta-cognition and reflection
- As a record of children's talking and thinking
- To bring the joy back into observing children
- To continually develop our knowledge, understanding and practice of children's development – it's great CPD

- To describe children's interests and retell an aspect of their play
- To show the quality of provision and practice
- So you can focus on the serve and return conversations
- To tune into who children are and what they think and feel
- To give visual clues especially for children learning English as a second language

Appendix 6

Characteristics of effective learning		
A unique child: observing how a child is learning		
Playing and Exploring – engagement	Active Learning – motivation	Creating and Thinking Critically – thinking
Finding out and exploring • Showing curiosity about objects, events and people • Using senses to explore the world around them • Engaging in open-ended activity • Showing particular interests	**Being involved and concentrating** • Maintaining focus on their activity for a period of time • Showing high levels of energy, fascination • Not easily distracted • Paying attention to details	**Having their own ideas** • Thinking of ideas • Finding ways to solve problems • Finding new ways to do things
Playing with what they know • Pretending objects are things from their experience • Representing their experiences in play • Taking on a role in their play • Acting out experiences with other people	**Keeping on trying** • Persisting with activity when challenges occur • Showing a belief that more effort or a different approach will pay off • Bouncing back after difficulties	**Making links** • Making links and noticing patterns in their experience • Making predictions • Testing their ideas • Developing ideas of grouping, sequences, cause and effect
Being willing to 'have a go' • Initiating activities • Seeking challenge • Showing a 'can do' attitude • Taking a risk, engaging in new experiences, and learning by trial and error	**Enjoying and achieving what they set out to do** • Showing satisfaction in meeting their own goals • Being proud of how they accomplished something – not just the end result • Enjoying meeting challenges for their own sake rather than external rewards or praise	**Choosing ways to do things** • Planning, making decisions about how to approach a task, solve a problem and reach a goal • Checking how well their activities are going • Changing strategy as needed • Reviewing how well the approach worked

Figures

1: What is Talk for Maths Mastery?

1.1 Process of practitioner inquiry used in the New Zealand Educational Leadership Projects — 10

1.2 (a) Kolb's experiential cycle of reflection; (b) observation cycle from Development Matters — 11

1.3 Maths Talk Is Everywhere – an example — 16

1.4 Example of a timeline from Pipworth Primary School, Sheffield — 20

2: Maintaining the momentum of children's mathematical development

2.1 Maintaining children's learning momentum — 28

2.2 Maintaining learning momentum with number lines — 30

2.3 Jacob following a rhythmical pattern — 33

2.4 Rainbows Nursery poses the question for their own reflections by asking, "Can you see the maths talk?" — 37

2.5 Exploration table — 39

2.6 George at 3.4 years old has carefully painted parallel lines, dots and circles in specific places which at first glance look like a pattern — 43

2.7 Keeley and Ruby had spent all morning in the box modelling corner, having found a sturdy box which they covered and decorated — 43

2.8 Schema into concepts — 50

Learning stories

Leo's story – experiencing spatial awareness, balance and speed — 35

Dylan experiments with Two by Two — 45

Milo is The Straight-Line Person — 47

3: What does mathematical mastery mean for young children?

3.1 Describing some mindset behaviours we may see in young children — 59

3.2   New Zealand learning story – learning
       dispositions   62
3.3   Key aspects of mastery orientation   71

Learning stories

       Numbered Footballs   64

4: Documenting children's mathematical talking and thinking through observation, learning stories and floor books

4.1   Using floor books – the process   83
4.2   Addressing misconceptions   99

Learning stories

       Floor book story: I Can Jump
       4 Metres!   86
       As Tall as a Camel   89
       Here, There and Everywhere   94
       Only Big Things Are Heavy   97

5: Building mathematical thinking through whole-class child-led learning

5.1   'Easter Maths Addition'   112
5.2   'Conker Fun'   112
5.3   Adult led/adult initiated/child initiated   114
5.4   Findings from the Maths Is Everywhere
       observations   118

Learning story

       How to Make a Love Monster Happy   122

6: Making their mathematical mark: understanding and supporting children's mathematical mark-making and thinking

6.1   Home learning partnership   141
6.2   The child's perspective   147
6.3   The adult's role   151
6.4   The enabling environment and continuous
       provision   152

Learning stories

Peyton – mark-making at 2 years old 143
Meryam's Shape House 154
Aadam's Treasure 157
Meryam's 3-D Shapes 159
Aadam and Farhaad's Big Numbers 161
Go Compare 164

7: How do adults support children's mathematical talk, thinking and mastery?

7.1 Role of the adult: "My mathematical thinking is supported by . . ." 172
7.2 How do young children learn? In a straight developmental trajectory? 174
7.3 How do young children learn? In an entwined and interwoven way? 174
7.4 Thomas makes a list 184
7.5 Harry's drawing of Luton station 189
7.6 Harry's drawing of Market Harborough station 189
7.7 Harry's map of his route from home to school 190
7.8 Harry's drawing of buildings he knew in Sheffield city centre 190
7.9 Observation cycle 193
7.10 Process of observing in the moment 195
7.11 Billy 196

Learning story

Makhi transforms a cutlery box . . . 180

8: Maintaining children's mathematical momentum into Year 1 – a case study

8.1 Maintaining children's learning momentum 199
8.2 Implementing the vision 203
8.3 Building on mathematical thinking through child-led interests from FS2 into Y1 211

Learning stories

One Is a Snail Ten Is a Crab 200
Let's Build a House 217

References

Abbott, L. and Moylett, H., eds. (1999). *Early Education Transformed*. London: Taylor & Francis.

Anning, A. and Ring, K. (2004). *Making Sense of Children's Drawings*. Maidenhead: Open University Press.

Atherton, F. and Nutbrown, C. (2013). *Understanding Schemas and Young Children: From Birth to Three*. London: Sage.

Athey, C. (2007). *Extending Thought in Young Children: A Parent-Teacher Partnership*, 2nd ed. London: Paul Chapman Publishing.

Bleses, D., Makransky, G., Dale, P., Højen, A. and Ari, B. (2016). Early Productive Vocabulary Predicts Academic Achievement 10 Years Later. *Applied Psycholinguistics*, 37(6), pp. 1461–1476. doi: 10.1017/S0142716416000060.

Bloom, B. S. (1968). Learning for mastery. *Evaluation Comment*, 1(2), pp. 1–12.

Boyd, P. and Ash, A. (2018). Mastery mathematics: Changing teacher beliefs around in-class groupings and mindset. *Teaching and Teacher Education*, 75, pp. 214–223.

Boylan, M., Maxwell, B., Wolstenholme, C., Jay, T. and Demack, S. (2018). The mathematics teacher exchange and 'mastery' in England: The evidence for the efficacy of component practices. *Education Sciences*, 8(4), p. 202.

Bright, R. (2012). *Love Monster*. Glasgow: Harper Collins Children's Books.

Brock, L. and Siraj-Blatchford, J. (2015). *An Investigation of Schemes and Schema in Emergent Mathematics*. Available at: www.researchgate.net/publication/283459307_An_Investigation_of_Schemes_and_Schema_in_Emergent_Mathematics [Accessed Dec. 2019].

Brodie, K. (2015). *When There's Meaning in Mathematical Mistakes*. Available at: https://theconversation.com/when-theres-meaning-in-mathematical-mistakes-42962.

Bromley, H. (2006). *Making My Own Mark: Play and Writing*. London: The British Association for Early Childhood Education.

Bronson, M. B. (2002). *Self-Regulation in Early Childhood: Nature and Nurture*. New York: The Guilford Press.

Bruce, T., ed. (2006). *Early Childhood: A Guide for Students*. London: Sage.

Bruner, J. (1960). *The Process of Education*. Cambridge: Harvard University Press.

Bruner, J. (1966). *Toward a Theory of Instruction*. Cambridge: Harvard University Press.

Carr, M. (2001). *Assessment in Early Childhood Settings: Learning Stories*. London: Paul Chapman Publishing.

Carr, M. and Lee, W. (2012). *Learning Stories: Constructing Learner Identities in Early Education*. London: Sage.

Carr, M., Smith, A., Duncan, J., Jones, C., Lee, W. and Marshall, K. (2009). *Learning in the Making. Disposition and Design in Early Education*. Rotterdam: Sense Publishers.

Carruthers, E. and Worthington, M. (2006). *Children's Mathematics Making Marks, Making Meaning*, 2nd ed. London: Sage.

Carruthers, E. (2017). Children's mathematics early. *Education Journal*, 83, Autumn. Available at: www.early-education.org.

Chesworth, L. (2016). A funds of knowledge approach to examining play interests: Listening to children's and parents' perspectives. *International Journal of Early Years Education*, 24(3), pp. 294–308. https://doi.org/10.1080/09669760.2016.1188370.

Chilvers, D. (2020). Our 'non negotiables'. *Early Years Educator (EYE Journal)*, Apr., pp. 32–34.

Chilvers, D. (2019). The observation tool kit: A pedagogical tool to support practice in observation, assessment and mapping children's progress. *WatchMeGrow*. Available at: https://watchmegrow.uk/observation-toolkit/.

Chilvers, D. (2018). Professionalising the process of observation and understanding children's development. *Early Education Journal*, 84, Spr. Available at: www.early-education.org.

Chilvers, D. (2017a). Mastering maths starts with a great deal of talking. *Early Years Educator (EYE Journal)*, Apr. 2017, 18(12), pp. 26–28.

Chilvers, D. (2017b). Recognising mathematical mastery in child-led play. *Early Years Educator (EYE Journal)*, July 2017, 19(3), pp. 22–26.

Chilvers, D. (2015). *Quality Teaching: Skilful Teaching in the Early Years, in Achieving Excellence in the Early Years: A Guide for Head Teachers*. Early Education. Available at: www.early-education.org.uk.

Chilvers, D. (2013). *Creating and Thinking Critically: A Practical Guide to How Babies and Young Children Learn*. London: Practical Pre-school Books.

Chilvers, D. (2012). *Playing to Learn: Accessed*. Available at: https://watchmegrow.uk/resources/resource-tools/playing-learn-guide-child-led-play-importance-thinking-learning/.

Chilvers, D. (2006). *Young Children Talking: The Art of Conversation and Why Children Need to Chatter*. London: Early Education. Available at: www.early-education.org.uk.

Chilvers, D. (2002). *Re-Thinking, Thinking on Reflective Practice in the Early Years*. Dissertation at the University of Sheffield, Sheffield.

Chilvers, D. and SSELP Schools. (2017). *Talk for Maths Mastery: Recognising Children's Mathematical Mastery in Their Child-Led Play in the EYFS and Year 1*. Available at: https://watchmegrow.uk/resources/resource-tools/talk-maths-mastery-maintaining-momentum-childrens-development-learning/.

Chugani, H. T. (1998). A critical period of brain development: Studies of cerebral glucose utilization with PET. *Preventive Medicine*, 27, pp. 184–188.

Claxton. G. (2000). Transcript of a lecture 'a sure start for an uncertain world'. *Early Education Spring Journal*. Available at: www.early-education. org.uk.

Cockburn, A. and Littler, G. (2008). *Mathematical Misconceptions: A Guide for Primary Teachers*. London: Sage.

Craft, A. (2010). Teaching for possibility thinking: What is it and how do we do it? *Learning Matters*, 15(1).

Craft, A. (2008). *Creativity and Possibility in the Early Years*. Available at: www.tactyc.org.uk/pdfs/Reflection_craft.pdf.

Craft, A. (2002). *Creativity and Early Years Education: A Life Wide Foundation*. London: Continuum.

Csikszentmihalyi, M. (1996). *Creativity: Flow and the Psychology of Discovery and Invention*. New York: HarperCollins.

DCSF – Department for Children, Schools and Families. (2010). *Finding and Exploring Young Children's Fascinations*. Available at: www. foundationyears. org.uk/wp-content/uploads/2011/10/Finding_Exploring. pdf.

DCSF – Department for Children, Schools and Families. (2009a). *Children Thinking Mathematically: PSRN Essential Knowledge for Early Years Practitioners*. Nottingham: DCSF. Available at: www.childrens-mathematics.net/childrenthinkingmathematically_psrn.pdf.

DCSF – Department for Children, Schools and Families. (2009b). *Learning, Playing and Interacting: Good Practice in the Early Years Foundation Stage*. Available at: www.foundationyears.org.uk/wp-content/uploads/2011/10/Learning_Playing_Interacting.pdf.

DCSF – Department for Children, Schools and Families. (2009c). *Numbers and Patterns: Laying Foundations in Mathematics*. Available at: www. foundationyears.org.uk/wp-content/uploads/2011/10/Numbers_and_Patterns.pdf.

DCSF – Department for Children, Schools and Families. (2008a). *Mark Making Matters: Young Children Making Meaning in All Areas of Learning and Development*. Available at: www.foundationyears.org.uk/files/2011/10/Mark_Marking_Matters.pdf.

DCSF – Department for Children, Schools and Families. (2008b). *Independent Review of Mathematics Teaching in Early Years Settings and Primary Schools, Final Report – Sir Peter Williams*. London: DCSF. Available at: www.standards.dcsf.gov.uk/national strategies.

DCSF – Department for Children, Schools and Families. (2008c). *Every Child a Talker: Guidance for Early Language Lead Practitioners*. Available at: https://foundationyears.org.uk/wp-content/uploads/2011/10/ecat_guidance_for_practitioners_12.pdf.

DCSF – Department for Children, Schools and Families. (2008d). *The Early Years Foundation Stage: Setting Standards for Learning Development and Care for Children from Birth to Five*. Nottingham: DCSF. Available at: https://webarchive.nationalarchives.gov.uk/20130321061516/www.education. gov.uk/publications/eOrderingDownload/DCSF-00012-2007.pdf.

Dewey, J. (1933). *The Later Works 1925–1953, Vol 8: Essays and How We Think*. Carbondale: Southern Illinois University.

DfE – Department for Education. (2017). *Statutory Framework for the Early Years Foundation Stage, Setting the Standards for Learning, Development and Care for Children from Birth to Five*, Apr. Available at: https://www.gov.uk/government/publications/early-years-foundation-stage-framework-2.

DfE – Department for Education. (2013). *Mathematics Programmes of Study: Key Stages 1 and 2 National Curriculum in England*. Available at: https://assets.publishing.service.gov.uk/government/uploads/system/uploads/attachment_data/file/335158/PRIMARY_national_curriculum_-Mathematics_220714.pdf.

Donaldson, D. (2016). *Spinderella*. Glasgow: Egmont UK Ltd.

Donaldson, D (2012). *Superworm!* London: Alison Green Books.

Dowling, M. (2013). *Young Children's Thinking*. London: Sage.

Dowling, M. (2005). *Young Children's Personal. Social and Emotional Development*, 2nd ed. London: Paul Chapman Publishing.

Drury, H. (2014). *Mastery Mathematics: Teaching to Transform Achievement*. Oxford: Oxford University Press.

Dweck, C. S. (2006). *Mindset, the New Psychology of Success*. New York: Random House.

Dweck, C. S. (2000). *Self-Theories: Their Role in Motivation, Personality, and Development*. Oxford: Psychology Press, Routledge.

Early Education. (2012). *Development Matters in the Early Years Foundation Stage (EYFS), DfE*. Available at: www.early-education.org.uk.

Education Scotland. (2020). *National Improvement Hub*. Available at: https://education.gov.scot/improvement/learning-resources/early-level-play-pedagogy-toolkit/ [Accessed 14 Aug. 2020].

Edwards, C., Gandini, L. and Forman, G., eds. (1998). *The Hundred Languages of Children: Reggio Emilia Approach – Advanced Reflections*. Norwood: Ablex Publishing.

Elliott, E. S. and Dweck, C. S. (1988). Goals: An approach to motivation and achievement. *Journal of Personality and Social Psychology*, 54, pp. 5–12. doi: 10.1037/0022-3514.54.1.

Emery, A., Sanders, M., Anderman, L. and Yu, S. (2018). When mastery goals meet mastery learning: Administrator, teacher and student perceptions. *The Journal of Experimental Education*, 86(3), pp. 419–441.

Ephgrave, A. (2017). *Year One in Action: A Month-by-Month Guide to Taking Early Years Pedagogy into KS1*. Abingdon: Routledge.

Ephgrave, A. (2015). *'In the Moment' at EYFS Matters*. Available at: https://eyfsmatters.wordpress.com/2015/04/16/anna-ephgrave-guest-blog-in-the-moment/.

Ephgrave, A. (2012). *The Reception Year in Action, Revised and Updated Edition: A Month-by-Month Guide to Success in the Classroom*. Abingdon: Routledge.

Evans, S. (2017). *Fluency, Reasoning and Problem-Solving in Primary Maths*. Available at: www.tes.com/teaching-resources/blog/fluency-reasoning-and-problem-solving-primary-maths.

Ferrara, K., Hirsch-Pasek, K., Newcombe, N. S., Golinkoff, R. M. and Lam, W. S. (2011). *Block Talk: Spatial Language During Block Play*. Available at: https://doi.org/10.1111/j.1751-228X.2011.01122.x.

Finch, S. (2018). Introduction. In: J. Grenier, S. Finch, and C. Vollans, eds., *Celebrating Children's Learning: Assessment Beyond Levels in the Early Years*. Abingdon: Routledge.

Fisher, J. (2017). *Talk for Maths Mastery Conference; A Developmental Approach to 'Mastering' Mathematical Understanding Through Play in the EYFS and Y1*. Conference –Talk for Maths Mastery: A Developmental Approach to Mastering Mathematical Understanding Through Play in the EYFS and Y1, 16th June, Sheffield.

Fisher, J. (2016). *Interacting or Interfering? Improving Interactions in the Early Years*. Berkshire: Open University Press.

Fisher, J. (2013). *Starting from the Child*, 4th ed. Berkshire: Open University Press.

Fisher, K. R., Hirsh-Pasek, K., Newcombe, N. and Golinkoff, R. M. (2013). Geometric knowledge through guided play. *Taking Shape: Supporting Preschoolers' Acquisition of Child Development*, Nov./Dec. 2013, 84(6), pp. 1872–1878f.

Fisher, J. (2010). *Moving on to Key Stage 1: Improving Transition from the Early Years Foundation Stage*. Maidenhead: Open University Press.

Goddard Blythe, S. (2008). *The Well Balanced Child: Movement and Early Learning*. Stroud: Hawthorne Press.

Gopnik, A., Meltzoff, A. and Khul, P. (1999). *How Babies Think: The Science of Early Childhood*. London: Weidenfeld and Nicolson.

Harvard University, Center on the Developing Child. Available at: https://developingchild.harvard.edu/science/key-concepts/brain-architecture/ [Accessed Dec. 2019].

Harvard University, Center on the Developing Child. (2018). *Serve and Return*. Available at: https://developingchild.harvard.edu/science/key-concepts/serve-and-return/.

Harvard University, Center on the Developing Child. (2012). *Serve & Return Interaction Shapes Brain Circuitry*. Available at https://developingchild.harvard.edu/resources/serve-return-interaction-shapes-brain-circuitry/

Haylock, D. and Cockburn, A. D. (2008). *Understanding Mathematics for Young Children: A Guide for Foundation Stage*. London: Sage.

Heyman, G. D., Dweck, C. S. and Cain, K. M. (1992). Young children's vulnerability to self-blame and helplessness: Relationship to beliefs about goodness. *Child Development*, Apr. 1992, 63(2), pp. 401–415.

Hirsh-Pasek, K. (2018). *PEDAL Seminar, a Prescription for Play: Why Play Fosters Social and Cognitive Development*. University of Cambridge. Available at: https://sms.cam.ac.uk/media/2833460.

Kant, I. (1724–1804). Available at: https://en.wikipedia.org/wiki/Schema_(Kant).

Karmiloff-Smith, A. (1994). *Baby It's You*. London: Ebury Press.

Kolb, D. A. (1984). *Experiential Learning: Experience as the Source of Learning and Development*. Upper Saddle River: Prentice Hall.

Laevers, F., ed. (1994). *The Leuven Involvement Scale for Young Children (Manual and Video)*, Experiential Education Series, No. 1. Leuven: Centre for Experiential Education.

Laevers, F., Declercq, B., Marin, C., Moons, J. and Stanton, F. (2010). *Observing Involvement in Children from Birth to 6 Years. A DVD Training Pack.* Centre for Experiential Education [Leuven] and Kent Council.

Laevers, F. Declercq, B. and Thomas, F. (2010). *Implementation of the Process-Oriented Approach in Early Years Settings in Milton Keynes.* Final report. Leuven, Belgium: CEGO Leuven University.

Lim, C. (2002). Public Images of Mathematics. *Philosophy of Mathematics Education, Journal*, 15, University of Exeter.

Lindon, J. (2007). *Understanding Child Development – Linking Theory and Practice.* London: Hodder Arnold.

Liu, C., Solis, L., Hanne, J., Hopkins, E., Neale, D., Zosh, J., Hirsch-Pasek, K. and Whitebread, D. (2017). *Neuroscience and Learning Through Play: A Review of the Evidence*, White Paper. Denmark: The Lego Foundation.

Malaguzzi, L. (1996). *The Hundred Languages of Children, Catalogue of the Exhibition, Reggio Emilia.* Italy: Reggio Children. Maths – No Problem! Available at: https://mathsnoproblem.com/.

Matthews, J. (2003). *Drawing and Painting: Children and Visual Representation*, 2nd ed. London: Sage.

Matthews, J. (1999). *The Art of Childhood and Adolescence: The Construction of Meaning.* Brighton: Falmer Press.

McCarthy, M. and Redpath, J. (2017). Open mathematics in early education: Teacher. *Early Education Journal*, 83. Available at: www.early-education.org.uk.

McNicoll. (2008). *New Zealand Coaching & Mentoring Centre.* Available at: www.coachingmentoring.co.nz/articles/peer-supervision-no-one-knows-much-all-us [Accessed 14 Aug. 2020].

Meade, A. and Cubey, P. (2008). *Thinking Children-Learning About Schemas.* Berkshire: Open University Press.

Moyles, J. R. (1989). *Just Playing? The Role and Status of Play in Early Childhood Education.* Milton Keynes: Open University Press.

Moylett, H., ed. (2014). *Characteristics of Effective Early Learning – Helping Young Children Become Learners for Life.* Berkshire: Open University Press.

NCETM. (2014). *Mastery Approaches to Mathematics and the New National Curriculum.* Available at: www.ncetm.org.uk/public/files/19990433/Developing_mastery_in_mathematics_october_2014.pdf.

NCB – National Children's Bureau. (2014). *Making Maths REAL: Working with Parents to Support Children's Early Mathematical Development.* Available at: www.ncb.org.uk/sites/default/files/field/attachment/NO20%20-%20ncb_making_maths_real_august_2014.pdf.

National Literacy Trust. (2019). *Language Unlocks Reading: Supporting Early Language and Reading for Every Child.* Available at: https://literacytrust.org.uk/policy-and-campaigns/all-party-parliamentary-group-literacy/language-unlocks-reading/.

National Numeracy Organisation. (2017). *The Essentials of Numeracy: A New Approach to Making the UK Numerate, Nationalnumeracy. org.uk.* Available at: www.nationalnumeracy.org.uk/sites/default/files/ nn124_essentials_numeracyreport_for_web.pdf.

Nutbrown, C. (1999). *Threads of Thinking. Young Children Learning and the Role of Early Education*, 2nd ed. London: Paul Chapman Publishing.

O'Connor, A. (2017). All about memory. *Nursery World*, 2–15 Oct.

O'Connor, A. (2008). Enabling environments: Continuous provision part 1 – Don't stop me now! *Nursery World*, 9. Available at: www.nurseryworld. co.uk/nursery-world/feature/1091648/enabling-environments-continuous-provision-dont-stop (requires Nursery World subscription).

Ofsted. (2015). *Teaching and Play in the Early Years – A Balancing Act? A Good Practice Survey to Explore Perceptions of Teaching and Play in the Early Years* (Reference no: 150085). Available at: https://assets. publishing.service.gov.uk/government/uploads/system/uploads/ attachment_data/file/444147/Teaching-and-play-in-the-early-years-a-balancing-act.pdf.

Parker-Rees, R. (1997). *Learning from Play: Design and Technology, Imagination and Playful Thinking.* IDATER Conference Paper, Loughborough: Loughborough University.

Pascal, C. and Bertram, T. (1997). *Effective Early Learning: Case Studies in Improvement.* London: Hodder and Stoughton.

Pascal, C., Bertram, T. and Rouse, L. (2019). *Getting It Right in the Early Years Foundation Stage: A Review of the Evidence.* Early Education. Available at: www.early-education.org.uk.

Pascal and Bertram in Abbott, L. and Moylett, H., eds. (1999). *Early Education Transformed*, New Millennium Series. London: Falmer Press.

Peacock, A. (2018). *Celebrating and Developing Expertise in Teaching and Learning.* 10th January 2018, Primary Early Years Conference at Sheffield Hallam University.

Piaget, J. (1968). *Six Psychological Studies.* London: University of London Press.

Pound, L. (2008). *Thinking and Learning About Mathematics in the Early Years.* Abingdon: Routledge.

Pound, L. (2006). *Supporting Mathematical Development in the Early Years*, 2nd ed. Maidenhead, Buckingham: Open University Press.

Project Zero, Harvard Graduate School of Education. (2001). *Making Learning Visible: Children as Individuals and Group Learners, Reggio Emilia.* Italy: Reggio Children.

Redding, R., Morgan, G. and Harmon, R. (1988). Mastery motivation in infants and toddlers. *Infant Behaviour and Development, Journal*, 11, pp. 419–430.

Rinaldi, C. (2006). *In Dialogue with Reggio Emilia: Listening, Researching and Learning.* Oxford: Psychology Press.

Robson, S. (2010). Self-regulation and metacognition in young children's self-initiated play and reflective dialogue. *International Journal of Early Years Education*, 18(3), Sept., Routledge.

Robson, S. (2006). *Developing Thinking and Understanding in Young Children: An Introduction for Students*, 2nd ed. Abingdon: Routledge.

Romeo, R. R., et al. (2018). Beyond the 30-million-word gap: Children's conversational exposure is associated with language-related brain function. *Psychological Science*, 29(5), pp. 700–710.

Rose, J. and Rogers, S. (2012). *The Role of the Adult in Early Years Settings*. Maidenhead: Open University Press.

Russell, S. (2000). Developing computational fluency with whole numbers in the elementary grades. In: B. J. Ferrucci and K. M. Heid, eds., *Millennium Focus Issue: Perspectives on Principles and Standards. The New England Math Journal*, vol. 32, no. 2. Keene, NH: Association of Teachers of Mathematics in New England, pp. 40–54.

Schweinhart, L. J. and Weikart, D. P. (1993). Success by empowerment: The High/Scope Perry Preschool study through age 27. *Young Children*, 49(1), Nov., pp. 54–58.

Siraj-Blatchford, I., Kingston, D. and Melhuish, E. (2015). *Assessing Quality in Early Childhood Education and Care: Sustained Shared Thinking and Emotional Well-Being (SSTEW) Scale for 2–5-Year Olds*. London: IOE Press.

Siraj-Blatchford, I. and Manni, L. (2007). *Effective Leadership in the Early Years Sector (The ELEYS Study)*. London: Institute of Education Press.

Siraj-Blatchford, I., Sylva, K., Muttock, S., Gilden, R. and Bell, D. (2002). *Researching Effective Pedagogy in the Early Years (REPEY)*. DFES and the Institute of Education (Research Report 356). Available at: http://dera.ioe.ac.uk/4650/1/RR356.pdf.

STA – Standards and Testing Agency. (2019). *Early Years Foundation Stage Profile 2020 Handbook*. Available at: https://assets.publishing.service.gov.uk/government/uploads/system/uploads/attachment_data/file/858652/EYFSP_Handbook_2020v5.pdf.

Stevens, J. (2018). *Let's Talk About Maths at Teach Early Years*. Available at: https://www.teachearlyyears.com/learning-and-developmentview/talking-about-maths.

Stewart, N. (2013). Active learning. In: H. Moylett, ed., *Characteristics of Effective Early Learning: Helping Young Children Become Learners for Life*. Maidenhead: Open University Press.

Stewart, N. (2011). *How Children Learn: The Characteristics of Effective Early Learning*. Early Education. Available at: www.early-education.org.uk.

Sylva, K. (2015). Foreword. In: I. Siraj, D. Kingston, and E. Melhuish, eds., *Assessing Quality in Early Childhood Education: Sustained Shared Thinking and Emotional Wellbeing (SSTEW) Scale for 2–5-Year Old Provision*. London: IOE Press.

Sylva, K., Melhuish, E., Sammons, P., Siraj-Blatchford, I. and Taggart, B. (2004). *The Effective Provision of Pre-School Education [EPPE] Project*, Technical Paper 12, The Final Report: Effective Pre-School Education. London: Institute of Education.

Thom, J. S. (2018). All about spatial reasoning. *Nursery World Journal*, 8–21 Jan.

Thom, J. S. (2017). All about embodied learning. *Nursery World Journal*, 27 Nov.–10 Dec.

Thornton, L. and Brunton, P. (2005). *Understanding the Reggio Approach.* London: David Fulton Publishers.

Tickell, C. (2011). *The Early Years: Foundations for Life, Health and Learning. An Independent Report on the Early Years Foundation Stage to Her Majesty's Government.* DfE. Available at: https://assets.publishing. service.gov.uk/government/uploads/system/uploads/attachment_data/ file/180919/DFE-00177-2011.pdf.

Trevarthen, C. (2018). *Communicative Musicality: The Intrinsic Musical Nature of Human Interaction.* Available at: www.wombtoworld.org/ previous-conferences/womb-to-world-2018/.

Vygotsky, L. and Cole, M. (1978). *Mind in Society: The Development of Higher Psychological Processes.* Harvard, MA: Harvard University Press.

Wenger-Trayner, E. and Wenger-Trayner, B. (2015). *An Introduction to Communities of Practice. A Brief Overview of the Concept and Its Uses.* Available at: https://wenger-trayner.com/introduction-to-communities- of-practice/.

Whitebread, D. (2016). Self-regulation. *Early Education Journal*, 80, Autumn. Available at: www.early-education.org.uk.

Whitebread, D. (2012). *Developmental Psychology and Early Childhood Education.* London: Sage.

Whitebread, D., Bingham, S., Grau, V., Pino Pasternak, D. and Sangster, C. (2007). Development of metacognition and self-regulated learning in young children: Role of collaborative and peer-assisted learning. *Journal of Cognitive Education and Psychology*, 6(3), pp. 433–455.

Whitebread, D., Coltman, P., Jameson, H. and Lander, R. (2009). Play, cognition and self-regulation: What exactly are children learning when they learn through play? *Educational and Child Psychology*, 26(2), pp. 40–52.

Wood, L., Professor of Education at the University of Sheffield. (2019). *Nursery World Conference: Delivering High-Quality Education Under the New Inspection Framework.* London: Intent, Implementation and Impact.

Woodham, L. and Pennant, J. (2014). *How Can I Support the Development of Early Number Sense and Place Value?* Available at: https://nrich. maths.org/10739.

Worthington, M. and Carruthers, E. (2011). *Understanding Children's Mathematical Graphics: Beginnings in Play.* Maidenhead: Open University Press.

Worthington, M. and Carruthers, E. (2006). *Children's Mathematics: Making Marks, Making Meaning*, 2nd ed. London: Sage.

Zosh, M., et al. (2017). *White Paper: Learning Through Play: A Review of the Evidence.* LEGO Foundation. Available at: https://www.legofoundation. com/media/1063/learning-throughplay_web.pdf.

Useful links

Children's Mathematics Network. www.childrens-mathematics.net/.
The Sheffield REAL Project (Raising Early Achievement in Literacy). www.real-online.group.shef.ac.uk/index.html with links to REAM (Raising Early Achievement in Mathematics) www.real-online. group.shef.ac.uk/ream.

Index

Note: Page numbers in *italic* indicate a figure.

abstract thought level *50–51*
accommodation: in cognitive development 41; in mark-making development 145–146
Action Plan 19, 231
action schema 42
Active Learning: in case study *211–213*; as characteristic of effective learning 48, 76, 77, 219, 232; in continuous provision 23, 24, 25; in mark-making development 145, 157, 162; mastery development 175
adult-initiated/adult-led maths *113, 114, 115*
adult roles in mark-making development 148–150, *151*; adult support of children's maths mastery 169–197; adult attitudes about maths 169–171; allowing time for problem solving and pursuit of interests 177–181; creating opportunities for children's talk 186–191; having knowledge of child development and how children learn 191–192; identifying children's maths thinking and potential for opportunities 173–177; knowing how to observe 192–196; providing combination of child-initiated and adult-focused teaching 181–186; role of adult *172*, 208–209, *212*
assessment: formative 193; ongoing 193; role of 193
assimilation: in cognitive development 41; in mark-making development 145

Athey, Chris 41, 42
attitudes: of adults on maths 169–171; and dispositions 60–62; in mindset 58
authentic contextual experiences 127–132; real-life environment 153

babies: cognitive development 41; developmental momentum of 33–34; mark-making experiences 138–140
baking and cooking 100, 126, 153
boys, and mark-making 159

Carruthers, Elizabeth 23, 117, 121, 137
case study, maintaining momentum into Year 1 198–220; challenges 207–208; continuing continuous provision 214–215; following children's interests 210–214; Foundation Stage meets National Curriculum 215–220; home learning partnership 215; implementing vision into Year 1 198, *203–207*; role of adult in Year 1 208–209; strong overall vision 199–202
characteristics of effective learning 48, 77, 144–145, 192, 232
child development 191–193; developmental momentum 36–37
child-led learning, whole-class 109–136; key questions 109; mathematical mastery in practice 121–134 (analysis of learning story 132–134; authentic contextual experiences 127–132;

enabling environment 124; Love Monster learning story 121–123; problem solving as key disposition 123; reflection and meta-cognition 125–127, 132–133; sustained shared thinking 123–124); reasons for learning stories 134–135; role of play in developing mathematical mastery 110–118; teaching by following children's interests 119–121

children's agency: and self-belief 79–80

children's interests: adult support of 149–150, 177; building mathematical thinking and mastery 119–121; defined 99–100; maintaining momentum into Year 1 210–214; planning for 103–104

children's talk: conversational talk, serve and return 72; children's mathematical 148

cognitive co-construction 74, 162

cognitive self-regulation 78, 210

cognitive structures: and schema 40–41, 48

concepts: connections in daily life 200, *205–207*; defined 48–49; and fluency 86–87; mathematical 48–49, 70, 80, 131–132, 164, 167, 214; and reasoning 87–88; and schema *50–51*

connections, making: in mark-making development 144

contextual experience, shopping as 127

continuous provision: documenting 102, 106; and enabling environments 17; maintaining momentum into Year 1 *212*, 214–215; for mathematical mark-making 139–140; principles of 23–24; in sustained shared thinking 123; in whole-class child-led learning 117

Creating and Thinking Critically: in case study *211–213*, 216; as characteristic of effective

learning 22, 48, 76, 77, 219, 232; in children's interests 119; in contextual experiences 127; in continuous provision 23, 24, 25; in mark-making development 145, 157, 162; mastery development 175; and sustained shared thinking 86, 123

developmental momentum 27–28; of babies 33–34; of toddlers 34–36; of young children 36–37

dispositions *60–62*; problem solving as key 123

documenting children's learning 81–108; children's interests 99–100, 103–104; children's misconceptions 98–99; children's schematic thinking and learning 100–102; fluency 87–88; importance of documentation 82; key questions 81; mastery and meta-cognition 104–107; problem solving 87; process of using floor books *83*, 84–87; reasoning 88–92; serve and return interactions 92–98; through learning stories and floor books 82–83

Dweck, Carol 55, 57

Early Years Foundation Stage (EYFS): on children's learning 175–176, 177, 193; Early Learning Goals 131, 162; mathematical mastery 56, 67, 76; and National Curriculum 215–219; philosophy of play-based curriculum 109; Statutory Framework 110

embodied learning 52

enabling environments: and continuous provision 17; creating a maths mastery 124–125; documenting 102, 103, 106; maintaining momentum into Year 1 *212*; in mark-making development 150, 152; in mathematical development 41; in whole-class child-led learning 117

enactive representation 148
equilibrium, in mark-making development 145–146
Every Child a Talker (ECAT) project 17
executive functions 77, 78
extended professional development initiative (EPDI) 8–11, 26

Fisher, Julie 23–24, 113
fixed mindset 57–59, 79
floor books: documentation through 82–83; Here, There and Everywhere 94–95; I Can Jump 4 Metres story 86–87; process of using *83*, 84–87
flow 76, 157, 178, 187, 217; Csikszentmihalyi, Mihaly 75
fluency 87–88
functional dependency relationships *50–51*
funds of knowledge 35

Go Compare learning story *31*, 164–167, 210, 221
Gopnik, Meltzoff and Kuhl 26, 32, 138
grounded theory 10
growth mindset 57–59, 63, 79

habits of mind 60
Harvard University: Centre on the Developing Child 72, 77
HighScope Perry Preschool longitudinal study 63
holistic development 35, 62
home learning partnership: and authentic contextual experiences 128; documenting 102, 107; maintaining momentum into Year 1 *213*, 215; for mathematical mark-making 140–142, *141*
Hot and Cold Spot audit 17–18
how children learn 56, 63, 191–192, 216

iconic representation 148, 153–154, 157

independent learner 200
intentional thinking 78
interests *see* children's interests
in the moment 195
involvement: levels of, and well-being 75

knowledge, and what children learn 56

learned helplessness 57–59
learning, process of 173, *174*
learning dispositions, five domains of 61, *62*, 76
Learning Environment Audit, Mathematics 18–19, 21–22, 226–230
learning momentum 28–29
learning orientations 60
learning power 60
learning stories: analysis of 132–133; children's agency and self-belief in 79; documentation through 82–83; maintaining momentum into Year 1 208; observation using 13–15; reasons for whole-class 134–135; uses of 232; with mathematical mark-making *141*, *147*, *151*, *152*, 161–162; *see also* narrative learning stories
Lego Foundation 76, 110
listening, pedagogy of 85

maintaining momentum 27–28; *see also* mathematical development, maintaining momentum of
Malaguzzi, Loris 5, 13, 34, 43, 93, 173, 197
Manni, Laura 9
mark-making, mathematical 137–168; adult interactions 148–149; adult support for developing interests 149–150; authentic, real-life environment 153; building on enabling environment 150, 152; children's mathematical conversations 148; continuous provision

and under-threes 139–140; development in 146–148, 153–155, 156–163; extended thinking for 145–146; home learning partnership 140–142; rotational schema 144; with birth to 3 year olds 138–139; with 2 year olds 142–145; with 3 to 4 year olds 146–148, 153–156; with 4 to 5 year olds 156–163; with 5+ year olds 163–167
mastery: and meta-cognition 104–107
mastery orientation 48, 55, 57–59, 63, 67, 68–71
mastery orientation, key aspects of 71–80; child-led play 73; children's agency and self-belief 79–80; conversational talk, serve and return 72; effective learning 77; meta-cognition 78; self-regulation 78; sustained shared thinking 74–76
mathematical babies 33–34
mathematical development, maintaining momentum of 27–54; about learning momentum 28–29; action schema 42; concepts 48–49; developmental momentum of babies 33–34; developmental momentum of toddlers 34–35; developmental momentum of young children 35–37; embodied learning 52; figurative schema 42–47; maintaining momentum 38–39; number line discussion, and transition of pedagogy 29–32; schema 40–42; schema underpinning concepts 48–51; spatial reasoning 53–54; talking and thinking 39–40
mathematical graphics 137, 147, 156
mathematical interests see children's interests
mathematical mark making see mark-making, mathematical
mathematical mastery 55–80; defined 55–56, 65–68, 70–71;

dispositions and attitudes 60–62; how and what of children's learning 56; mastery orientation 48, 55, 57–59, 63, 67, 68–71; mastery orientation, key aspects of 71–80; role of play in developing 110–118; see also whole-class child-led learning, and mathematical mastery in practice
mathematical toddlers 34–35
mathematical vocabulary 186–189
Maths is Everywhere observation review 15–16, 117–118, 150, 224, 225
meta-cognition 78; and mastery 104–107; and reflection 125–127
mindset behaviours 57–59, 60, 79
misconceptions: addressing 98–99; revealed by talk and play 96–98
momentum see mathematical development, maintaining momentum of
motor or action level 50–51
motor skills 139, 146, 148

narrative learning stories 12, 13–15; see also learning stories
National Centre for Excellence in Teaching of Mathematics (NCETM) 100
National Numeracy 169
New Zealand: Early Childhood Curriculum dispositions 60–62, 76; educational leadership projects 10; Te Whariki curriculum 60–61, 76, 134
Numbered Footballs learning story 31, 64–65, 75, 78, 177, 187
number line discussion: and transition of pedagogy 29–32
numerosity 25
Nutbrown, Cathy 52, 99

observation: adult support of children's learning 192–196; observation cycle 11, 193; observe, wait and listen (OWL) 191; observing in the moment

195; and pedagogy of listening 85; in research 9; as strategy 12; using narrative learning stories 13–15; *see also* Maths is Everywhere observation review
Ofsted 110, 113
One hundred languages of children 34, 43, 93
Open Mathematics 24

pedagogy 8; of listening 85; responsible 149; transition with number line 29–32
planning in the moment 195
play: child-initiated 42, 181; child-led 40, 41, 73; directed 73; free 73; key features/essentials of 113, 117; playful learning/playful teaching 182–187; playing and exploring (in case study *211–213*; as characteristic of effective learning 48, 73, 76, 77, 219, 232; in continuous provision 23, 24, 25; in mark-making development 145, 157, 162; mastery development 175); Play Spiral 73; in process of using floor books 86–87; role in development of mathematical mastery 110–118
possibility thinking 96, 122, 164, 187
practitioner action research 9–10, 20
problem solving 87, 122, 123, 177
professional development initiative *see* extended professional development initiative (EPDI)
professionally informed practice 149

Ready, Willing and Able 60–61, 76
REAL (Raising Early Achievement in Literacy) 142
REAM (Raising Early Achievement in Maths) 142
reasoning 88–92
reflection: analysis of learning story 132–133; and meta-cognition 125–127

Reggio Emilia 82, 84, 108, 173
research findings 20
research-in-action 9
responsible pedagogy 149
Rinaldi, Carlina 82

schema: action 42; defined 40–42, 100; figurative 42–47, 51, 144, 160; and mathematical development 40; rotational 144
schematic thinking and learning 100–102
science, technology, engineering, and mathematics (STEM): and spatial reasoning 53
self-belief of children 79–80
self-regulation 78, 210; emotional 78
sense of agency 35
sensorimotor schema level 144
serve and return conversations: documenting support of learning 92–98; in Hot and Cold Spot audit 17; as key aspect of mastery orientation 72; in mathematical development 41; role of adult implementing in Year 1 208
Siraj-Blatchford, John 9
spatial reasoning 53–54
sustained shared thinking (SST) 21, 22, 54, 64, 74–76, 123–124; serve and return conversation and 28, 37, 45; Sustained Shared Thinking and Emotional Wellbeing scale 126
symbolic representation *50–51*, 148, 149–154, 157

talk: and thinking 39–40, 41, 186
Talk for Maths Mastery (TFMM) 7–26; about 7–8; continuous provision principles 23–24, 117; exemplification 24–26; extended professional development initiative (EPDI) 8–11, 26; getting started 11–12; implementing in Year 1 202, *203–207*; learning stories as basis 83; and mathematical mastery 66; our

story 21–22; perspectives of mathematical development 172; questions 22–23; schematic thinking and learning 101; tools and strategies in practice 12–20; use of research findings 20
talking and thinking 39–40, 41, 186
teaching: Ofsted definition 113; through adult-led whole-class sessions 120
Te Whariki 60–61, 76, 134
timelines 19–20
toddlers: developmental momentum of 34–35; mark-making development 142–145

understanding of knowledge 56

vision, in maintaining mathematical momentum 199–202
vocabulary, mathematical 188–191

Well-being and Involvement Scale 75
what children learn 56, 192
Williams Review 171, 177
working theories 35
Worthington, Maulfry 121, 137

Year 1 children: in mark-making development 163–167

zone of proximal development 75